D0952086

A BATTLE FOR THE SOUL OF ISLAM

AN AMERICAN MUSLIM PATRIOT'S
FIGHT TO SAVE HIS FAITH

DR. M. ZUHDI JASSER

THRESHOLD EDITIONS
New York   London   Toronto   Sydney   New Delhi

Threshold Editions
A Division of Simon & Schuster, Inc.
1230 Avenue of the Americas
New York, NY 10020

First Threshold Editions hardcover edition June 2012

THRESHOLD EDITIONS and colophon are trademarks of Simon & Schuster, Inc.

For information about special discounts for bulk purchases, please contact Simon & Schuster Special Sales at 1-866-506-1949 or business@simonandschuster.com.

The Simon & Schuster Speakers Bureau can bring authors to your live event. For more information or to book an event, contact the Simon & Schuster Speakers Bureau at 1-866-248-3049 or visit our website at www.simonspeakers.com.

Designed by Renata Di Biase

Manufactured in the United States of America

10 9 8 7 6 5 4 3 2 1

Library of Congress Cataloging-in-Publication Data

Jasser, M. Zuhdi, 1967—
  A battle for the soul of Islam : an American Muslim patriot's fight to save his faith / M. Zuhdi Jasser.
    p. cm.
  1. Islam—21st century. 2. Islamic fundamentalism. 3. Islam—United States. 4. Jasser, M. Zuhdi, 1967– 5. Syrian Americans—Biography. I. Title.
BP161.3.J37 2012
305.6'970973—dc23

                                                    2011047714

ISBN 978-1-4516-5794-4
ISBN 978-1-4516-5798-2 (ebook)

To my children, Zachariah, Zaina, and Zaid
With eternal gratitude to my wife, Gada

CONTENTS

CONTENTS

A BATTLE FOR THE
SOUL OF ISLAM

INTRODUCTION

As a Navy veteran, I have wondered at times what it was like for my country when the Japanese attacked Pearl Harbor, what it really felt like to hear such shocking news over the radio. It was not until 9/11 that I had any real sense of what that day must have been like. However, in many ways I believe that history will view the 9/11 attacks as far worse than Pearl Harbor. The attack on Pearl Harbor, as terrible as it was, was military in nature and largely targeted our U.S. Navy, those whose duty it is to serve and protect their country, while 9/11 was an attack by terrorists upon civilians, and it was executed by men who claimed to do so in the name of God. As a Muslim, it is hard for me to put into words just how horrific this is, how deeply I believe it betrays my faith, and the depth of sorrow I feel for the victims. Like all Americans, I feel that that day will always be with me, and as a Muslim it forced me to confront certain realities.

Once the shock of the attack wore off, my next response was pure rage. I wanted to get even with the bastards who had done this, and what added to my fury was that they had done this in the name of my faith of Islam. I had to find a way to address how angry I was about what had been done, and at the same time make it clear to my fellow Americans that true Islam, our Islam, was not what was represented by these madmen. I had no idea

1

what a big job that would really be; that, in fact, it would become a second calling for me, the need to make the world aware of the difference between Islam and Islamism. To that extent, President George W. Bush was right: they *do* hate us for our freedom.

I waited for other Muslims to come forward, to unequivocally denounce the actions of the 9/11 terrorists and to protest the very idea that Islam could be used as the excuse for such acts. There were Muslims who came forward to denounce the nineteen terrorists and their acts, but there were more than a few times when it was done with the caveat of "Yes, I believe it is terrible what happened, but one must look at U.S. policy in the Middle East, its support of Israel . . ." and so on. The very idea that one could invoke and blame U.S. foreign policy for what these men did on 9/11 was absurd. Whatever disagreements any of the terrorists may have had with U.S. foreign policy in the Middle East, how does that justify killing innocent civilians? How could civilized American Muslims, rather than put the blame squarely on their supremacist ideology, find excuses and explanations for them? Bin Laden's conceit that all Americans are guilty of our government's "crimes" in the Middle East—having troops in Saudi Arabia and supporting Israel being the primary ones, in his view—and are all therefore deserving of death is not at all supported by the Qur'an or the Islam I knew, had learned from my family and teachings, and practiced as an officer in the U.S. Navy. As an intensely patriotic Muslim physician in the Navy I had always believed that one of our primary missions was to protect the innocent from the very kind of evil that attacked innocent civilians on 9/11. For him to twist things so that all Americans became fair game in his terrorist ambitions was a complete betrayal of the basic principles of Islam, a betrayal I swore to confront head-on.

On the first anniversary of the 9/11 attacks on our homeland, I wrote an advertisement directed at all Americans. The leadership of the mosque my family and I attend in Scottsdale, Arizona, agreed to run it in the state's largest newspaper, *The Arizona Republic*:

Members of the Islamic Center of the Northeast Valley in Scottsdale on this solemn day of remembrance, prayers, and meditation recall that a year ago today, barbaric acts of murder and destruction fell upon our citizens and our cities.

On September 11, 2001, nineteen criminals and their organization directed a sneak attack upon our nation and everything for which we all stand. The perpetrators of this act violated the laws of God and outraged the sensibilities of all. They cowardly murdered thousands of our fellow citizens—innocent men, women, and children. They only succeeded in strengthening our resolve and in pulling us together.

Our freedom was the target and we shall defend it. Our democracy was their enemy and we shall maintain it. Our unity was their envy and they shall continue to suffer from it. We shall neither forget nor forgive in this life, and they shall contend with the judgment of God in the next.

To the victims belong our sorrow and tears. To their families we direct our prayers to God for his favor and blessing in easing their pain and healing their injuries. To our country we stand by all our fellow citizens in unity and prayer for our national strength, justice, freedom, and peace.

While at times scores of Muslims would voice some agreement with the frankness of my commentary, for the most part it was slow going finding those with the resolve, courage, and focus on ideology. In the immediate weeks after 9/11, it soon became obvious to me that I needed to make my own voice heard as someone who both loves his faith and his country and wanted to draw a clear line between the Islamists' interpretation of Islam and mine. My father felt as passionately as I did on this subject, and I felt grateful to be joined by him as we both raised our voices in protest against the Islamists. I was very proud when *The Arizona Republic* reached out to him and published his op-ed piece on September 13, 2001, in which he aimed squarely at the sort of Islamist thinking that led to 9/11. My father had been a well-respected physician in Phoenix at the time, while I had been in the Phoenix Valley for only a little over two years, since leaving the Navy. But in the weeks and months that followed, the apologetics from Muslims began to flow. I reached my limit when an article appeared on November 4, 2001, on the front page of the *Republic* titled "U.S. Muslims torn between Love of Islam and America," by Dennis Wagner and Tom Zoellner. After reading the long and painful story, I quickly called the reporters and let them know how offended I was and asked them where they found the litany of radical Muslims they interviewed. Among many radicals, they interviewed a local Muslim university student at Arizona State University who said that the USS *Cole* bombing was deserved and "not necessarily wrong" because Americans were intruding and unwelcome in those Muslim countries. The student additionally stated:

> In the final analysis, America offers me one of two choices: either I submissively accept perpetual enslavement and oppression, or become an Osama bin Laden. Honestly, there is not a third choice.

A local leading imam in the Phoenix Valley area, Ihsan Saadeddin, asserted the classical Islamist denial, stating with confidence that the perpetrators were not Muslims and most likely were Mossad agents. Another local Valley imam, Omar Shahin, who would later be head of the North American Imams Federation (NAIF), blamed American foreign policy, hinted at conspiracies, and flaunted a sign in his office that stated, "Those who are persecuting you have the same ignorance, hate, and evil in their hearts as the (Sept. 11) terrorists did." Words cannot express how infuriated I was that the reporters could not find a single patriotic, liberty-loving Muslim among the many representatives and leaders they interviewed to give them an alternative American Muslim response. After my anger sank in, I realized that we as American Muslims had a major problem. Now I just had to figure out how to address it. My deepest fear was that if we did not do it well, American security would remain in increasing peril and my children would grow up in a nation whose acceptance of Muslims would only degenerate toward a deeper and deeper fear.

I had no such struggle in my life between being American and Muslim, and questioned why were there no Muslims like me included in the article, those who clearly had no problem with loving their country as well as their religion and were able to keep both in perspective. Ultimately, the reporters simply went to the "lowest-hanging Muslim fruit"—searching the local yellow pages or Google for "Muslim" or "Islamic." Unfortunately, the current paradigm of the organized American Muslim communities would inevitably lead them to Islamists, groups that politically or tribally organize under the banner of "Islam" and "Muslims."

Phil Boas, one of the editorial page editors at *The Arizona Republic*, showed just how fair-minded he was when he encouraged me to write an opinion piece that elaborated upon my feelings about loyalty to country and religion. In that piece I wrote:

The seditious and treasonous ranting and raving of a few ungrateful Palestinians brings an unspeakable revulsion from me and all Muslims with an inalienable love for America. If I had been aboard the USS *Cole*, I would have had no hesitation in sending the approaching murderers to their martyrdom. Any U.S. citizen calling an attack on a ship of his own country that killed 17 sailors and fellow citizens, an attack by martyrs or "not necessarily wrong" is outrageous. A pager, a cellular phone, and a big house do not make a Muslim an American. . . . American freedom and liberty in all its glory is at the core of an Islamic life and principles. From this Muslim's perspective, American Muslims would certainly fully endorse and enlist proudly in every aspect of Operation Enduring Freedom. The U.S. Constitution embodies the one and only form of government that allows them to practice their faith like no other country in the world. Those who are uncomfortable with being unequivocally loyal should be honest enough to simply leave. (*The Arizona Republic*, Nov. 9, 2001)

While I had no second thoughts about writing the piece, in retrospect I should have. To my disbelief, there were actually those in the local and national Muslim community who were opposed to what I had to say, who put Islam (specifically its global political movement) above their country. I was at a loss to understand how they could do this, since it was actually the United States, more than any other nation, that gave them the right to worship in whatever way they chose. That was part of my point in the piece, that my religion is very dear to me, and because I live in a country that offers the freedoms and rights the United States does, I can actually practice my religion the way I choose. Who could argue with that? The Islamists, that's who. With this, my first op-ed piece on the issue, I found myself the recipient of a flurry of gratitude from scores of American Muslims and non-Muslims as well as a flurry of disdain and hate from Islamists. On November 12, 2001, Riad Abdelkarim, M.D., the Western Region communications director for the Council on American Islamic Relations (CAIR), sent me unsolicited email after email proclaiming his defense of the Muslims I critiqued. He then went on to tell me that "justice [for the 9/11 murderers] should not be paid for with the blood of innocent Afghan civilians . . . think about what you say before you do so." He then, out of left field, complained to the leadership of an unrelated national medical organization about my fitness to lead. He wrote to the president, "Of course, he is entitled to his views—no matter how obscene they may be—but do we really want him representing (or leading) our Arab-American physicians?" His cheap attacks were soundly rebuked by the organization, but it did demonstrate that Islamists like Abdelkarim have no boundaries.

I should not have been surprised. I had been doing battle with the Islamists well before 9/11, and expecting them to have changed their attitudes because of 9/11 was like expecting a zebra to change its stripes. Still, Muslims in the long run are the only ones who can address this radical strain within the faith. It involves a deep change in consciousness, and this is part of what led me eventually to form the American Islamic Forum for Democracy (AIFD).

It was my general lack of satisfaction with my fellow Muslims' response to 9/11, and the lack of enough visible opposition to political Islam overall, that eventually led to my decision to form AIFD. I kept waiting for the leaders in the American Muslim communities locally and nationally to take a strong stand against Islamist terrorism, and to make it clear that Islam is a spiritual and personal way of life, not a political belief system. I continued to be disappointed at the lack of any sort of consistent voice in that arena.

So I struck out on my own, with the philosophy that imbues the classic movie *Field of Dreams*: "If you build it, they will come." We officially formed our organization in our living room on March 3, 2003, with eight other Muslim families in Phoenix and agreed upon bylaws, a board of directors, and founding principles that we all shared. We hammered out the principles we felt would treat and counter the root cause of Islamist-inspired terrorism— the theo-political separatist ideology of Islamism. Those principles included a founding mission to *"advocate for the preservation of the founding principles of the United States Constitution, liberty and freedom through the separation of mosque and state."* We came together and proclaimed that "we believe that the American citizenship pledge, the Constitution and Bill of Rights, and support of our armed forces are central to countering the root cause of Islamist terrorism: Islamism." Our whole organization was founded upon the belief that the defeat of Islamism is the only pathway toward American security from radical Islamists. And the only way to defeat Islamism is to advocate for liberty, inoculating Muslims with the ideas of universal freedom within the Islamic consciousness. We also agreed on the following principles:

1. We explicitly and fundamentally reject any justification whatsoever for any form of terrorism (the targeting of civilians and noncombatants).

2. We will intellectually and morally invalidate the Islamist (Muslim supremacist) belief system. We reject the association of Islamism with Islam.

3. We will openly name and challenge Islamist organizations and their enablers in order to clearly demarcate

organizations that exploit the religion of Islam for their own political purposes.

4. We recognize the fact that there is no clergy in Islam, and we accept the Qur'an as our main reference for discussions regarding our faith.

5. We will promote our belief that pluralism and moderation are fundamental principles of the Holy Qur'an.

6. We recognize and honor the principles of individual liberty and freedom. We believe that the practice of religion and its laws are a matter of free choice within an individual's beliefs and conscience only. Our governmental laws should be based upon our Constitution and Bill of Rights, and derived from reason.

7. We believe that every Muslim is equally entitled to his or her opinion concerning the religion of Islam, in an environment free of ostracism, intimidation, and reprisal. While we recognize the value of scholarship and learned discourse in Islam, we believe that all Muslims should play an active role in the debate and *ijtihad* of our own faith.

8. We will work to educate the public regarding the special historical relationship between Judaism, Christianity, and Islam.

9. We will publicly affirm our belief that the primary threat to America is from both violent and nonviolent Islamists who exploit the faith of Islam, and who use

identity politics, victimology, tribalism, and intimidation to further their goal of Islamist hegemony.

10. We believe in the equality of the sexes, which is well established in the Qur'an.

11. We will work to promote and enhance the understanding of spiritual Islam in America, and clearly differentiate it from the dangers of political Islam (Islamism).

12. We will work to express the consistency of the principles of Islam with economic principles of free markets, individual choice, and capitalism.

13. We will work to educate Muslims about both the positive contributions of Islamic history and the need for a second enlightenment of Muslims that recognizes the universal principles of freedom, individual rights, separation of religion and state, and limited, constitutional government.

14. We will work to instill in young American Muslims a clear understanding of, and appreciation for, liberty, the U.S. Constitution, and the distinctively positive impact that America and American ideals of freedom and liberty have had upon the world.

15. We will work to formulate principled positions on specific areas of American foreign and domestic policy as they relate to the vital national interests of the United States and the principles of freedom.

16. We specifically stand in support and unqualified recognition of the state of Israel and its right to exist behind secure borders as do all free nations. (*While as Muslims and American citizens we will take stands on many diverse foreign policy issues, we feel that the recognition of Israel has proven to be one of the litmus tests for Islamist demagoguery. Thus we feel it is important to make a foundational statement about the recognition of the state of Israel.*)

17. We also support the right of the Palestinian people to live peacefully and be represented by an anti-Islamist government that unequivocally recognizes the state of Israel and is free from radical ideologies that justify acts of terror.

The first major event we organized at AIFD was a public protest against Islamist-inspired terrorism that we planned for April 24, 2004. It received unprecedented national attention for a Muslim-led event, including supportive editorials from *The Arizona Republic* and the *Washington Times*. Two weeks before the event, *The Arizona Republic*, in fact, admonished all local imams to join us in the rally or be perceived as not being vocal against terrorism. We chose the aptly named Patriots' Square in central downtown Phoenix to hold the interfaith event, which we called "Standing with Muslims Against Terrorism." After four months of planning, more than four hundred people showed up, and to my great satisfaction, they included hundreds of Muslims, joined by Christians, Jews, and a broad representation of faiths. Sadly, the local imams from the eleven mosques in town never ended up joining us at the event, despite their leadership's being involved in our preparations. In fact, the interfaith sponsor for the event ultimately withdrew a few weeks before the rally because of the stark division we created between the corrupt apologetics of Islamist leadership of some mosques and other Islamist groups like CAIR's Arizona chapter in Phoenix. The interfaith leaders certainly came to the rally and supported us, but they understandably had to step away from cosponsoring what was clearly an internal conflict in the Muslim community. AIFD forged ahead with the rally regardless. We stood firm against the Islamists and their local imams. We refused to give them any right to pollute our Muslim statement against terrorism with their empty denials and insulting moral equivalencies, which detracted from our moral message by falsely invoking their Islamist message of so-called American terrorism in such places as Iraq, Afghanistan, and Israel. The local leadership of imams and their Islamist choir preferred to remain united behind an empty generic statement against "all forms of terrorism" rather than make a clear moral statement for the world to hear against all Muslim-inspired terrorism, something I will cover more in depth later on in the book.

The event got some pushback both from Muslims locally and nationwide. CAIR, unsurprisingly, made a point of singling me out for criticism, as though trying to unite Muslims against Islamist terrorism was a threat to the American Muslim community at large. Did they think it was somehow better to pretend, as they did, that the Islamists did not exist? CAIR, simply, was hatched from the Islamic Association for Palestine in the mid-1990s. It is one of a number of American Muslim groups of Islamists that sprouted from the ideas of political Islam as embodied in the teachings and platform of the Muslim Brotherhood. The ideas of any anti-Islamist movement threaten their very power structure, and the ideology from which they derive fuel. They were so enraged by the success of the event that the hate speech against my work spiked on almost every front, including a major half-page cartoon in the local Islamist rag, the *Muslim Voice*, portraying me as a dog at the end of a leash held by the staff of *The Arizona Republic*. Needless to say, the use of the word "dog" ("*kelb*" in Arabic) is a vicious statement of hate. Our own mosque leadership in Scottsdale removed the paper, chagrined by the defamatory tactics against our work and a respected member of their community. However, within a month, the paper (with no other Muslim competition in the Phoenix Valley) soon returned, as if nothing had happened, distributed to every mosque in the area.

CAIR-AZ, in fact, did everything it could to subvert the rally in the months leading up to it, only to make a play forty-eight hours before the event, insisting that they wanted to participate and give an antiterror speech. Our board decided that it would be hypocritical to allow CAIR representation when they had spent months siding against the rally, with the local leading imams who insisted upon making the rally about Israel and U.S. policy rather than about a clear moral statement of Muslims against terrorism. Per routine, they wanted to take a statement of moral courage and render it useless with geopolitics and conspiracy-laden moral equivalencies.

Hamas came out of the Muslim Brotherhood (MB) in the Middle East and thus shared its vision of political Islam and its goal in government. In fact, the Holy Land Foundation (HLF) trial, which convicted five board members of financing terror through Hamas, laid all of this out with no objections to the evidence introduced by the Department of Justice. The evidence, publicly available, documented an organizational meeting in Philadelphia in 1991 of the founders of the MB movement in the United States with the organizations they viewed as their progenitors, unindicted coconspirators to the trial: CAIR, the Islamic Society of North America (ISNA), and a host of other organizations and individuals. When you are propped up with such blood

13

money and apologetic ideologies, anyone who brings attention to that fact is definitely not considered a friend. While they continue to deflect public identification as a Muslim Brotherhood legacy group, their silence about the core ideals of the MB as well as their own obvious platform of political Islam speaks volumes. But in a way my battles with such groups had just begun, and I would soon learn just how far their tentacles spread.

As an American Muslim who loves his country, for me 9/11 raised questions that were not common for the average American. While before 9/11 there were people who had inquired curiously about my religion and how it perhaps made me "different," I never had to contend with the question: Why did Muslims do this to us? For many Americans the word "Muslim" began to take on a dangerous connotation after 9/11.

President George W. Bush certainly tried to quell such fears when he referred to the 9/11 terrorists as figures who had twisted "a great and peaceful religion," but such good intentions on his part still left many unanswered questions for many Americans about Islam. Others in the American political community followed Bush's lead, and there were those in the American Muslim community as well, including such high-profile figures as Muhammad Ali, who tried to make it clear that the acts of the nineteen hijackers did not reflect the teachings of true Islam. Platitudes, however, did not answer many Americans' basic concerns. If the nineteen hijackers on 9/11 did not reflect true Islam, some asked, then how is it that they came to commit such horrific acts? From where did they get the idea that their final, murderous acts somehow reflected the teachings of our scripture, the Qur'an? Many, many books have attempted to answer that question. Some take the stance that the 9/11 terrorists, and others before and after who have committed terrorist acts in the name of God ("Allah" in Arabic), have taken their orders directly from the Qur'an, that all the violent verses are there that can be interpreted in such a way as to inspire extremism. Some books and commentators have even taken the stance that there is no such thing as a "moderate Muslim" (a term I have never liked, since it means something different to everyone), that Islam's true nature is violently opposed to the "infidel," and that history easily backs this up. For them there is no real difference between Islam and Islamism, which essentially holds that Islam is not only a personal faith, a religion, but also a societal political system, and calls for Islamic states across the world with Islamic hegemony among them to unite into a new or a neo-Caliphate-like system.

Some of the books have been more balanced in their approach, and clearly differentiate between the majority of Muslims worldwide who peacefully practice their religion and the minority of radical Muslims. At the same time, most of these post-9/11 books have one thing in common: they're written by non-Muslims. While I can deeply respect the scholarship of someone like Bernard Lewis or the journalistic integrity of investigative reporter Steven Emerson (of the Investigative Project on Terrorism) or Daniel Pipes (of the Middle East Forum), there is at the same time the need to hear from traditional American Muslims, particularly those of us who embrace not only our religion but our country as well, and see no conflict whatsoever between the practice of Islam and our great respect and love for the United States Constitution and all the attendant rights and liberty one has as an American citizen. For Muslims like my parents, who immigrated to America from Syria in the latter half of the twentieth century, their hopes and dreams were no less great than those of immigrants who arrived generations earlier. The Statue of Liberty makes many of us American Muslims misty-eyed, and we raise the flag on national holidays and feel a surge of pride when the national anthem is played.

Still, ten years after 9/11, the question remains for some Americans and others around the world, sometimes unspoken, when it comes to those identified as Muslim Americans, "What kind of Muslim are you? The 'good' kind or the 'bad' kind?" While I certainly feel that the 9/11 terrorists committed acts that did not reflect true Islam, I can understand why such questions remain for many Americans about the real nature of Islam. Theirs may not be "my Islam," but it is a deep denial from Muslims who refuse to acknowledge that it is "an Islam." The truth is that while America is a multicultural melting pot, it is also still a predominantly Christian country. Those who are raised Christians are not generally taught the tenets of Islam any more than I was schooled in the New Testament while being raised a Muslim in Wisconsin. In less volatile times, this would not likely be an issue, but 9/11 put Islam under a spotlight and raised that question for many people, "Can a good Muslim be a good American as well?" and once again that very common question, "How can people who claim to practice the same religion have such radically different takes on it?" The same might be asked of Christians, Jews, Buddhists, and others. Different interpretations of religious beliefs are the norm, not the exception. In my eleven years of service in the U.S. Navy, not once did I feel a conflict between my orthodox practice of Islam and my service as a naval officer.

Still, it remains incumbent upon us in the American Muslim community to answer that question for our fellow Americans, "Is Islam compatible with the concepts of the U.S. Constitution, of liberty and human rights?" The short answer is "yes," and the longer answer to that question is why this book has come to be.

I am not simply an American Muslim, but a conservative with some libertarian leanings and someone who studied existentialism (along with medicine) and lives by Plato's credo that "the unexamined life is not worth living." As you will see, such belief systems are not in conflict with "my Islam," but actually in harmony with it. You will also, I hope, come to understand how political Islam and Islamists, as its adherents are more commonly known, run directly counter to the true teachings of Islam. More to the point, I want America and the world at large to understand why violence and extremism are only part of the problem we face in relation to radical Islam. The bigger problem is Islamism, a belief system that holds Islam superior to all other world religions and political systems and seeks for it to dominate the world. While many religions have suffered from supremacist thinking through the ages, the difference is the real and present danger Islamism in its most violent form currently poses to world stability. Islamists, however, are often not violent, and one of the greatest threats they pose comes in a deceptively innocuous form in which they seek to establish shariah law as a separate legal system for Muslims in the West. This is every bit as dangerous as terrorism, in its own way, because separatism is part of what drives a true Islamist. Islamism must be defeated because it is completely at odds with Western secular values of liberty and separation of church and state, most specifically our Establishment Clause that no one religion can hold sway over government and become a ruling force for the public.

I have always been particularly attracted to Jeffersonian principles of democracy, as embodied in his first inaugural speech from 1801. This vision of government's responsibility to its citizens and the essential equality of all mankind was part of what originally inspired both my grandparents and my parents to seek a better life in America. It also clearly establishes that government must be free of any religious partiality and that states' rights must be respected, in line with the philosophy that the "government is best which governs least." For the Islamists, of course, all these points are moot, since for them Islam must rule over all, whether insidiously or in the most totalitarian way imaginable. We underestimate this threat at our peril.

As a doctor, it is my responsibility not only to tend to the needs of my patients, but to respond if I see a stranger in life-threatening physical distress, arresting or "coding" as it is known in medical parlance. To that same extent, I have had to respond to the accelerating and impending "coding" that I see happening to my religion because of the Islamists. There is a malignancy in such a politicized, radicalized version of Islam that threatens not only all free-thinking Muslims but the world at large. It will not do, as some in the world community think, to simply try to eliminate this threat through arrests or a declared war on the tactic of terrorism. We must get to the root causes, the poisonous thinking that allows one to think that one's religion must dominate above all others at all costs, where balanced thinking on such matters is dismissed as a compromise with the infidel. Radicals and militants do not become so overnight. There is a common pathway, an ideology that leads them down a conveyor belt of radicalization. That common path is political Islam. Some end up as militants believing that the ends justify any means, but most continue through lawful means of advancing their global vision of pan-Islamism. Sadly, over ten years after 9/11 our public focus generally remains on "violent extremism," a generic, meaningless term, rather than on the treatable ideology that only Muslims can reform: Islamism.

The Islam I was taught was full of balance, first in its insistence on man's free will, his ability to accept or reject faith in God, and all the consequences that went with such a decision. Beyond that, the Islam I learned from my parents and grandparents, and others in my Islamic community, taught me respect for everyone: for my elders, for those of different religious beliefs (or no religious belief at all), for women, and for the laws of my country. Long before I could ever understand the history and exegesis of our scripture, or the existence of "other Islams," the Islam I held in the depths of my soul taught me to have compassion, to be mindful of the less fortunate, who are my equal, and to reach out to them because their needs are more important than my own.

For me, there was never any inherent contradiction between my obligations to my religion and my duties to the country that had allowed me the freedom to worship in the way I chose. On the contrary, if anything, I owe the United States a profound debt of gratitude and service for all the rights and blessings it has bestowed upon me and my family. In that sense, I see myself as an American first, a Muslim second. This in no way ascribes an inferior status to my religion and most definitely not to God, but puts faith in the proper community context that our Founding Fathers intended. The point for Jefferson, Washington, Adams, Franklin, Madison, and the others was that one's religious beliefs were one's own business, but that they had to come to consensus on the rights, freedoms, and laws that applied to all citizens, regardless of their religion.

For Islamists, the thinking is reversed: Islam comes before all else, and everything should be done to make this religion the dominant one in the world and for laws to be based not on secular agreement but purely on shariah ("the way to the watering hole," or Islamic jurisprudence). The goal is not liberty or democracy but some form of theocracy. To understand clearly what such a society might look like, think of Saudi Arabia or Iran, where the rights of man are second to very narrow religious dogma, where women are second-class citizens with few or no rights, and where punishments tend to be extremely brutal—beheadings, cutting off limbs, stonings, and so on—because of their reliance on fourteen-hundred-year-old religious laws. Many Islamists who profess moderation will try to say that those societies "just screwed up the implementation of shariah and if done right it can be like the United States if not better." They are missing the essence of why the United States remains the most successful economic and humanitarian society in the history of mankind—as a result of our Constitution and its Establishment Clause—and why Islamist societies have always and will always be failures when it comes to the rights of the individual and the vibrancy of their communities.

The problem with the Islamists is that they are not an idle threat. They are very determined and extremely well funded, thanks in large part to Saudi and Gulf State oil money. Make no mistake about it, we are no less at risk from the Islamists now than we were on 9/11. In fact, in many ways we are more at risk, because the threat is not merely of violent acts of terrorism, but also of devious and well-orchestrated domestic and global plans to force American isolationism and supplant American values of freedom and human rights. If the Islamists have their way, the United States will find itself with a nation within a nation, one governed by the precepts of the U.S. Constitution, the other under the sway of shariah. More important, abroad, if the Islamists have their way, U.S. power (soft and hard) will wither and the fifty-seven states of the Organization of the Islamic Cooperation (OIC) will flourish vis-à-vis Islamic states. We already see this materializing before our eyes in the wake of the Arab Spring. It remains incredible that the West challenged the entire existence of the OIC as a faith-based bloc of nations, a neo-Caliphate, in a postmodern world.

One must clearly understand that terrorism is merely a tactic for the Islamists, that their overall goal is the spread of their ideas throughout the world, and that they are mounting a propaganda war worthy of the Nazis or the Soviets. Those of us who love our country as well as Islam must be heard above the noise these dangerous men and women are making, for they threaten the United

States and the world as well as those of us who wish to practice Islam with the sort of freedom that is still largely unknown in most countries of the Middle East. This conflict has always been eminently clear to me, but as I have traveled across the nation speaking on this issue to hundreds of groups, I have realized that the very essence of this conflict is rather nuanced to most, whether Muslim or non-Muslim.

Over and beyond the threat of Islamism to national security, it is important for Americans and the world to understand that one of the things needed to defeat Islamism is nothing less than a Muslim reformation. We Muslims must take action to modernize our interpretation of Islam and bring it into harmony with liberty so that the more antiquated aspects of shariah law, such as cutting off the hand of someone who robs, ascribing second-class status to women, or killing those who leave Islam, become things of the past. In addition, we must turn away from the narrow Wahhabi practices of Islam, with its anti-Semitic, anti-Christian, and anti-freedom agenda, and its tendency to misinterpret Qur'anic verses to support a supremacist position. Instead, we must examine the Qur'an more closely, as it gives all the necessary guidelines for practicing one's faith, as well as respecting others' religious beliefs without necessitating any interference in government. As we will see, the verses that the Islamists use to justify their anti-Christian and anti-Semitic stances have been twisted to suit their own agenda. In line with all this, the real threat to Islam is not external but internal, and it is embodied by the extremists who preach hate and violence in the name of God (Allah).

In many countries in the Middle East, merely stating these things would be enough to get me killed, and even in America and Europe such a position puts me at risk, as the fatwas (religious legal opinions that sometimes translate into death sentences) on those who have challenged the Islamists have shown.

21

However, if we in the so-called Muslim world are not willing to speak out, particularly those of us in America who have the luxury of liberty, then how will the Islamists ever be defeated? They will not. In fact, without liberty-loving, devout Muslims' taking on the Islamists about the essence of Islam, they will never be defeated. The time to take such a stand is now, and for the sake of my children, and my children's children, I can hope for no greater legacy than one that clearly shows them how their religion and freedom work hand in hand.

PART I

MUSLIM IN AMERICA

1

AMERICAN PATRIOTS FROM SYRIA

After World War II, it looked as if freedom had finally come to Syria. All of a sudden independent and no longer under French control in 1946, Syria apparently would finally be free of foreign influence. What Syrians did not count on was the slide into massive corruption, fights for power, and military coups that would become the norm.

My grandfather Zuhdi Al-Jasser was one of the community leaders after the war who believed ardently in his country's ability to become free and prosperous. At the time, he earned his living primarily as CEO of a prominent vegetable-oil company he owned, but he was also heavily involved in Syrian politics. With the end of French colonial control, he saw the possibility that Syria might at last know freedom and democracy. Before the French, Syria was subjugated for several centuries by the Turks as part of the Ottoman Empire, a brutal regime that came to a close after World War I, at which time the Syrians hoped for independence, only to be taken over shortly thereafter by the French. So, after France relinquished control of Syria, the country in the late 1940s formed a functional parliament in a Western-style democracy. My grandfather's hopes grew that his own vision, and that of so many modern Syrian intellectuals, of a free Syria might actually come to be. Influenced greatly by Western ideals of freedom, his dream for Syria was that along with political modernization and liberal democratic ideals, economic, technical, intellectual, and industrial progress might follow, as it did in the West.

My grandfather's greatest contribution to the dream of a Syrian democracy was made through his pen. He began to write regularly for a major Syrian newspaper, *Al Nazir*, during the late forties and fifties, making his political opinions as a freedom-loving Syrian readily known. He was also active in the People's Party (*Hizb al-Shaab*) but later broke off from it when it was hijacked. He eventually had to write most of his work under the pseudonym *Kareem* ("generous and the truth"), as he took the prevailing political leadership to task for its sacrifice of principles of democracy and freedom. While most Syrians probably knew that Kareem was Zuhdi Jasser, his reputation and political status in Syria made it difficult for the thugs of the month in the Syrian regimes to do much about him other than exact recurrent periods of imprisonment, most often at home under house arrest. That degree of separation allowed his ideas to have more impact than tagging them to his own political identity. He and our family paid a heavy price for those ideas.

From a prominent, well-respected family in Aleppo, my grandfather was a respected businessman, devout Muslim, intellectual, politician, and journalist. He believed in a philosophy that on the one hand embraced his Islamic faith and on the other called for the sort of freedom and rights known in the United States and much of Western Europe. His admiration of Western-style governments ultimately influenced my father, Mohamed Kais Jasser, who went on to undergraduate study at London University around 1960 in part because of his own deep admiration for British government. Both my grandfather and my father were fond of Churchill's famous statement "It has been said that democracy is the worst form of government except for all the others that have been tried." Little did my grandfather know that his own quest for justice and liberty would eventually and unjustly cost him his freedom. The People's Party and ultimately most political blocs in Syria would descend into military rule, corruption, and tribalism.

Genuine parliaments and democratic rule in Syria were a fleeting apparition for my grandfather and his colleagues of the late 1940s and early 1950s. I recall my father telling me how my grandfather, or "Juddo" as I'd affectionately call him in Arabic, lamented over experiencing those refreshing few years of successful democratic growth and a burgeoning parliament only to see early Syrian presidents replaced in military coups and the government descend into tribal power struggles, rather than the rule of law that he and others had worked so hard to see implemented. The first few years of independent governance with Presidents Shukri al-Quwatly and then Husni Al-Zaim were authoritarian and military-controlled. But then Hashim al-Atassi, a friend of my grandfather's originally from Homs but close to many intellectuals from Aleppo, tried to plant the seeds of a parliamentary democracy. He created bulwarks against military control, gave women the vote, and began implementing true civilian democratic reforms. But this progress was fleeting, since the military could not be controlled. Colonel Adib Shishakly seized power in another military coup in 1951 and abolished all parties by 1952, declaring martial law. There were efforts to restore democratic constitutional governance, but by 1957, the pro-Western democrats had been pushed out by far left socialists and Ba'athists bolstered by Soviet influence and the emerging cooperation with Gamal Abdel Nasser, the strongman of Egypt. Syria was turned over to a union with Nasser from 1957 to 1962. My grandfather and our family protested this in every way possible. My grandfather found himself in and out of house arrest as he wrote his columns for democratic change against the icons of Ba'ath Party and socialist authoritarianism. But then the Ba'athists withdrew from Nasser's union and followed that with a violent coup on the streets of Syria as they cleansed any hope for moderation from their ranks and from the citizenry. The Syrian Ba'athists consolidated control in late 1963. Urban unrest worsened, and my grandfather and grandmother had to leave Syria once the ascent of the socialist Arab nationalist Ba'athists became a fait accompli. Soon thereafter occurred a massacre of thousands, in the ill-fated town of Hama, Syria, in 1964 (unfortunately followed by another more publicized massacre in 1982). Syria deteriorated, with coup after countercoup. All those military coups hijacked the aspirations of free-thinking Syrians. Syria's opportunity for democracy, the vacuum left behind after French withdrawal, was squandered by a complete inability of the Syrian people to check their military and its ascendant populist, socialist, pan-Arabist ideologies. My father's family intellectually fought against the ideas of Ba'athism and pan-Arabist Nasserism, which anesthetized so many Syrians to the vicious autocracy that would embody Syrian Ba'athists and Nasserists. But it was all to no avail. Minority gangs of thugs inside and outside the military and the political apparatuses of Syria ended up vying for control in a rat race of cycles for decades until the Ba'athists consolidated power in the 1960s. Governmental, political, and military leadership in Syria changed more frequently than the dirty water of a hookah pipe at the corner hookah lounge for over twenty years until the most oppressive and evil despot of them all, Hafez Assad, took over in 1970.

These decades of political and military chaos left the majority of Syrian citizens, a generally diverse, vibrant, moral community of intellectual democrats like my grandfather, struggling futilely against insurmountable odds.

Many pundits today seem to have forgotten the fact that the

postcolonial Middle East of the 1940s, fifties, and sixties was so chaotic, with at times monthly if not quarterly turnover of governments like that of Syria (three presidents in 1949 alone) due to an inability of the intellectual and moderate class of citizens to check the power and corruption of the military and its political accomplices. As Syria became overrun by military rule and despots, my grandfather turned from participatory and constructive political activism within Syria's fleeting democracy to being a leading voice for the opposition against the military and political despots and autocrats of the day. As he wrote his columns under his pseudonym he tried to expose the oppressive socialists and fascists who were destroying Syria. In return the government ultimately stole his businesses and property, "nationalizing" them, and tried to silence his pen and all those of others like him. He never acquiesced. Due to the financial pressures, my father had to return from study at London University to finish both his undergraduate studies and then medical school in Damascus.

In the United States, and in many countries of Western Europe, his columns would not have been considered radical. They proposed that Syria now had the chance to be a free and prosperous democracy and should take advantage of the opportunity. Such a view grew increasingly popular, and as he continued his commentaries on the political scene and his concern that tribal factions were gaining increasing power, his popularity as a writer grew.

However, the economic progress Syria had begun to make reached a standstill, and the succession of military governments began to take away more and more rights from the citizens. When able and not under arrest, my grandfather expressed the ideas of the majority of Syrians who were oppressed by the thuggish minority.

The Ba'ath Party took power in the early 1960s, and it was the final nail in the coffin of liberty for Syrians. With the Ba'athists, the rule of totalitarian socialism solidified in Syria, and became ossified under Hafez Assad and his fascist reign. As the Ba'athists consolidated their power, they took over all private businesses, including my grandfather's property, and finally put an end to his writing and his newspaper.

It was this struggle of honest Syrians against the forces of oppression and evil, and against the fascist gangs in power within the Syrian military, that drove my father and grandfather to instill in me at a very early age an intense love for the American military. They taught me that one of the cornerstones of American stability, and the success of American liberty that they so admired, is the moral and representative nature of the American military officers and enlisted ranks. I remember my grandfather and father frequently discussing the fact that the American military was a genuine cross-section of a moral American citizenry. They taught me that the U.S. Constitution would be meaningless were it not protected by a population that not only believed in the rule of law but believed that the military should always defer to the control and direction of the civilian government. It was this legal and cultural subservience of the military to the civilian political power structure that my family dreamed of for Syria and never saw come to be in their lifetimes.

This passionate attachment to the American military structure and associated national fealty drove me to seek a military scholarship for my education. I remember my father telling me how much pride he had in the honor of the American generals and admirals who loved their nation to the point that they gave an undying loyalty to the American legal system and their elected civilian government, regardless of its current political persuasion, serving at the pleasure of the American citizens and our government, no questions asked. That spirit and culture protected Americans from ever seeing their freedoms vanish at the hands of the military, as happened in Syria over and over and over again.

I must add that my family's description of how the completely unarmed and untrained Syrian citizenry provided a green light for the generally bloodless coups that were the mainstay for the Syria of the 1940s, fifties, and sixties was always a central reason for my passionate belief in the Second Amendment to our U.S. Constitution, and the right to bear arms.

Fast-forward to 2011. Many shortsighted pundits lamented the beginning of a new era of so-called instability due to the rather heroic uprisings of the citizens of so many of the Middle Eastern nations against their despotic governments. The so-called stability in the Middle East of the late twentieth century was an unbelievable façade that masked deep, festering pathologies. Beginning with Tunisia in December 2010 and Egypt in January 2011, continuing with Libya, Yemen, Bahrain, and Syria, the Arab uprisings and revolutions of 2011 finally manifested citizenries that were taking back ownership of their own government and resisting the inhuman oppression of the military rule by which they were enslaved. My grandfather used to tell my father that despite how much suffering the people of Syria endured over decades, at the end of the day, as the French philosopher Joseph de Maistre observed, "Every nation has the government it deserves." A harsh statement, but the courage of the Syrian people in 2011 suggests that they have finally stepped forward to change their own condition. I so wish my grandfather and father had been alive in 2011 to see the unbelievable awakening of the courage the people of their motherland, Syria, demonstrated month after month against the military thugs who shot them in the streets in cold blood simply because they chose to demonstrate against their own government. Thousands upon thousands died and more were tortured and displaced in 2011 after over forty years of oppression by the

Assads. The Bashar Assad regime, like that of his father, Hafez, looked upon the Syrian people as subhuman slaves who deserved the boots and bullets of their military, until they were tortured into silence. The Assad family and its rule deserve a place in history right next to Stalin, Hitler, and Pol Pot.

In 2011, the Syrian people finally decided to pay the ultimate price for their legacy, for their children—in a revolution attempting to change their miserable condition. We will look at the so-called Arab Spring of 2011 in much greater detail later on, but for now, let's return to the mid-twentieth century, when my grandfather and father found themselves mired in a very repressive Syria.

For my grandfather and his family, life in Syria became intolerable. The freedom and democracy he dreamed of for his country seemed like a distant illusion, and his own life became a daily struggle for survival. My mother's parents and her family in Damascus were just as devastated by the absence of freedoms, though they were generally left alone since they were not politically active. My mother was also from a well-respected intellectual family in Damascus. Her father, Subhi Sabbagh, visited us in Wisconsin a few times in my youth and was a shariah family court judge who ultimately became the head of the Supreme Court of Syria from 1975 to 1985.

My grandparents and their other two children left for Beirut in 1963 while my father completed his medical studies and my mother completed her pharmacy studies in Damascus. My parents met around this time and were soon married. They also eventually left Syria for Beirut (on the day that my father was scheduled to graduate from medical school in 1966). While he worked as an intern at a hospital in Beirut and made plans to emigrate to America with my mother, my grandfather was then working for one of the more progressive newspapers in Beirut. My grandfather by this time had given up trying to reform Syria directly and now tried to do so from the outside, but his work on the newspaper was very much in line with his belief in trying to change the corrupt, totalitarian governments that were more the norm than the exception in this part of the world.

At the same time, my father and mother finally got their visas to go to the United States. They left Beirut in 1967, and my father's parents followed them a few years later. For all four of them, from the very first moment they stepped onto U.S. soil, they were patriots. America was everything that Syria was not: free, prosperous, and overflowing with opportunities, regardless of one's faith or national origin.

I was born in Canton, Ohio, in late 1967, soon after my parents' arrival here. Shortly thereafter, we relocated to New Orleans, where my father finished his medical training and my mother her master's in pharmacology at Tulane. After that, we settled in the small town of Appleton, Wisconsin, where my dad joined a private practice. My grandfather joined us there and spent quite a bit of time with me, and I could always tell he loved me dearly. He talked to me often about their days in Syria, his dreams for his country's freedom, and how the United States ultimately came to fulfill for him the dreams that Syria could not. While he held out the hope that Syria might someday become a free and prosperous nation, he was realistic enough to know that it would not likely happen in his lifetime.

From my grandfather, whom I remember in my youth poring over the telex machine in his basement in Appleton, I learned just how powerful words are, that the quest for freedom can sometimes cost you your liberty, and I developed an enormous appreciation for the gifts my country offers. He also taught me the value of faith, for during all his political struggles, and even after losing everything he had worked for all his life, my Grandfather

Zuhdi never lost his faith in God. His belief in God's ultimate mercy and benevolence was borne out for him by the fact that he and his family were able to have the life in the United States that they couldn't have in Syria.

My family's story, of course, is not unique. In fact, the number of Syrian expatriates worldwide today is greater than the current population of Syria. In many Arab countries similar struggles have been repeated over and over again through the years. Few Americans are aware of just how great the struggle for freedom was among countries in the Middle East during the twentieth century and just how great the Arab people's disappointment has been to see repeated coups and corrupt leaders and thuggish militaries whose thievery, deceit, and oppression have resulted in the lack of any real economic or political progress. Many Arabs have come to the United States in search of the freedom and prosperity that was largely unknown in their own countries. They also came here to escape the kind of genocide practiced by Assad, such as the massacre in Hama back in February 1982, in which almost forty thousand innocent Syrians were killed by their own government and military in just a few weeks. I remember my father lamenting, in tears, as we lived comfortably in Neenah, Wisconsin, that the genocide of Syrians in Hama was covered in but a few pathetic paragraphs in the back of *Newsweek*. He asked me, where was the moral outrage of the freest nation on earth?

The problem often is that once the original generation settles in and is able to achieve the dream of freedom and prosperity in the United States, it is not uncommon for the next generation and succeeding ones to take such benefits for granted. I can definitely say that was not the case with my family. My grandfather and my parents always made it very clear that we had much to be grateful for, for a way of life that was really possible only in the United States. Here, said my grandfather, you are free to be as Muslim as you want to be, or to practice any other faith. By that, he meant that you had freedom to worship in the way you wanted, that unlike in Syria, where you were classified as a Sunni or a Shia Muslim, or an Alawite, or Druze, and so forth, here in the United States, you were an American first and a Muslim second.

It struck my grandfather as very ironic that he should have more freedom to practice his faith in the United States than in Syria, which is a predominantly Muslim country. Never take such a thing for granted, he emphasized to us, for it is why so many millions of people from around the world seek a new life in America. He added that Americans are so used to freedom, they often do take it for granted, like oxygen, but that we should never become so complacent. I remember learning from my parents and grandparents something we mentioned every year during Ramadan: that our daily fasts from sunrise to sunset, our prayers five times a day, our choice of *zakat* (charity), our choice of community, and our assembly inside and outside the mosque were more purely Islamic and closer to God in Wisconsin than they had ever been growing up in Syria. To them, while the ethnic and cultural atmosphere of Syria felt more Muslim, the subtle and overt coercive forces there made for a far less pure belief and a far less genuine relationship with God. That reality of personal faith can be felt by free people, as we are as Americans.

Though my grandfather passed away when I was nine years old, he was very much with me in spirit when I joined the Navy to serve my country, and years later when 9/11 happened. The spirit of liberty and of Islam I had learned from his example, my father, and other Islamic teachers had everything to do with freedom, respect, and doing the right thing, not the barbarism, intolerance, and evil embodied by the Assads or those nineteen terrorists on September 11. There were those who criticized President Bush's statement at the time, "Freedom was attacked today," but for those of us whose families have truly known what it is like not to be free, the statement resonated. My grandfather would have understood exactly what the president was talking about, for he knew all too well how totalitarianism in all of its forms, secular and theocratic, worked in the Middle East, and would have likely seen the Islamists as having sprung from the same sort of fascist seeds as secular nationalist dictators like Assad and Saddam Hussein. My grandfather would have been able to explain that, unfortunately, the rise of secular, corrupt, and oppressive dictatorships like Assad's and the resulting disenchantment of the people became a fertile ground for Islamist supremacists to grow a following. He could have told President Bush and the rest of the nation that his journey to the United States had everything to do with fulfilling a dream of religious and political liberty that neither the Islamists nor the dictators respect. In addition, my grandfather might have been able to say to his fellow U.S. citizens, "Please understand that as terrible as these attacks have been, and all the loss of life, it is only a small taste of just how bad things can get if the Islamists are not stopped. You must understand that just as a fanatic like Saddam Hussein had to be stopped in Kuwait before he could invade Saudi Arabia, these Islamists are no less determined, and because they do not have a formal army they can sometimes be even harder to recognize. You must begin to see that this is part of a worldwide pattern designed to completely destabilize the West and to force Islamic states upon the world."

My grandfather would have been able to say these things because he knew that fascism is fascism, whether it comes in the form of a politician or of a religious leader. Our struggle today and that of my grandfather in the middle of the twentieth century are the same—for liberty, but against different forces at different stages of maturation. When armed guards are stationed around your house so that you cannot distribute your columns about freedom, when the government muftis insist that only their vision of Islam is valid—and compare Christians and Jews to apes and pigs—and when such political and religious oppression becomes the norm throughout many countries in the Middle East, one who survives such a system develops a very fine appreciation for freedom and open-mindedness and an incredible disdain for and resistance to tyranny. That was definitely the case with my grandfather.

Many Americans can take liberty for granted because they are used to having it. But 9/11 reminded all of us just how precious freedom and human rights are. The problem is that for many Americans that day is now part of the distant past. Many Americans now see the threat as remote at best, and concentrate on other things, like the current economic problems.

However, as difficult as our economic problems may be right now, we must not lose focus when it comes to the goals of the Islamists. We must see 9/11 for what it was: a tipping point in which the terrorists brought their war to our shores, an event that should force Americans to understand not only who the terrorists are but who is behind them and the environment in which they arose. Those terrorists are a violent offshoot of a deeper global ideological struggle between Islamism and Americanism. My grandfather and anyone else truly familiar with the overall goals of the Islamists would strongly advise Americans against being complacent about this threat, for it is exactly what the Islamists want, for us just to sit back and pretend they pose no real danger, even as they try to advance their draconian interpretations of shariah law for Muslims over secular laws and our Constitution, and even as their adherents are foiled again and again in their efforts to attack our stateside military bases, airports, and subways. My grandfather, who was overly familiar with how tenacious fanatics can be, would likely say that one must look at the record, that over eight years passed between the first attack on the World Trade Center and the second one in 2001, but that ultimately, through incredible cunning, patience, and planning, the Islamists succeeded in their goal of destroying immense symbols of U.S. power and causing enormous loss of life in the process.

In their very randomness and insinuation into the daily life of civilians, acts of terror provoke great fear among citizens. In relation to the West, the hope of the Islamists is that enough such attacks will undermine Western economies and freedoms (with draconian law changes that could allow the government to do away with standard privacy rights and law enforcement procedures) while driving them toward an isolationism that takes the ideas of liberty out of competition for hearts and minds in Muslim-majority nations. For Islamists to succeed, they must first find a way to topple the system as it stands or at the minimum remove the influence of Western ideas of freedom on Muslim-majority nations and communities.

Related to the Islamists' overall agenda, my grandfather would have probably told his fellow Americans to look not just at terrorist acts, but also at the very underhanded propaganda techniques the Islamists use and how they seek to dismantle the Western world from within, one brick at a time. This is the "Grand Deception" of Muslim Brotherhood legacy groups and their ideological ilk that Steven Emerson and others have spoken and written about extensively, which involves apparently innocuous, unrelated acts, like those of Islamist groups that insist on footbaths for Muslims in airports, or insist that Muslim men and women must have separate exercise facilities on university campuses, or the acts of Muslim cab drivers in Minnesota who refuse to transport passengers from the airport who carry liquor or pork products—all behavior that no one in my family could ever recall seeing in Syria or the Middle East. But in the West, Islamist groups push these separatist requests in order to amplify their control and incubate their ideas among Muslims under their sway. In a case I will address later, Attorney General Eric Holder's Department of Justice even had the temerity in December 2010 to file suit against an Illinois school district on behalf of a Muslim teacher, barely on the job a year, who was denied three weeks of vacation in order to make her once-in-a-lifetime hajj (pilgrimage) to Mecca at the age of twenty-eight. Never mind union contracts, or leave requirements, or the floodgates of special leaves of absence anyone can ask for in the name of religion.

Make no mistake, the Islamists want Muslims to have rights that no other religious groups have because in the long run they do not believe in the separation of religion and state. This is one of the reasons my grandfather was so focused on the necessity for public debate, where ideas can be contested, because he knew from experience that no one group should hold too much power. For the Islamists, total power is the ultimate goal. They will feign a respect for "democracy" (e.g., elections), but ultimately their path is one that seeks to change the rules of the game to an Islamocentric system rather than one centered in reason, under God, with unalienable rights for all. They want an Islamic state, but here in the United States, as in the United Kingdom, the Netherlands, and other Western countries where Muslims are a minority, the idea is to sneak shariah in a little at a time. It's akin to putting a frog into a pot of cold water on the stove, then increasing the heat a little at a time, so that before the creature knows it, it has been boiled alive.

All of us American Muslims came to the United States because our families escaped Arab fascism and prefer the American political system to political Islam, a system run by Islamists whose goals we know all too well. The first people to boil are always liberty-loving Muslims. Once they disappear, the West will be left with no allies within Muslim communities. Our Muslim allies are indispensable if the West is going to have any hope of countering Islamism and promoting liberty within the Muslim consciousness.

The essence of Islam is *not* fascism or theocracy, but free will, the right of individuals to choose their faith (or the lack thereof), not to have it imposed on them from without, or to have interpreters of the Muslim faith decide that it must rule the legislature as well. For those of us in various American Muslim communities, Islamism is a very real threat to our religion and our freedom to practice it as we want, and by its very nature it has no real respect for those of other faiths or non-Islamists within the faith.

If my grandfather were alive today, I'm sure he would be in the forefront of this fight for our liberty and basic rights, but since he is not, the best I can do as his namesake is to try to honor his legacy and carry on the work he began all those years ago in Aleppo.

In the small town of Neenah, in which I spent most of my early, formative years, the fact that I was a Muslim was generally always second to the fact that I was Zuhdi, just another Wisconsin kid. In fact, it was my name that was generally of interest to my fellow students, rather than my religion. You know how kids are. If your name is somewhat different, they're bound to make fun of it. In the era before cultural sensitivity had taken hold, this was just something that people with "foreign" names had to deal with frequently. These days, such behavior would probably earn one a reprimand for being "culturally insensitive." While I have many problems with the so-called politically correct mentality, I have to say that it is a definite plus that people are generally more accepting these days of those whose names are somewhat different or who have different cultural traditions.

At the same time, the only ones who made fun of my name were the sort who typically pick on people for any perceived differences. For my circle of close friends, my name and religious background did not make any difference. My friendships growing up reflected, even in the small town where I lived, how cultural and religious differences are so often accepted in America. My closest friends were Christian but also Jewish, Hindu, Buddhist, and atheist. What mattered was our common ground, how much we enjoyed each other's company, and that is still true today, as I continue to be friends with several of them.

My boyhood was like that of many midwestern kids in small towns. We built forts and treehouses, played with model rockets, and played all sorts of games. I remember laughing a lot and just generally having a very good time.

While I enjoyed the company of my friends, I also had my paternal grandparents close by, who had joined us shortly after we moved to Wisconsin, since they had left Syria even before my parents did. One of my fondest memories is of the time my grandfather Zuhdi spent with me as he helped me learn to ride my bike. He was very generous with both his time and his affection. He actually often seemed more affectionate to me than he was to his own son, my father, who had paved the way for him to come to the United States.

We were definitely one of the few Muslim families in our town in Wisconsin. Because there was not a mosque in our area for several years in my youth, I initially learned about my religion almost wholly from my parents and my grandparents.

One of the very first things they emphasized was that honesty and humility were paramount values, that God is very much aware of our actions and is watching us, and that to lie dishonors not only oneself, but one's family and, most important, God and his creation. My mother in particular taught me that one has two angels on one's shoulders, one who writes down the "good" things one does, the other the "bad" things. Eventually, she said to me, if the tally is in favor of good things, it will mean a better place in the afterlife, but if bad acts predominate that will result in a very undesirable position in the life that comes after this. I was also taught about the "Verse of the Chair" (*Ayatul Qursee*) from the Qur'an, how God sits metaphorically in his chair on high and watches everything and is aware of all that goes on all the time. My mother gave me as a young child a gold chain of that verse for protection, which I still wear to this day.

This acute and constant awareness of God in my life had a huge impact on me early on, as I felt even then an overpowering urge to do the right thing, not to disappoint God or my parents, to be honest, do the very best that I could in everything, and be kind to others. The Golden Rule had to be in my nature if I sought God's love and protection. My father also taught me that competition was a good thing, that it helps us be the very best we can be, and that was also in the forefront of my mind when I began school. I wanted to excel, as my parents had taught me that knowledge is power, and how we learn about the world God created, and my healthy sense of competition spurred me to want to be the very best student I could be.

At the same time, I was taught that one must choose one's faith, that it must be a conscious choice and commitment. This emphasis on self-responsibility and free will was key to me, even at an early age, because it implied on the one hand that I was free to make my own choices, but on the other that I must be aware that God is always watching. In my choices I was directly accountable not only to my parents and society but also, most important, to God.

There was never, ever any mention of *taquiyya*, the previously esoteric but now ubiquitous corrupt idea that a Muslim can lie to non-Muslims if doing so promotes the cause of Islam. The Islamists often practice *taquiyya* in the mistaken belief that their interpretation of God condones lying or deceiving if it serves Muslims' needs over the "infidel." An example of this would be claiming that shariah law and U.S. constitutional law are not in conflict with each other. The Islamist knows very well that shariah law is based on Islamic scriptural exegesis of Muslim legal scholars—religious law for Muslims only—and that alone puts it in conflict with American law, which has a secular basis in reason universal for all citizens equally. In addition, much of shariah law dates back to the eleventh, twelfth, and thirteenth centuries and very much needs to be modernized.

I mention all this because U.S. governmental traditions and history were also a very important part of my growing up, not just at school, but at home. For as long as I can remember, my parents and grandparents talked about how grateful one must be to live in a country such as the United States, where so many freedoms were guaranteed: of speech, assembly, religion, and the press. While I grew up loving God and our faith of Islam, I never had the idea that we were here to bring Islam to the West, but rather to learn about freedom and liberty and bring those American ideals into our own lives and modernize the interpretation of our faith.

As I was born in the United States, it would have been easy for me to take such things for granted had my parents and grandparents not emphasized their importance. But the mental image of my grandfather, confined to house arrest in Syria merely because his newspaper disagreed with the regime, was something I never forgot. Much of the world is like that, my family taught me, not just Syria. But here in the United States, I learned freedom is a right, not just something one dreams about.

So, for me, Islam and liberty have been conjoined for as long as I can remember. At around the same time I was being taught specific Qur'anic verses at home, I was also learning the Pledge of Allegiance, the story of our Founding Fathers, and what it meant to be an American. I remember the profound impact the Wisconsin American Legion's Constitution contest had on me when I finished in the top fifteen in the contest, which pitted high school students against one another in memorization of the U.S. Constitution. One might say that it is only natural that Muslim children learn U.S. history along with their religious beliefs, just as other children do, whether they are Christians, Jews, Buddhists, or Hindus, and are able to be Americans first and to keep their religious beliefs in perspective in relation to the wider society.

Yes, that is true, unless one is being raised in an Islamist environment where one is taught that their religion comes first, that a worldwide hegemony of Islamic states is the "Will of Allah," and that U.S. constitutional law must make way for shariah. Such children learn from an early age that their country is here to serve them and their religion, and grow up with an outrageous sense of entitlement. For the Islamist, there is really no such thing as "fellow Americans" unless fellow Americans offer a pathway toward the Islamization of America. There are Muslims and non-Muslims and eventually "infidels," and any such non-Muslims are viewed as innately inferior due to their rejection of Islam.

My Muslim upbringing taught me to respect other religions, and, in line with Qur'anic teaching, I was specifically taught to appreciate the common religious legacy of all messengers of the Word of God, such as Abraham and Jesus. This made it easy for me to feel at home with students of other faiths or those of no faith, and this respect for differences also helped me when I joined the debating team in high school. Because I had been taught that the world is full of divergent opinions and beliefs, I was able to passionately disagree with others' political positions, but at the same time respect them and their right to have a different position. The famous statement often incorrectly attributed to Voltaire, "I disapprove of what you say, but I will defend to the death your right to say it," resonated with me as a Muslim and as an American.

In many ways, life was very idyllic for me in Wisconsin. I lived in a beautiful area, had close friends, was a huge Green Bay Packers fan (and still am today, though as an Arizonan the Cardinals have grown on me), and enjoyed school as well as some of the big musical acts of the day, such as Billy Joel, U2, Peter Gabriel, and Bruce Springsteen. I also developed a very large pro-football card collection, which I have to this day. Many of the cards I collected trading with close friends or at flea markets near our home. Someday, when they can appreciate it, I look forward to showing my sons with pride Walter Payton's rookie card, which I got for pennies and which is now worth thousands of times that.

There was plenty of time to enjoy the prosperous life my parents had built for us, but at the same time there was a very serious element to our lives as well. My two sisters and I were expected to always put a premium on two things: Islam and education. Those two things were related, since the quest for knowledge was the way not only to get ahead in life, but also to understand God's world. So we excelled in school as part of honoring our commitment to God and our parents and society, very much as those of other faiths did. At the same time, we continued to receive our religious education as well. While my close friends clearly saw that we shared common family values, which was all that really mattered to them, there were some hurdles to cross when it came to some of the perceptions of others, and how they viewed Muslims.

For the most part, my family had found great acceptance from others as one of the few Muslim families in town. However, no situation is perfect, as we soon found out when we sought to change the status quo. My father encountered unexpected resistance when he and a group of other Muslims planned to build the first mosque in the Appleton and Neenah-Menasha area of Wisconsin in 1980. This was after the 444-day American hostage crisis at the U.S. Embassy in Teheran, because of which there were some Americans who were suspicious of Muslims. There were also people who plain and simple did not want a mosque in town, and, having some political muscle, they planned to do all they could to prevent its construction. While this surprised my father and his group of four other Muslim families, since they had not as a rule experienced discrimination because of their religion, they did not let such resistance discourage them from trying to reach their goal. Until the mosque was built, we had been having weekly services at a large Catholic church in Appleton, whose head priest was my father's patient, which opened its doors to our community. My father took full advantage of freedom of expression and freedom of religion and took our case to the media. Long story short, public sentiment began to tilt in favor of the mosque's being built as the story became more widely known in the larger community in northeastern Wisconsin through television and newspapers. The overriding opinion became that freedom to practice one's own religion is a basic right, and the building of the mosque proceeded.

For my father and others in his group who had been used to the government oppression in their home countries, it was an extraordinary thing, as immigrants and relatively new citizens, to be able to take on the powers that be and win without violence or lawsuits. My parents always told us that the struggle and uncertainty about Muslims were human but their victory for religious freedom was American. Upon completion of the mosque, a rather humble structure that resembled a one-story ranch home, it was a very emotional day when we were able to pray there. "Never forget this day," my father said to me. "Never forget what we accomplished here and how it is because of this country we live in that this was possible." Interestingly, I recall my mother mentioning to me that the humble nature of the mosque made it all the more spiritual, Islamic, American, and ours, unlike many other mosques in the West that were funded heavily by haughty, materialistic, autocratic tribes (such as the House of Saud) living not off their own creativity but off confiscated national property—petroleum. I recall my parents stating that even if the Saudis offered their monies out of the sky they would send it back and demand that these corrupt monarchs use it to reform their own societies and release their own people from enslavement and poverty. Little did I know what a profound impact my parents' disgust for the corruption of so many royal families in the Middle East would have upon my own empowerment later to directly take on their Islamist proxies in the United States.

I never did forget that first day at the mosque. I also never forgot what happened the time my mother tried to vote in an election in the town of Menasha and was not allowed to do so. She had taken my younger sister with her to witness her pride in voting, but when she arrived for registration, the polls were near closing and they told her that she would have to have naturalization papers in addition to her regular identification to be able to vote. She didn't understand, since natural-born citizens were not subjected to such scrutiny or to demands for their birth certificates. The officials held firm, and she was turned away from the voting booth.

Eventually, my father hired an attorney and my mother, though usually nonconfrontational, sued the town of Menasha and the state of Wisconsin in federal court after the state refused to mandate that the town change its requirements. My parents could not understand why naturalized citizens must carry papers that natural-born citizens did not. It became a landmark case for the state, which ultimately found in her favor, deciding that neither she nor anyone else should be subjected to more stringent standards regarding voting identification. My father, though he had spent just over twelve years in the United States, had a deeply passionate and lifelong understanding of "equal protection" under the law, a passion that he instilled in me and that lives on in my own passionate opposition to Islamism.

These victories taught me much as a child and adolescent, namely that our system works here in the United States, not that it's perfect, but that it does work, particularly if one takes the time and trouble to exercise and defend one's rights. In the case of the mosque, my father and his group could have given in to local resistance to building the mosque. They could have just decided, to heck with it, it's not worth it, these people are bigots. They could have become bitter over that. But they didn't. They took action, and the resistance crumbled in the face of overall public opinion, which favored fair play and freedom of religion.

When it came to the voting incident, we could have chosen to be passive. We didn't. My family stood up for what we believed, and the state sided with us. We made a difference not only for our family, but for the entire state. Foreign-born, naturalized voters would now be treated the same at the polls in the town of Menasha and the state of Wisconsin as natural-born citizens. Instead of falling into the trap of feeling that one is a perpetual victim, we stood up, and it made all the difference. One must understand that in many Arab countries standing up for one's rights can get one killed. For my grandfather, it curtailed his freedom, and eventually to live the way he wanted to, he had to leave Syria behind. My grandfather and my parents made a decision early on that they had to live somewhere where liberty was a given, and for that reason no place appealed to them more than the United States. Though they were haunted by the memories of repression in their home country, and all the mistrust and paranoia that are a part of daily life in a totalitarian regime, they decided to take it on faith that things were different in America.

This sort of liberty, these kinds of rights, were what my grandfather and his family dreamed of for Syria. To date, this has not come to be there, but at least he got to witness it in action in America. At the same time, I'm sure if he were still alive he would be appalled by some of the ways the Islamists have tried to exploit such liberty here in the United States. He would be outraged, for example, about the "flying imams" case, in which these individuals brazenly behaved strangely at an airport, audibly praying on their prayer mats in Arabic in the waiting area before a flight, once on board asking for seat belt extenders when their weight did not justify such a thing, and in general behaving in ways that could have easily been seen as inappropriate and threatening to the crew and other passengers, and then claiming discrimination when they were thrown off the flight. They later sued U.S. Airways and won, another travesty of justice that we can add to the many unjustified lawsuits initiated by CAIR. This sort of thing is not in the great American tradition of rights and liberty, but is an abuse of the system and feeds the narrative of those who say that Muslims cannot be trusted. In the Arab American and American Muslim communities, we must reject the transparent, deceitful manipulations of our justice system by groups like CAIR. The American legal system is vitally important to our freedoms, but the CAIRs of the world use it to defend the Islamist collective while liberty-minded Muslims use it to defend individual rights. We should as Muslim communities be standing up against Islamist terrorism and underhanded manipulation of our freedoms. We should applaud and champion reformists who want to modernize shariah law and bring it into the twenty-first century. We should show Americans by our actions that we believe in liberty, not in being perpetual victims.

One of the first steps in that direction will be to reject the ideology of political Islam, something that I was not even really aware existed until I reached the University of Wisconsin–Milwaukee.

2

TWO ISLAMS

I was very much unaware of political Islam until I reached the University of Wisconsin–Milwaukee as a freshman. It's not as though I didn't know about the conflicts in the Middle East between Israel and neighboring Arab countries, but until I got to college, I never knew that there were people who used the mosque and Muslims to espouse and advance their political views. It took some time, however, before I saw firsthand how this brand of fanaticism worked.

The transition to college is one of those milestone moments for any young person. In my case, it was a very exciting time as I embarked on the most independent time of my life to date and also determined my courses of study. While I knew that I wanted to go into medicine and premed (zoology) was my major, I wanted to make sure that I was fairly broad-minded in my overall course of studies, and for that reason I enrolled in the honors track with an emphasis on philosophy, specifically courses in existentialism. Many medical students opt strictly for courses in the sciences, but my religious and family background encouraged me to explore as much knowledge and as much of a liberal education as possible. My family's interest in Western thought went back to my grandfather's days in Syria, and I knew I could only benefit from learning how thinkers like Sartre, Kierkegaard, Nietzsche, Rousseau, and Voltaire influenced modern Western thought. Also, because the Islam I was taught encouraged one to embrace knowledge in general, I thought it would be important for me to have a focus beyond the sciences.

Many students struggle in their first year with being independent of their parents for the first time, very often liking certain aspects of independence and not others, and I was no different. Part of the reason I chose to attend school in Wisconsin was that I believed in remaining close to my parents. I had grown up in a traditional, conservative Muslim household, and my parents had great concern about the culture shock of my living in a dorm where a good amount of drinking and even drug use might take place. Growing up in a small town, I had managed to keep myself away from all such temptations. I hadn't even smoked a cigarette, much less pot, or drunk beer. It was not as though it was really an issue, however, as I never had an interest in such things. My father, despite being a cardiologist, was quite overweight and for some time had been a heavy smoker. This was my first indication that there might be a contradiction between what my father preached and what he lived. My father's morbid obesity and cigarette addiction, if anything, encouraged me to be diligent about taking care of myself physically and avoiding bad habits such as smoking. Beyond that, the Qur'an is very clear about the need to take care of one's physical health, and that also influenced me very heavily in the choices I made regarding my physical health.

While my parents had faith in my ability to make the right decisions about such things, they didn't think it would be good for me to be in a dorm where people who drank, used drugs, or did not share my core values might be present. Because of this, I got my own apartment off campus and learned to live independently at eighteen. I generally ate on campus, but had to learn the basics of cooking so I could make a simple meal on occasion, and also learned how to clean, do laundry, and perform other household tasks.

Then there was the whole issue of the opposite sex. While I had dated briefly in high school, I was committed to not having sex outside of marriage, as it would have gone against all my religious beliefs and instruction on the institution of marriage. Beyond that, my little experience with dating while I was in high school presented a lot of conflicts for me. For one thing, the girls I had dated were not Muslims, so while I had feelings for them, I couldn't be really committed because I had decided that my future wife must share my religion. While Islam permitted me to marry from among "people of the Book," which included Jews and Christians, I believed this to be for the best, in terms of overall common ground in a marriage. So, even as a teenager, I had problems with the idea that I was taking advantage of someone's feelings in a way, even if that was not my intention, since I knew no serious commitment was involved. It made me determined not to repeat the same mistake in college.

I knew the external pressures to date would probably only increase, since, if anything, there were even more couples on a college campus, and it was no secret that sex was more the norm than the exception. Despite that, I didn't even date in college. I think I knew that the best way to stay away from temptation was not to invite it in, so the most I would do was attend an occasional night out with my clique of college friends who "dragged" me to the clubs near campus. I did have a good time dancing, joking around, and being the "token" Muslim designated driver. Trust me, I was no Travolta on the dance floor, which was just as well, since it probably decreased the likelihood of my getting into any mischief.

One thing I really had to consider while away at college was where to worship. The University of Wisconsin–Milwaukee in the late 1980s was not exactly the capital of multiculturalism. However, it turned out that there were a few small groups of Muslim students at the university, and that the school and some Muslim students had set aside a loft that we could use as a gathering place for prayer (a sort of makeshift mosque). I ended up gravitating toward the students who were of Malaysian and Indonesian origin as it seemed to me their gatherings and camaraderie were more about the spiritual aspects of Islam and our holy days than about geopolitics or Muslim identity politics. My forays with Muslims of Arab origin dominated by Palestinian students were less successful, since I was repelled by their obsession with political movements, anti-Semitism, and foreign policy. I could understand neither their political orientation nor their religious literalism. Despite initially engaging them, I ended up distancing myself spiritually from not only the Arab Muslim cliques but the Islamists and their Muslim Students' Association (MSA).

But my other Muslim friends were more than welcoming, and I never felt judged for my politics or my religious opinions. As we gathered on the weekends and, when our class schedule allowed, nightly for meals in our month of fasting in Ramadan, it was a time that this group of Muslims set aside differences and remembered God and our frailty. I remember nightly Taraweeh prayers that a few of the students led and read our Qur'anic recitations nightly from cover to cover once through by the end of the month. I'd race home from the library or our college newspaper's offices to join them when I could at sunset and break our fast from all food and water together. At times, since sunset was after 7:30 p.m., the student cafeterias were closed—a stark reminder that very few non-Muslims knew it was our holy month of daily fasting and nightly meals. So if I had to eat in the cafeteria, I'd strike a deal with a cook to set aside some food for me to heat up at sunset. And on the weekends I ate with my Malaysian and

Indonesian friends together in the makeshift mosque that we shared. This meant that I not only had a regular place to worship, but was also able to connect with other Muslim students. Often on the way back to my apartment I'd stop and do my daily prayers in our "mosque" with the group rather than alone at home. While I was able to easily form friendships with non-Muslim students as well, it was good to find other students with whom I had common religious and spiritual ground.

Politics played no part in the small mosque at the school. We were not there to discuss such issues, but to pray, and discussions typically centered on specific religious and spiritual concerns and challenges. This was exactly as it had been for me back home, so there was a great deal of comfort for me in having a similar experience at school.

In addition, my social circle expanded beyond the members of my mosque as I got to know other students in various classes. The honors program I was in allowed me to take some small, specialized classes, and I very much enjoyed the courses I took in existentialism. This led to lots of interesting discussions both in and out of class about Kant, Nietzsche, Sartre, Camus, and so on, and rather than conflicting with my Muslim beliefs, the conversations actually remarkably complemented them. While many people might believe that such philosophies were not the province of a traditional, conservative Muslim, the real common ground was that I was taught as a child that I had free will, and could choose whether to believe in God and to follow the teachings of the Prophet Muhammad. While I was taught that there were dire personal consequences with God for not having faith, I was at the same time taught that it was a choice or else it would not be faith. So, in actuality, existentialism, and the concept of man having to search for his own meaning in life, fit very well with what I had been taught as a child. All around, with my circle of fellow worshippers, and my mind challenged by courses in philosophy and the sciences, I found college a very rewarding and stimulating experience.

It was not until I left the campus to seek out a larger mosque at the suggestion of my mother that everything changed. The imam at the Islamic Society of Milwaukee was a young man in his thirties, and the mosque was led by a number of well-known Muslim leaders in the Milwaukee Muslim community. But the imam, whose ideas must have reflected the sentiment of many who sat respectfully week after week listening to him, was no spiritual leader. He was a political leader. One who made me ill. Within two Fridays, I became incensed at his vitriol and obsession with attacking American foreign and domestic policy. But even had he said something with which I agreed, I was deeply offended that I had taken time from my studies and classwork and left campus to come and listen to his theo-political drivel. I remember lamenting incredulously to my mother and father that a supposedly spiritual man had found it appropriate to hijack his *minbar* (pulpit) for the advancement of his own political agenda. I had a quick education that the agenda was not his own but that of a global movement of Islamism (political Islam). He made it a point always to address how situations in the world affected Muslims. This was 1985. I was a freshman at UWM. He talked about the Soviet invasion of Afghanistan, and how, while it might be true that the CIA was helping the Afghan rebels, the United States was not to be trusted and that its goal was to imperialize Afghanistan and control or convert Muslims. From there he would usually go on an anti-U.S. tirade that condemned the country for its support of Israel, and in the process would manifest his deep-seated anti-Semitism, usually lambasting Jews in general and Zionists in particular.

All of this shocked me. For one thing, as a Muslim, I was raised to believe that Christians and Jews were my brothers and sisters, "People of the Book," so I had a natural affinity for members of these religions, not antipathy. I was not raised to hate Israel, but was rather taught that the Jews had a right to their homeland. More specifically, my father taught me that it was wrong for the Arab world not to accept the United Nations partition back in 1948, that more than likely had they done so it would have prevented much of the bloodshed between Arabs and Jews that followed. Was he or my grandfather happy that Syria lost the Golan Heights to Israel? Of course not, but at the same time neither man was naïve enough to believe the Arab world had been blameless in the Six-Day War; on the contrary, the constant desire of these countries to wipe Israel off the map had done nothing but create more wars and more problems.

I didn't understand how any of the imam's polemics had any relevance to being a Muslim and our worship of God. It wasn't as though the Muslims who attended the mosque back in my hometown didn't have political opinions. They had plenty of such opinions. We're talking, after all, about Arabs, one of the most politicized peoples on the planet. The difference was that none of the people who attended the mosque in my hometown considered it a place where one should have political discussions. If anything, the attitude among them seemed universal: At the mosque, one could put aside such things for the time being and focus on one's spiritual state and relationship with God. In that sort of environment, it made no more sense to discuss politics than it did to discuss sports or the state of the economy. You were there to be with God and your fellow Muslims, not to spout politics, which was fraught with divisiveness and issues most often entirely unrelated to being Muslim.

In the Milwaukee mosque, however, these political discussions were the norm, not the exception. I wondered how it happened. Can it be, I wondered, that they just don't understand that this sort of thing is not appropriate? When I raised the issue with the imam at the mosque, and said I didn't want to know if someone I was praying with was a Republican, a Democrat, a socialist, an Islamist, or a communist, or whether they supported the creation of a Palestinian state, or thought the mujahideen were being exploited by the United States, I was met with both vacant stares and outright resistance. No, I was told, it is *you* who are wrong. You are not trained as an imam, they told me, and therefore you are not qualified to say what is and is not Islam. The imam, they told me, knows these things because of his training. He gives them a spin on the news about Muslims they cannot get anywhere else. It was his brand of Islamism they could not get elsewhere. But I had yet as a freshman to have a firm grasp of Islamism.

Rather than get into arguments that I thought would lead nowhere, I eventually made a decision to leave the mosque, as it offered much too much politics and far too little spiritual sustenance. My venture out into the wider world had opened my eyes in a way I had never expected. I returned quite happily to the small "mosque community" I had at school and was at least able to placate my mother on the phone that I had tried to venture to the "big city" mosque and learn more about Islam from senior leaders. When I expressed to her my experiences and discontent, she seemed to know exactly what I had faced. She understood it and understood my frustration, but wondered if I could have ignored the politics. That was the difference between my mother's side of the family and my father's. My father's family could not ignore it.

On campus, however, I was slowly introduced to political Islam all over again, this time through the school newspaper—the *UWM Post*. There were Palestinian students, most of them Muslims and members of GUPS (General Union of Palestinian Students), who had made it their mission to make the newspaper their forum for their anti-U.S., anti-Israel views. Some of them took a rather secular stance in their opinion pieces; others definitely felt that God and Islam were on their side. They wrote about both countries as being imperialist and singled President Reagan out for particularly harsh criticism. Their essays and letters made it seem as though Palestinians were the perpetual victims, and the United States and Israel had it in for Arabs and Muslims. Beyond the Palestinians and their views, the general tenor of the paper was very liberal and very anti-Reagan.

As a passionate supporter of President Reagan, I took exception to such views, especially their one-sided nature. There were other conservatives who felt the same way, and we were able, through the funding rules we uncovered at the university, to help ensure that the school also started subsidizing a right-leaning newspaper, which the students who formed it called the *UWM Times*. It offered students more conservative views. I was already then a conservative Republican, having had a column for a few years in the Neenah High School newspaper, which I edited, called "On the Right Track." I found my ideas shaping up very much in line with the president's. In regard to the Middle East, I supported the idea of dialogue between Palestinians and Israelis, as well as a two-state solution. This, of course, put me at odds with the Palestinian faction that wanted to "drive Israel into the sea." Still, even though I caught some flak from those who disagreed with my conservative views on things like entitlement programs, economics, anticommunism, and military defense, and from Palestinian students who thought I was a "sellout," it was good to have a forum—through these different newspapers—where divergent points of view could be expressed.

One incident in particular with the Palestinians stands out. We had an International Culture Day scheduled for the university in October of my sophomore year, normally a very festive event, where students of all different nationalities could bring a native dish to be shared with the rest of the school. The only thing we needed to do was to make sure there was some variety and that not all of us brought in the same dishes. Unbelievably, some of the Palestinian students got into major disagreements with the Jewish students because they wanted to have baklava and a few other "contestable" recipes be one of their own ethnic dishes. No, said the Palestinian students, baklava is a native Arab dish, and the Jews therefore have no right to claim it. I wish I could say I was making this up. That's how absurd it sounds to me even now. I wrote a column in the liberal campus paper about it, chastising the Palestinians for their childishness, and focusing on the absurdity and unfairness of the Palestinian position. How, I reasoned, can there ever be hope for peace in the Middle East when there is such fanaticism over such a small matter? In retrospect, I guess it was good that the Greeks didn't get into the debate over baklava!

While I received flak from some of the Palestinian students over my columns, I continued to have the freedom to express my views. This was proof once again of my country's basic sense of fairness. Instead of the school's trying to squelch our views, it encouraged them, even helped us get our own newspaper to express our opinions. This is the essence of liberty and democracy, encouraging a host of different views, and very much the opposite of what I experienced at the Islamic Society of Milwaukee. I did not pay any price for having more conservative political views or having my differences with Palestinian students. I was not ostracized, or graded differently, or told in so many words to keep my mouth shut. How different this was from what my grandfather and family had experienced for having a different point of view in Syria!

Still, the whole experience with the mosque in Milwaukee gnawed at me. It made me aware that there was such a thing as political Islam, and from my first experience of it, it seemed to be a force unto itself, very tenacious, and not at all open to free debate.

As someone who had been taught to defend my religious views with reason, and not to blindly accept dogma, this was not something I was used to, or for which I had any convenient reference points. I tried to console myself with the idea that within a generation or so this sort of thing should be worked out, that a solution must be at hand that would put such fanatics on a different track. What can I say? I was quite young, naïve, and idealistic in my own way.

Still, I do believe a solution is at hand, but now am more realistic and think it will probably take a lot longer than what I originally had in mind and need far more poking and prodding in the right direction, more than likely for several generations, not one or two. The age-old wisdom applies here: it won't change unless we take a stand to change it, which is a big part of the reason why years later I eventually started the American Islamic Forum for Democracy (AIFD).

At the same time that my eyes were being opened to the reality of political Islam, my relationship and later experiences with my father reminded me in very visceral ways how the legacy of patriarchy and a rigid adherence to both Arab tribal traditions and one's perceived version of the Qur'an could have a drastic impact on family relations.

The legacy of my father is a complex one. If anything, the older I get the more I come to feel that it is not possible for any relationship of any real depth to ever be simple, certainly not the one we have with our parents. In the case of my father, I have no doubt how much I loved him, but at the same time, I am very clear that there were aspects of his character that I did not want to make my own, while there were other very admirable traits and beliefs that he passed on to me that helped me persevere at the most challenging times of my life. When I was in the Navy, for instance, the advice I sought from him at different points, which he willingly shared, did more than just help me through, it ultimately helped me succeed in circumstances that were anything but easy.

My father had an iron will. In many ways, it is part of what allowed him to leave Syria and successfully go through all the struggles inherent in making a new life for himself and my mother in the United States. He believed ardently in liberty and was willing to do whatever it took to make sure his family had a better life than the one he had in Syria. As a doctor, he was an inspiration to me, someone who was brilliant and a true healer, and who was absolutely devoted to his patients, who for good reason felt the same way about him. My father never pushed me to go into medicine. He didn't have to. The inspiration of his example was enough to make me want to pursue that course.

His devotion to the faith of Islam was another inspiration for me. I could not help but absorb into my personality his near-daily obsession with discussing overriding principles of our faith and the challenge of navigating the often murky and confusing waters of *ilm* (knowledge) in Islam. With extensive training and deep understanding in both classical Arabic and English, my father was able to explain interpretations of our Qur'anic scripture in a way that allowed us to stay true to the authenticity of the Arabic script while giving us a way of interpretation from within modernity. He was a physician by profession but he had inherited his father's deep love of language, linguistics, politics, and debate. My father and I spent countless nights in my youth addressing what many critics of Islam today have called the "troublesome" passages of the Qur'an that Wahhabis and other extremist Muslims use to oppress minorities and women. He spent many of the last years of his life completing his own sentence-by-sentence interpretation of the Qur'an. He put almost ten years into finishing that work, which emanated from his own frustration

62

with most Muslim leaders and intellectuals being unable to give interpretations compatible with modern society. His passionate understanding of both languages uniquely positioned him to give me a sense early in my religious development that my personal understanding of my faith could be compatible with Western values and ideals—a challenge that my father and his father before him had also fulfilled in their own soulful engagement of their scripture and faith of Islam. Ultimately as I matured I grew far beyond my father's ideas and developed my own distinct Islamic positions and identity. We certainly had our intellectual disagreements. My own Islamic ideas were influenced by a host of others in my life, from the deep spiritual grounding of my mother and her father (a retired Supreme Court judge and expert in shariah) to many of the non-Islamist imams I was able to find who nurtured my faith. In my own readings I was influenced by such leading reform-minded Islamic thinkers as Muhammad ibn Al-Arabi, Muhammad Sa'id al-Ashmawy, Bassam Tibi, Abdolkarim Soroush, Abullahi An-Na'im, Muhammad Abduh, Fatima Mernissi, Abdurrahman Wahid, Elijah Izetbegovic, Nasr Abu Zayd, and Fazlur Rahman.

When I also witnessed how generously my father gave of his time to make sure the mosque got built in our small town in Wisconsin, his actions taught me more about priorities than anything he could ever say. It helped me understand that while professional success had its place, we could not lose sight of the reason for such a blessing or any of the gifts we're given: God. The need to constantly give thanks to the Almighty, to pray, worship, and reflect. All of that was embodied in the messages my parents conveyed about my faith, country, and the way they made that mosque and our Islamic life a reality.

My parents believed in me and expressed a pride in my accomplishments throughout my youth and into early adulthood that provided my soul with a fuel to which words cannot do justice. For an Arabic father, who I am told due to tribal "machismo" can often be less than warm, he was often remarkably affectionate. He did remind me that his affection was partly intended to make sure that the more formal, lukewarm relationship he had with his own father, Zuhdi Jasser, did not continue to our generation. Interestingly, my grandfather was rather affectionate with me despite his cool relationship with my dad. He also, according to my father, gave his daughters far more love and compassion than my dad had ever received. My father seemed to have turned the tables on our generation, telling us that he loved all of his children equally, even if his treatment of my sisters revealed double standards. His dysfunction, however, would also ultimately manifest in my relationship with him after I came back to live near my parents again and practice medicine with him.

There was more to this man than simple goodness. In our Arabic and Muslim culture people never discuss intimate details about familial relationships and the stresses they manifest. That is not only part of who I am, but reveals a great deal about the depth of the honest challenges that Muslims and especially Arabs face in coming to terms with modernity and open society.

Many writers have addressed just how deep the roots of patriarchy go in Arab as well as Muslim culture, and while I take issue with that view, as far as what the Muslim faith actually teaches, or at least taught me, the dominance of patriarchy in Arab culture is well established. One must remember that Arab culture is much older than Islamic culture, and just as patriarchy runs deep in Jewish culture, in part due to the thousands of years of that particular tradition, Arabs face similar challenges when it comes to feminism and equal rights for women. The difference, I believe, is that Jews have a much longer history of assimilation with Western values, whereas the Arab world has been more isolated, relatively speaking, from such cultural differences and stimuli for change.

My father had a great deal of exposure to Western values. He studied in London for several years and was an Anglophile who greatly admired Western icons like Winston Churchill, and Western values of liberty, democracy, and human rights. As a member of the more prosperous class in Syria, at least until totalitarian socialism robbed my grandfather of his businesses, he was taught that women should have the right to education and even professional careers if they so choose. This, of course, was quite forward thinking for the time, since not that many years before, under the Turks, Syrian women were not allowed to go to school, and Syrian men could go only through the third grade. My grandmother was one of the first Syrian women to be educated in Paris and then return to teach higher education in Syria. She was a strong woman whose relationship with and equal treatment from my grandfather were quite exemplary in their time. In my mother, my father saw an independent, educated, and intelligent woman who attended the University of Damascus School of Pharmacy, attaining her graduate degree in pharmacy, and who hailed from a prominent Damascus family that walked the walk of women's rights and equality.

When my parents came to this country, my father supported my mother in furthering her professional goals by getting an additional master's degree here in the United States at Tulane University. But it is one thing to be egalitarian on that front, and quite another to extend such largesse, if it can be called that, to the domestic front. My mother is no shrinking violet, but simply put, my father did not share power at home. His word was the final one, and his decisions, whether they involved me, or my sisters, or a financial issue, were all made unilaterally.

This caused a lot of arguments, as my mother is a strong person and did not unquestioningly accept his totalitarian domestic stance, whether it involved such things as the purchase of a new car or the expansion of his medical practice. The idea that she was an equal partner did not seem to register with him. Even though he encouraged her professional independence and external equality outside the home, internally no such equality existed. There were times when he became emotionally and verbally abusive with my mother, which caused me great anguish, as on the one hand I felt a desire to protect my mother, and on the other I was intimidated by the prospect of confronting my father. As I got older, I did speak up, but it was always difficult for me to do this in view of the level of intimidation he wielded, as much as I loved my mother and wanted to protect her.

I also didn't understand how my father could behave this way, based on what our Islam taught and on what he had taught me about how to treat women equally. The Qur'an had many verses about the reverence that must be accorded women as the life givers, and very particular advice about how a man should treat his wife and daughters. For instance, in the opening of Chapter 4, titled "Women," God tells Muslims:

O' People, be mindful of God who created you from a single soul, then from it He created its mate, and from them He created many men and women. Be mindful of God in whose name you swear to one another, and be respectful of the mothers from whose wombs you were born. God is watchful of what you do. (4:1)

This verse speaks to a Muslim about the equality of men and women in every facet of life before God:

Muslim men and women, believing men and women, men and women who dedicate themselves to God, faithful men and women, enduring men and women, men and women who give in charity, fasting men and women, men and women who keep their purity, and men and women who mention God frequently; to all God prepared forgiveness and huge reward. (33:35)

Lastly, on the central importance in our lives of marriage and its love, God tells Muslims:

One of His signs also is that He created for you from yourselves spouses that you can feel comfortable with, and He created between you a loving and caring relationship, and in that there are signs for those who think. (30:21)

These verses and many others validate the notion that men and women are equal between each other and before God. This is not to say that there are not other passages of the Qur'an and the Prophet Muhammad's hadith (sayings and examples of the Prophet Muhammad) that have been used as tools of oppression by militants and misogynists and those who reject equality, but those passages can also be interpreted in a moderate light. But many of our leaders do not do that. In fact, the head of the largest Muslim group in the United States, the Islamic Society of North America, Dr. Muzammil H. Siddiqi, stated in a fatwa at one of the most trafficked Islamic sites in the world (Islamonline.net, a primary outlet for the ideas of the Muslim Brotherhood) in April 2004:

It is important that a wife recognizes the authority of her husband in the house. He is the head of the household, and she is supposed to listen to him . . . a husband may use some light disciplinary action in order to correct the moral infraction of his wife, but this is only applicable in extreme cases and it should be resorted to if one is sure it would improve the situation. However, if there is a fear that it might worsen the relationship or may wreak havoc on him or the family, then he should avoid it completely.

There is a large debate within Islamic communities over the meaning of parts of Chapter 4, Verse 34. This debate gives a window into modernist methods of maintaining scriptural authenticity while modernizing interpretations. In that passage most current translations state that the verse ends with the following:

. . . And the righteous women are the truly devout ones, who guard the intimacy which God has [ordained to be] guarded. And as for those women whose ill-will you have reason to fear, admonish them [first]; then leave them alone in bed; then beat them; and if thereupon they pay you heed, do not seek to harm them. Behold, God is indeed most high, great!

Here is the translation my father shared with me:

Good righteous women are dignified and keep covered what God kept covered (and different) of their anatomy. Those who you have reason to fear their deviation, reason with them, punish them by refusing to have relations with them, and some you may have to get going on their way. Once the deviation is corrected do not ever take advantage of them; God is Supreme and Exalted. (4:34)

Note here that the term most scholars translate as "beat them," "*daraba*," is in classical Arabic a term that can mean "separate from them" or "get going on their way" apart, much as the word "strike" in English can mean "hit" or go "on strike." These nuances and this understanding of classical Arabic allow Muslims the freedom to modernize the interpretation of our faith without violating the orthodox sanctity of our scriptures to the word. While I spoke Arabic fluently, by using the logical analyses of reasoned thinkers, I did not personally need to be an expert in classical Qur'anic Arabic to be able to parse interpretations of that and other passages.

The equal treatment of men and women also has many hadith that support this belief. Fatima Mernissi, a well-known Islamic feminist scholar, quoted a hadith that states, "The Prophet never raised his hand against one of his wives, nor against a slave, nor against any person at all." And she also quotes, "The Prophet abhorred violence toward women and stubbornly adhered to that attitude."

My father was one of the primary people who taught me these verses, so at a certain age, I had to conclude that my father knew right from wrong as far as how to treat my mother, my sisters, and women in general. But he often let his emotions get the best of him, and chose time after time to do the wrong thing.

Part of the problem is that his very willful way of being ended up undermining him in his own family. Behind the scenes, my mother made it clear to my sisters and me that his emotional and verbal abuse of her was not something that any of us should emulate or tolerate. This stance, of course, created a lot of confusion for me, and likely for my sisters, because she was doing one thing but telling us to do another, in her own way unintentionally reflecting the contradiction my father embodied, to some extent. But looking back, I have a deep empathy for my mother's predicament over the years of dealing with my father. On the one hand, she selflessly sacrificed her own independence just to keep our family whole, and I certainly benefited from any measure of stability that offered me. I'm not sure how I might have turned out without the regular presence of my father in my life, however flawed he was. On the other hand, her acquiescence to his tyranny and her own victimization made her in the end obviously unequal, sending confusing messages to her children about the equality of women. Their relationship ended up in divorce anyway, albeit after thirty-seven years of marriage and after her children had already grown and left home.

Still, I regret the way my mother suffered under what was at times my father's tyrannical reign, and wish that she could have found a way to effectively stand up to him and put him in his place. The forces against women in our culture are profound and overwhelming. Fealty to male dominance has deep historical, cultural, and religious roots. Overcoming them is not easy for any woman, no matter how strong she may be. In my own understanding of Islam, the oppressive challenges she faced from my father did not necessitate her own self-victimization, and his pathologies did not have to become all of ours. But then again, sacrificing the individual for the tribe, the family, is the Arab and Islamist way that has yet to give way to wholesale reform and modernization to protect the individual. Ultimately, many families like ours will realize that protecting the individual may seem more costly to the family or the "tribe" up front, but it will protect an investment in the truth that no other tribal system could ever support.

Overall, though, my mother provided an example for which I will always be grateful, and that was her kind, selfless, compassionate, and humble way of being, truly reflective of the core of Islam. How she dealt with my father was problematic, but how she treated her daughters, me, and the world at large truly inspired me. It was she, in fact, who inspired in me the simplest clarity about the essence of Islam in my life.

Setting aside family dynamics and the stressors of life, when I put my head down alone in prayer or on my pillow, Islam, to me, is both everything and nothing. It is all that is left after I peel away everything tangible, material, physical, and human on this earth, and yet it is everything that gives my soul (*rouh*) purpose, life, and connection to God. In this life, whether I am completely free or in solitary confinement, I will always have Islam. Islam to me is that deeply personal submission to God and relationship with God that I (*nafs*) am left with after I do everything in my power to accept and meet the challenges God created for me, for us, on this earth.

In regard to my father, for me it was a bit different than for my mother or sisters, because in keeping with certain cultural norms, as the only son in an Arab family it seemed to me that I was accorded a special status by both my parents.

My father in particular singled me out for special treatment, was much more affectionate with me than with my sisters, and was more concerned with giving me the freedom to shape my own destiny. All of this made it easier for me to maintain a basically respectful, albeit blind, relationship with my father while I was growing up, whereas my sisters seemed to find it easier to question his judgments and pronouncements. His very willful, domineering way of being also adversely affected my father in the outside world. He was a very hardworking, ambitious man, who wanted to expand his medical practice and open other offices. His problem was twofold: His ego caused him to overextend himself, and his bull-in-a-china-shop approach to potential partners, lenders, and so on turned off a lot of people. The Qur'an teaches us to treat everyone with the same respect, whether they be rich or poor, powerful or powerless, and this sort of humility is one of the cornerstones of Islam. From what I know of other religions beyond Islam, the idea of blind, all-consuming pride going before a fall seems fairly universal. The concept of hubris is at the heart of some of the greatest Greek dramas and definitely made an impact on me when I read plays such as *Oedipus Rex*.

I believe my father's tragedy was that at times his own personality and emotions ruled over the great truths of living that he knew from the Qur'an and our faith of Islam. This is not to say that his religion was unimportant to him, but that emotionally he had a hard time applying what he knew to be true intellectually: that we must keep extreme emotions at bay and through the spiritual balance of Islam also achieve physical and emotional equilibrium.

His willfulness and temperamental nature left him in a vulnerable position with his marriage, family, and the world at large, which was ironic as well as paradoxical since he sought control through his domineering ways. However, while one may initially give in to someone who dominates or manipulates one, inevitably resentment builds, and very often such a person finds himself alone, since it is just too much of a struggle to get along with such a troublesome person.

One of the symptoms of my father's chronic unhappiness was that he was morbidly obese and for many years smoked heavily, something that I know was very painful for him personally, even more so since he was a cardiologist, and was rather embarrassing for my sisters and me when we were children. His was the ultimate case of the wounded healer. It was others' wounds and illnesses that he healed, not his own. At times, he felt free to inflict emotional wounds through control, verbal terror, and abuse. He, of course, was not alone in this, as one can go through history and find many cases of great but troubled souls who were able to inspire and sometimes heal others, but were less able to tend to their own psychic and physical ailments. Freud comes to mind, whom Carl Jung once described as a man unable to face his own unconscious religious conflicts. My father's hero, Winston Churchill, struggled his whole life with what he called his "black dog," his own euphemism for depression. Some of our own more recent political leaders, such as Bill Clinton, John Edwards, and Arnold Schwarzenegger, all of whom had shown uncanny vision and inspiring leadership qualities, were also beset by personal demons, which later became public knowledge. All of us want our parents to be superheroes when we are young, able to help us with anything. As we grow older, and they are revealed in the full scope of their humanness, it can be quite sobering.

After my sisters and I were grown and on our own, it was a very sad day for the family when my parents divorced, but in some ways predictable, based on the unresolved conflicts that marked their marriage. After leaving the Navy and my last billet with Congress as a congressional physician, I left the fast track in Navy medicine in order to work side by side with my father in his medical practice. Within a few years, a father-and-son practice that started out embodying the proudest days of our lives turned into deep disappointment. After a certain point, I found that I simply could not bear it. Sadly, the term "indentured servitude" came to my mind due to the daily financial oppression as my workload grew, my pay shrank, his false promises grew, and our relationship deteriorated. I always loved my practice and the patients to no end, and they were what kept me there. But he was simply too egomaniacal, a "control freak" completely unwilling to be transparent in business, and unreliable in anything related to the economics of his practice. I was married with children by this time, and this made the situation even more difficult. All of a sudden the realities of my father's behavior were no longer simply emotional but included financial, professional, social, and familial dimensions I had never experienced before. After just five years with him in practice, rather than leave him to his almost certain economic and professional collapse, since I was primary care and his referrals depended for the most part on me, I stayed with him in the same office and severed all financial connections and opened my own medical practice.

Things only got worse from there. As his health began to fail, he blamed his doctors for his problems, even though they had provided the very best care possible for him. His irrationality increased, and he spent the last two years of his life consumed in what I saw to be a highly inappropriate lawsuit he initiated against the very doctors and hospital that did so much for him. Given my close attention to all of his cares, he expected me to testify on his behalf. He again seemed to expect me to subordinate my own opinions to his as the dutiful son. But I could not do that, because I knew the truth and the level of care the doctors had provided. It was devastating to see someone who had taught me the value of upholding the law and the truth in the end circling into the vortex of victimhood, ultimately forcing me to testify on behalf of the doctors against his claims. But as the Qur'an says, "O You who have attained to faith! Be ever steadfast in upholding equity, bearing witness to truth for the sake of God even though it be against your own selves or your parents or your kinsfolk" (4:135). This was absolutely painful to do, but since the only other option was to lie, I was left with no real choice.

This, of course, led to a major rupture in my personal and business relationship with my father that was repaired only somewhat as his health failed further and I and my family tended to his end-of-life cares. Our relationship may not have been totally healed, but we were at least father and son again, right up to his final days. My father was a man who helped thousands of patients through the years, but the problem was that he was simply too proud to let anyone help him. In part, this is just the way my father was, but I look back now and realize that there was a cultural piece at play as well. I don't believe in trying to stereotype a whole culture, but we Arabs are in general a very proud people, particularly the men, and that pride has often cost us dearly on a personal level as well as politically. My father, for instance, could see clearly how much the Arabs hurt themselves when they refused to sign the United Nations partition agreement with the Israelis in Lake Success, New York, in 1948. He could clearly point out how prideful and foolish this was, and what a terrible tragedy it was for both sides in the long run, with wars and loss of life, and constant recrimination. At one point he even referenced Abba Eban's famous statement: "The Palestinians never miss an opportunity to miss an opportunity."

And yet, for all his intellectualism, his encyclopedic knowledge of Churchill's works, his medical brilliance, and above all how much he loved his family and cherished being a Muslim, he somehow could not humble himself to simply be a partner to my mother, instead of an overbearing, insufferable egomaniac. Ultimately, this tragic flaw taught me that one must be willing to truly embrace the meaning of Islam, to submit to God's will, for it is in such submission that we ultimately find peace both within ourselves and with those around us.

Our parents are the ones who primarily teach us how to be in life, or how not to be, and it is up to us to learn as best we can from them and then make our own way. From my father's willfulness, I did learn a certain persistence, which definitely has a place in life, but at the same time I do my best not to be overbearing or domineering in my quest to accomplish goals. From my mother, I learned compassion and gentleness and humility, which are such important parts of being a Muslim. On my best days, I am able to take the best parts of both my parents, and be driven yet compassionate, goal-oriented yet giving.

My father taught me what his father had taught him: never be afraid to speak out. My father was not afraid to fight for the right to build a mosque in our little town in Wisconsin, any more than my grandfather was afraid to speak out for liberty and democracy back in Aleppo. Deep within my father was a personal strength that taught me that one of the most important aspects of life is our legacy of character and honor for having stood firm against corruption and for the virtues of morality. It was this moral courage that was his greatest gift to me. Whether I was right or he was right in all our areas of disagreement and conflict will be for God to judge. Without his and my grandfather's examples, I could not take on the very strong, well-organized forces of Islamism that I have.

In the eulogy for my father, I wrote, "Heroes are a funny thing, one day we aspire to be them, the next day we know better than them." I also wrote, "So often when I was young he gave me a fuel, a confidence that I could get from nowhere else on this earth." Beyond that, I can say that the dream my father had for his own children, for us to enjoy a level of liberty, prosperity, and openness that were unknown in Syria, came true not just because of what the United States offers, but because of my parents' efforts to help us live such lives.

3

A MUSLIM IN THE U.S. NAVY

For as long as I live, I will always look back with great pride on the years I served in the United States Navy. My father had said many times that if he was younger he would have wanted to honor his country by serving in the armed services. I was always taught that there were many things to be grateful for about my country, and this made service in the Navy an honor for me, a way to try to give something back to the country that had given my family so much.

Still, making that commitment was one of the most difficult things I ever did. It was not that I did not want to serve. I knew how grueling the training could be, and I was well aware that to make the commitment meant I would give up my independence as I had known it. As a Muslim, I was taught that my word is my bond, so I did not want to enter into such an agreement lightly. My father was a great help to me as I made this decision, and was, in fact, the one who most encouraged me to pursue scholarship and career opportunities with the armed services. This was motivated in part by his deep patriotism, and in part by the stark financial circumstances in which he found himself when I was getting ready for medical school. I can say that if our economic conditions had been better, I still would have chosen to go into the Navy. In what turned out to be a prescient statement, I remember my father specifically telling me in the summer of 1987 as we weighed my decision to accept a U.S. Navy scholarship for medical school, "Not only is it a natural decision for you and your love for this country but it will provide you invaluable experiences and a track record that will be indispensable to you, your family, and American Muslim communities that are sure to have many challenges in your lifetime." How true that was. I wish he were alive today so that I could thank him for that advice.

All through college I knew that this day of service would eventually come, as I was on a scholarship in a special seven-year accelerated medical program, in which I would complete my medical studies and then owe four years of service to the Navy. Of all the branches of the armed services, the Navy always held a certain mystique for me. And I'll admit it, I really liked the movie *An Officer and a Gentleman* with Richard Gere and Louis Gossett Jr. It took the high opinion I already had of the Navy and only increased it through the drama of seeing all the sacrifices these men made to become officers.

Under the terms of my scholarship, the Navy would pay for my education to any American medical school and provide me a modest monthly stipend. I was already headed to the Medical College of Wisconsin, in Wauwatosa near Milwaukee (formerly Marquette University's medical school), but now the tuition and expenses would vanish, thanks to the American taxpayers, in exchange for a four-year commitment on my part to the U.S. Navy. What a great deal! I got to serve my country and finish medical school with no loans. I also had the distinct pleasure at the end of medical school of completing the Honors in Research program, studying bench research on rheumatoid arthritis and its correlates with cancer on and off for four years in summer and many evenings. I also graduated medical school as president of Alpha

Omega Alpha Medical Honor Society, which will always be one of the achievements of which I am proudest.

For residency training, I headed off to Bethesda Naval Hospital (National Naval Medical Center) in Maryland, one of the very best places any doctor could learn his profession. I did my internship at Bethesda and then was called off to serve as medical department head aboard the USS *El Paso* (LKA-117). Throughout medical training, I found that Islam, whether in my relationship with God or in that with my family, gave me all the strength and discipline I needed to be the very best resident and naval officer I could be. Residency can be a grueling time, with very long hours and little financial compensation, but my faith kept me strong and focused. Like many Muslim students of medicine, I believed that my field of study gave me a way to better understand the miracle of life, so no matter how tough things got in training, I was always able to keep that at the forefront of my mind and push ahead.

The focus and strength of purpose that my faith gave me also came in very handy in my first foray with the Navy before I started medical school, when I went through Officer Indoctrination School (OIS) in Newport, Rhode Island. OIS was housed in the same base and training facility as the Officer Candidate School (OCS). OCS was a much more grueling program—six months, while OIS was six weeks of training. While my program was nowhere nearly as tough or as long as OCS, it was definitely not easy.

While it was a tremendous honor to complete such difficult training, for me the greatest reward I received was my parents' appreciation. When we spoke by phone, both of them would tell me how proud they were of me, and what tremendous honor I brought to the family by serving this great country, and then, without fail, they would cry. It is emotional for me even now to remember those calls, because I know that they meant every word. After my medical internship at Bethesda, I received orders to serve as the general medical officer (GMO) for the USS *El Paso* (LKA-117). I had to complete further surface warfare training in preparation for joining the ship and deploying in the summer of 1993. My most exciting Navy days lay ahead as GMO aboard the *El Paso*.

Anyone who has ever been on board a U.S. naval ship knows just how impressive they are. They are a world unto themselves, both technologically and organizationally. The *El Paso* was the fifth and final Charleston-class amphibious cargo ship. I was pulled from the last few days of surface warfare training to fly out to the Mediterranean and begin my service with the crew that was returning from Operation Restore Hope in Somalia. The "doc" I replaced had to go earlier than expected to his next duty station. I served on board from July 1993 to May 1994.

Some people have asked what it was like to be a Muslim officer aboard a U.S. naval ship, particularly since this was right around the time that Somali Islamist terrorists had killed several U.S. soldiers—the infamous "Black Hawk down" helicopter incident— and in a particularly brutal display of barbarism dragged the corpses of our fellow soldiers through the streets of Mogadishu like some sort of trophies. I can answer quite honestly that I did not see myself as a Muslim officer but as an American officer who happened to be a Muslim. I served alongside others of various religions and I can assure you that what was most important was the uniform we wore and the country we served. As the general medical officer and head of the medical department on board ship, I was one of only a handful of department heads who reported to our executive officer (XO) and commanding officer (CO). The health of each and every one of the crew was what mattered most to me on any given day—that and my decisions about the general health of the crew and the operational urgency of any acute health issues that could ultimately affect a wide-ranging operation. As always, I did my best to pray five times a day, fast during the month of Ramadan, and read the Qur'an, which can be quite challenging with the grueling schedule of a ship at sea, but once I made the effort, I found it sustained me and gave me all the strength and focus I needed to serve the crew in the best way possible. At port or in travel I always tried to find a local mosque in which to learn about other Muslim communities around the world.

More "uptight Muslims" have asked me if it was difficult to serve alongside men who are known not only to work hard but to play very hard as well. Some call the U.S. Navy the biggest drinking fleet in the world. It is definitely true that some in the Navy appear to have a limitless thirst for booze and an insatiable passion for women from all over the world, but I can say that whatever appetites and habits any in the crew had, they very much respected my lifestyle. I didn't drink, smoke, gamble, or chase women, but despite that, the crew had great respect for me. I did smoke a cigar with some of the crew, but that hardly qualified me for "wild man" status. What matters most on a ship is not what one does while on liberty or in one's spare time, but what one does when one is on duty. My faith taught me to respect the word of my CO, Captain Christopher Cole, and XO, Commander John "Joe" Daly, which was not hard to do, since they were such terrific leaders, and to serve my fellow crew members with all my heart and soul. I took my duties very seriously, and the crew quickly got to know me as someone who looked out for them, no matter what their rank was. Yet this still understates the great quality and character of those who serve in our armed forces. I would have entrusted every service member I knew well with my life, and it is sorely underreported how dedicated to family, community, nation, and personal integrity our service members are. Though I have since left the military for the private sector, I can still say that there is no more professional organization I have ever had the honor of working with than the U.S. Navy.

Some have asked, post-9/11, is it safe to have a Muslim in the armed services? Can Muslims put country above religion, or is there the danger of having a Mohammed Atta in the ranks? Or put more poignantly, which Muslims are a possible Major Nidal Hasan, the Army psychiatrist who turned upon his fellow soldiers and massacred thirteen and injured over thirty at Fort Hood, Texas, on November 5, 2009? I typically answer that of course it's safe to have a Muslim in any branch of the armed services, but what is a clear and present danger is to have a Muslim who is an Islamist serve, in the same way you would not want someone like Timothy McVeigh, with a political stance that threatens his loyalty to country, in your regiment. The vast majority of Muslims serve proudly in our armed services, but it is that small but significant subset of Muslims who embrace the Islamist narrative about the world, the West, and the United States who pose a risk.

With all the sophisticated questioning and psychological tests one can administer, one of the easiest ways to know if you're dealing with a fanatic or fascist of some sort is to find out whether they have a sense of humor. Nobody remembers guys like Hitler, Stalin, or Saddam Hussein for their jokes, but on the other hand, great leaders like Churchill and Reagan were definitely known for their wit. Beyond that, if you have to tiptoe around someone because of his or her religion or politics, chances are good that person is not going to be much of a team player in the Navy or anywhere else.

My experience overall in the Navy was that we were focused on what made us a strong, cohesive team, not on our differences. Because of that, there was a sense of unity that transcended where one was from, one's politics, or one's religion. My friendships reflected that as well, as one of my best friends in the Navy was a Mormon, another a Catholic, another a Jew, another a Protestant.

We cared about getting the job done, about doing right by our country. The rest was all extraneous details.

After about a year aboard the *El Paso*, politics intervened to take me off the high seas. President Clinton was instituting reductions across the board in the armed services. This included the closing of military bases and, in the case of the Navy, ships' being recalled and brought back (permanently in some cases) to port and often mothballed. Our ship's deployment was its last, as it was decommissioned upon our return. As a result, I had an opportunity to go back to Bethesda Naval Hospital for the completion of my specialty training in internal medicine from 1994 to 1996.

While I missed the close friendships and the tight-knit environment on board ship, getting back to specialty training and my core career progress at Bethesda Naval Hospital was a fortunate development. Back in Bethesda, I quickly returned to the intensities of residency training in internal medicine and focused on becoming the best internist I could. I developed close friendships with a number of other senior medical officers and colleagues. I had a great admiration for all of my mentors in the department of internal medicine, from the chairman, Captain Angeline Lazarus, MC USN, on down. They helped shape me as an internist and fostered the professionalism that characterizes the physician and specialist that I am today. One of the senior medical officers at Bethesda with whom I was close was Captain Mohammed Shakir, MC USN. He ran the department of endocrinology for many years and was also Muslim. As most of our attendings at Bethesda did, he had pictures in his office of military and government leaders who entrusted him with their care, including a previous president. It often caused me to pause and ponder how great that simple message about the American dream was, that an immigrant like Dr. Shakir could come to the United States, join the Navy, and end up caring for the highest echelons of our government's military and political leaders.

As the only two Muslims whom I knew of in the department, we became close on some issues. During my residency training, I finished some medical research on hormonal regulation with Dr. Shakir. He asked me if I was interested in presenting the paper at a national meeting. We thought it would be special on many levels to present it at the annual meeting of the Islamic Medical Association (IMA) in addition to a few other traditional medical venues. My paper was very well received at the IMA meeting, and I also got to hear other papers presented on other compelling medical issues by some leading American Muslim physicians. I remember having some disagreement with a few of the papers presented on medical ethics, since that was one of my areas of expertise and I am always quick to get my dander up when traditional Islamist narratives and scriptural interpretations supplant a reasoned discourse on medical science and modern interpretations of faith-based principles. But that is par for the course, and it is not surprising to hear theocratic narratives in medicine over reason-based arguments from a faith-based medical organization. If I had left then, all would have been well.

However, I discovered at the time that the IMA was intimately close with the Islamic Society of North America (ISNA), the largest American Muslim organization. Their conventions occurred sequentially in the same location, and attendance at one allowed attendance at the other. So we stayed for the opening day of the ISNA convention, a much larger event that had at least fifteen thousand Muslims in attendance. There were a few other Muslims there in uniform who belonged to different branches of the armed services, but they stood out from all the other attendees, who were civilians.

After the opening prayers and welcoming, ISNA's leadership invited the keynote speaker, Imam Siraj Wahhaj, to open the convention with a speech. I had never before been to a meeting of ISNA. The mere mention of ISNA evoked a visceral response from me due to a letter I had received from them burned into my memory from 1991. That was my only previous contact with them. The letter was addressed to me from ISNA and other so-called leading American Muslim organizations, and it beseeched all active-duty U.S. military Muslim personnel to refuse to participate in the Persian Gulf War on the grounds of "conscientious objection." But that was just a letter, which I angrily destroyed.

Four years later, I now found myself at their convention. I was pulled into listening to Siraj Wahhaj's address to the gathered Muslims. He was a slick, magnetic speaker who used anecdotes and sarcasm to subtly talk about his love of Islam, which I found compelling. But he also insinuated a subtle Islamic supremacist undertone that made me rather uncomfortable and disgusted. Nothing enraged me more than when he not so subtly began talking about the U.S. Constitution. He picked up the Qur'an and said, as I recall, "You know, I was sitting on an airplane minding my own business, reading my Qur'an, and imagine, a Jewish passenger sitting next to me asked me about the Qur'an I was reading—she asked me if Muslims became a majority in America, would we replace the U.S. Constitution with the Qur'an?" He laughed out loud and said, "Can you imagine someone wondering if a document made by humans would be superior to a document made by God?" He went on to describe our duty as Muslims to bring the Qur'an and its teachings and legal system to the United States.

I got lightheaded from how upset I became and sat down. After he was done with his speech, the president of ISNA and their board, all apparently delighted with his speech, then gave an opportunity for Muslims to come to the microphone and announce events during the convention or ask the leadership questions. These were usually platitudes. I went to the microphone and said, as I stood there in my Navy whites, "I cannot believe the silence in this room after that offensive speech by Imam Wahhaj. Not only as an American military officer, but as an American Muslim I am summarily offended. I'm not sure if you understand American law, Imam Wahhaj, but as I understand it you have just violated the Sedition Act. You're free to disagree with foreign and domestic policy, but you cannot talk about the overthrow of the U.S. Constitution and its wholesale replacement by another document as if we are an insurgency." I then encouraged other military personnel in the audience to leave and all members who disagreed with his sedition to publicly dissociate themselves from ISNA because they were violating their citizenship oath to this country. I then made it abundantly clear that to whatever extent my presentation at the Islamic Medical Association afforded me any membership in ISNA, I was publicly renouncing that membership. Even more concerning than Wahhaj's speech and ideas and the pleasure of ISNA's board at his thoughts was the reaction of the thousands in attendance. It was disturbingly silent. The few who came up to me seemed to think I was "overreacting to something Wahhaj mentioned and would never happen," but their muted response exuded deep guilt. I thought to myself, what does this have to do with the real purpose of this event, to bring together Muslims from all over the country to socialize and to appreciate how Islam unites us spiritually wherever we may come from? That is, unless there were other theo-political evangelical purposes at play.

This event stayed with me for a long time. If my time at the University of Wisconsin was an eye-opener as far as Islamism was concerned, this event with naval officers present let me know just how brazen the Islamists could be and the depth of their ideological conflict with their chosen nation. Did they not feel the least bit embarrassed to air such views in front of U.S. armed services personnel and other patriots who might be there? Apparently not. From what I could tell, they definitely believed that those in the room valued religion, political Islam, and Middle Eastern geopolitics over loyalty to our country. It made me wonder if there were members of the armed services present who agreed with the speaker. This awakened me to the organized threat to our nation of the ideologies of political Islam and the Muslim Brotherhood legacy groups like ISNA in America. This was 1995. The events of 9/11 were still several years away, and while I could never have predicted such horrific events, I was worried about the level of animosity such Islamists showed. I felt in my heart that while they may have been nonviolent, their separatism and inherent disgust for American freedoms and liberty were part of a deep animus for Western society permeated with a dangerous superiority that was bound to create a cadre of disaffected youths and disenfranchised communities. They were here in the United States, but seemed to have no real ideological loyalty to their adopted country, much less gratitude for all the liberty and rights it had given them. Their politics and religion seemed inseparable, and just as with the imam back in Milwaukee, there was no room for discussion. It was obvious by the glares I got from others in the room that my point of view was considered completely out of line. How dare I question such a position? And even if I was right, how dare I say it publicly, take on the "real" Islamic scholars, and air dirty laundry? I was learning that not only were our problems ideological, they were compounded by tribalism and groupthink.

Just as in Milwaukee, I held out the hope that such conflicts would be resolved by Muslims in a generation or so. Call me an eternal optimist.

There was another incident that prodded my concern over

Islamism when I was a resident at Bethesda Naval Hospital, National Naval Medical Center (NNMC). NNMC had never had an imam to lead Friday prayer services for Muslims, and in fact our gathering of four or five Muslims was an informal gathering that we arranged on our own at the hospital chapel on Fridays. But then, entirely unsolicited, the head of the hospital chaplain corps at NNMC, Captain Jane Vieira, spontaneously approached me and Captain Shakir, asking us if we would be interested in helping her department interview and secure an imam to provide Friday prayer services on contract and also tend to the spiritual needs of Muslim naval personnel. She put out the word in the D.C. metro area that NNMC was in need of a Muslim chaplain. Once she had a slate of candidates, we helped her conduct interviews. One came highly recommended from the largest mosque in the area, Dar Al-Hijra in Northern Virginia. I was not familiar with the mosque, but the department had high hopes that he would be the ideal choice.

During each of our interviews I posed questions about the specifics of how the imam would render advice to vulnerable Muslims stationed with us. By posing certain scenarios I was able to see on what side of the fault lines between Islamism and Americanism the imam sat and would direct the American Muslim soldier. I asked the imam from Dar Al-Hijra, for instance, how a Muslim officer should respond when he was obligated to attend an open Navy function that might involve the consumption of alcohol by his shipmates. He answered point-blank that the officer should simply not attend unless he was ordered to attend by the CO! He emphasized that a devout Muslim sets an example, and by not attending any function where alcohol was being served and consumed he would send a message that it is better that they not drink. And if they decided to cancel the availability of alcohol for the entire command, "all the better." When I asked him whether he ate at American restaurants, whether he understood the principle of free will in Islam free of coercion, he responded with an ossified form of binary thinking suitable to the Wahhabis of Saudi Arabia. When I asked him if he understood the ethical difference between consuming alcohol and being present when other free individuals consumed alcohol, he spoke of the importance of community morality in Islam, belying an understanding of free will and tolerance. When asked about the value of unit cohesion, he responded again with an obsession about implementing his interpretations of shariah over living and understanding liberty. Now think about this for a minute. We're talking about the Navy, which historically speaking is not exactly known as a place for teetotalers. Then, when asked what came first, one's country or religion, he answered unequivocally that Islam came first no matter what, even if the person was in the Navy. He did qualify the answer by saying that a sailor should never refuse a direct order, but that in his heart Islam must come first over any nationalism. *Taquiyya,* or dissimulation, anyone? Needless to say, we did not hire him. It was sobering nonetheless to see how deep this man's Islamism, his separatism from this society, went and how self-justified he felt in all his positions. It was almost as if he and I lived in separate countries: in his case one where all that mattered was Islam, notwithstanding the diverse religious and ethnic nature of America, and in my case one where my faith defined my life personally, but I felt perfectly content and privileged to share my country with people of all sorts of different beliefs and habits, including fellow naval officers who enjoyed a few shots now and then. It should be no surprise that only a few years later that same mosque, Dar Al-Hijra, would hire another imam, the now infamous Imam Anwar Al-Awlaki. Awlaki was naïvely interviewed by the *Washington Post* and *The New York Times* in the wake of 9/11 as a "moderate" American-born imam. During the Iraq war

Awlaki slid down the proverbial Islamist slope of radicalization, leaving the United States, declaring war on the United States, and helping stimulate a number of acts of terror against our homeland—most notably, the Fort Hood massacre committed by Major Nidal Hasan on November 5, 2009.

I'm happy to report that the role of part-time imam for NNMC was eventually filled by someone who at the time had a very balanced attitude toward God and country.

As I neared the completion of my residency I recall throwing my hat in the ring for the position of chief of residents, a leading teaching billet for the internal medicine training program at NNMC. After a number of interviews, I remember calling my parents to tell them that Captain Lazarus had selected me to be her chief of residents. I was humbled, and my parents were even more excited than I was. The plaque in the department office that lists all the previous chiefs at Bethesda was like a Who's Who in Navy medicine.

Then, during my year as chief resident, I received a call from the Office of the Attending Physician (OAP) for Congress at the U.S. Capitol asking me to throw my hat in the ring for one of the two positions as a staff internist at the OAP, the U.S. Navy medical clinic charged with the primary care of members of Congress and the U.S. Supreme Court, and 911 response for the Capitol Hill police jurisdiction. After a rigorous Navy-wide selection and vetting process, security clearances, and my own personal prayers, Admiral John Eisold, the attending physician to Congress, called and asked me to work for him at the OAP. I immediately thought back to when I joined the Navy, accepting my medical school scholarship when I was a junior at the University of Wisconsin–Milwaukee. I had never even imagined that I'd eventually be offered one of the most sensitive assignments for a Navy internist, or physicians anywhere for that matter, working for the United

States Congress as one of its doctors. After two years of service at the OAP, it was surreal to realize where I had served as a Navy doctor. At my departure ceremony at our medical office near the Rotunda, my parents, beaming with pride and shedding a few tears, had lamented that my grandparents were not there to see just how achievable an American dream is for anyone in the United States, regardless of faith or national origin, who believes in his nation, loves what he does, and works hard.

Aside from being entrusted with the care of so many members of Congress and our Supreme Court justices, we also provided emergency response for the Hill. I was the doc on duty on Friday afternoon, July 24, 1998. I was seeing patients, seated with a senator discussing his symptoms, when we both heard gunfire, as if it was right outside our door. We immediately responded to a 911 call and I led a team of corpsmen quickly around the corner toward Majority Leader Tom DeLay's (R-TX) office near the entryway through which the perpetrator shot his way. We attempted to provide immediate resuscitative support to those hit by the armed rampage of Russell Eugene Weston Jr. Weston ended up killing two Capitol Hill police officers in addition to Mr. DeLay's security detail. To this day, the notes and personal thanks our team received from the families of the slain officers who paid the ultimate price for service to our nation remain as one of my most cherished and emotional memories of my naval career and service.

In April 1999, my years of active duty came to a close, which coincided roughly with another big step in my life: marriage.

4

ISLAM IN MY LIFE

Many people not very familiar with the Muslim religion tend to assume that traditional, conservative Muslims opt for arranged marriages. My wife and I are proof that is not necessarily so, and we are certainly not an isolated case. In fact, if anything, the tradition of arranged marriages is much older than Islam itself, and can be directly tied to ancient Middle Eastern practices that far predate the Prophet Muhammad. My instruction in Islam was quite traditional, but it was never suggested that I had to agree to a marriage arranged by my parents, nor did anyone ever imply that I should have more than one wife. I have never met an American Muslim who had his marriage arranged nor one who was married to more than one wife. In some ways, it might have been easier if an arranged marriage had been my lot, as free choice has its own somewhat paralyzing challenges. It was a long road for me to find the right partner, just as it is for many people, whether they are religious or not.

The challenge, as I felt it, was for me to find someone who was a traditional, conservative Muslim, with whom I also shared enough personal compatibility to sustain the lifelong commitment that I learned from my faith and God's word in the Qur'an that marriage should be. Romantic attraction and love were also part of what I sought, though not the sole criteria, as I believe the responsibilities of marriage are very serious and require us to consider our values and our own level of maturity and spirituality as well as the other person's. While I believe it is possible for me to share much common ground with a woman who practices Christianity or Judaism, my desire to marry another Muslim was part of who I am. It was my gut instinct that with all the challenges a nuclear family faces through the generations, the foundation should be built upon a common faith and a shared spiritual practice. While I understood God's permissiveness in intermarriage between Jews, Christians, and Muslims, I just could not fathom for myself a marriage and a home where we could not worship in the same way and with the same scripture and message, celebrate our holidays together, fast in Ramadan together, and bury our dead with the same traditions, scripture, and spirit. I wanted the comfort of knowing that with whatever challenges life might throw our way, my wife and I could share a common spiritual, scriptural language and anchor.

My way to seek a life partner was basically through my parents' network of other Muslim and Syrian families, since it became a given that I was not going to "date."

There were times when I definitely envied those who dated, just as I occasionally felt that those in arranged marriages had it easier. It got lonely at times, since my approach to a relationship was that it had to be a lifelong commitment, and because of that there was a lot more work involved to find that right partner. It took several years of visiting with various Muslim families across the United States, looking not only for that person with whom I would be comfortable sharing my life but also for someone whose family was a good fit for me. I believe strongly that you marry not only the other person, but that person's family, and if there is not a strong degree of common ground, especially with regard to family values, faith, and morals, there's likely to be continuous conflict.

In one case, I met with a family with whom I shared many things, from faith to medicine to our Syrian heritage. I felt quite comfortable speaking to their daughter, as we also seemed to have many things in common and many shared values. However, there was a big problem right away, as her father, who was a prominent Syrian American doctor, proudly displayed in his living room a picture of himself and a group of physicians with President Hafez Assad. To my father, grandfather, and every honest Syrian I've ever known, Hafez Assad is one of the most evil and militant tyrants of the twentieth century. Assad and many members of his family robbed and raped his country and Lebanon shamelessly, committing repeated crimes against humanity in towns such as Hama and Tadmur (Palmiyra). The Syrian Human Rights Committee and many other human rights watchdogs have chronicled many of these atrocities and have repeatedly listed the Assad regime as one of the worst violators of human rights in the world. Did he not live through that? He certainly knew many families that had. I was not visiting this family behind the walls of iron-fisted Syria. They lived comfortably and freely in the United States. These photos were not mandated by anyone. I couldn't understand why anyone with a conscience could be proud to be seen with him let alone actually meet with the despot during a visit to their motherland. When I asked her father about the photo, I said as much to him, and a political argument ensued that effectively ended any prospect that his daughter and I might ever get along, let alone marry. I asked him how all those self-respecting doctors from an Arab-American Medical Association could allow themselves to be hosted, photographed, and led around by evil. I received no answer.

My mother quickly found out about my frankness with the father, and she was very unhappy that I had behaved in this manner. "What were you thinking?" she said to me. "Why do you always have to make such a big deal of politics? Couldn't you just let that go?"

It took me a while to answer, but finally I said, "You know very well I can't let such things go. Such issues are testimony to her father's character and the integrity of the family that they would allow such a thing. He can claim to be as traditional and pious a Muslim as it's possible for anyone to be, but if he can be proud of meeting and being photographed with a crook and despot like Assad, what does that say? If his daughter had voiced her discontent with her father's appeasement of the Syrian thug, I would have ignored her father's apologetics. But she did not, so I could not contemplate being married into such a family. And after all, it was you and Dad who passed on these values to me. Otherwise, we might still be in Syria."

While she couldn't really argue with that, she did make the point that if I looked for both the perfect mate and the perfect family, I might never get married. As she very much wanted grandchildren, that prospect wasn't at all appealing to her. She asked me to try to be a little less picky, and while I tentatively agreed to that, I knew the likelihood was that I would not jump into any commitment precipitously.

Years passed. I continued to make the rounds, so to speak, and talk with various families that had been referred to me by various associates, friends, and relatives. And then I met Gada, and everything changed.

When you meet the right person for you, it isn't always easy to put into words what makes that person so. If someone had asked me the first time I met Gada, did you know she was the one for you, I would have answered "yes," but it would have been hard to put my reasons into words. I think that's because love goes beyond reason and things we can easily explain. I did know from the very first that there was a sense of comfort and ease with her, as though

I'd always known her. Any initial awkwardness or shyness on my part was easily overcome, which says a lot, as I've never been a very forward person, at least not when it comes to the opposite sex. I think part of the compatibility I felt with her right away had to do with the fact that she was also somewhat shy, and that put me at ease.

But there was more, of course. It turned out her family was originally from Aleppo, the same as mine. Just as one finds that certain attitudes tend to prevail in particular parts of the United States, the same is true in Syria. The "big city" attitude that one often finds with New Yorkers, the belief that their city is the center of things, and their tendency at times to look down their noses at "simpletons" from smaller, less cosmopolitan cities, and even more so if one is from a rural area, can also be found in people from Damascus, and, I imagine, in other countries' centers, such as Paris or Beijing. Aleppo is one of Syria's biggest cities in size and population, though it is not as metropolitan as Damascus, and as a result there is less of a tendency to put on airs or be focused as much on material things. These are generalizations, to be sure, but sentiments consistent with my experience nonetheless.

So, whether it was because her family was from Aleppo, or just the way she was raised, from the very first it was obvious that Gada's values went far beyond material comforts. She was thoughtful, intelligent, humble, and considerate as well as beautiful. And while she respected my opinions, she was not afraid to have her own, and to question mine on occasion. I did not want to share my life with a woman who felt a need to be constantly deferential based on some perceived sort of religious obligation. I wanted to be with someone who shared my values, but that didn't mean that she had to be my mirror. It was important to me that she be her own person. That's just part of the way I view relationships, but it's also supported by the teachings of my faith of Islam as I learned them and found them in the Qur'an, which teaches mutual respect between partners. And I knew from the start that Gada had no problem being her own person.

After several trips to visit with Gada and her family, I knew for sure that this was the woman I wanted to marry. At the time, I was stationed at the Office of the Attending Physician at Congress in Washington, D.C., and she was doing postgraduate research at Case Western Reserve. So between my trips to visit her and her family we spent quite a bit of time getting to know each other on the telephone. The sense of comfort we had with each other only increased, as we had long talks about religious and spiritual values, America, my military service, the West, culture, music, politics, and our beliefs about charity, raising children in a tumultuous world, and the need to balance professional goals with commitment to family. Beyond these deep talks, I felt a magnetic attraction toward her, and before I knew it, had fallen deeply in love with her.

It was a bit awkward to try to express such feelings, as I simply was not used to it. As we were not yet engaged, our get-togethers ("dates") had to take place in public places. Such was the behavior of a couple during courtship in the Islamic tradition we both respected. This actually did afford us a bit of privacy, and it was at one of our dinners together after almost six months that I made it known to her that I wanted to spend my life with her. Fortunately, she felt the same way, and when I asked her parents for permission to marry her, they also made me quite happy by making it clear that I would be a welcome addition to their family.

Once our engagement was official, we shared even more romantic feelings with each other. Since she was in Ohio and I was in Washington, D.C., much of this happened via email or over the phone, but just the same, we shared our feelings in a deep way.

We had many discussions about faith in the months leading up to our marriage, including a discussion with the imam who would marry us. This also brought us closer together. He very much emphasized the mutual respect that needed to be at the heart of our marriage, and how we each must cherish the other. His comments, especially his formal comments quoting the Qur'an and relevant hadith at our Kittab (written marriage contract) reemphasized what I had learned as a child about how I must treat my wife and the equality of our relationship based upon the Prophet's teachings. The imam, though he may not have realized it, also reminded me how I did not want to make my father's mistake and be domineering or manipulative in my marriage. Based upon Gada's strong sense of self, it didn't look as if she would tolerate such a thing anyway.

Our marriage ceremony in many ways reflected our blending of East and West in our new life. Our vows were taken in a traditional Islamic manner with the imam, and we were married on Valentine's Day 1998. It was paradoxical for us, since there are many in the Islamic world, such as the Wahhabi sect of Saudi Arabia, who reject the concept of Valentine's Day as a corrupt Western tradition that promotes extramarital love, but for Gada and me this holiday appropriately celebrates the romantic spirit that we had both waited for so long in our lives, and as such there is absolutely nothing innately corrupt about it. It remains our favorite holiday.

The reception celebrating our wedding in Phoenix afterward included not only our families and friends from the Arab, Syrian, and Muslim communities, but also such notables as my commanding officer, Admiral John Eisold, the attending physician to Congress, and then-representative J. D. Hayworth (R-AZ). Representative Hayworth was a patient, and he and our families became close friends during my tour with the U.S. Congress and especially after our move to Arizona upon my leaving the Navy.

The wedding was very much a reflection of our cultural heritage as well as our immersion in American life. There was some traditional Arabic food and music, but there was also techno music, which we danced to with quite a bit of enthusiasm. My family still threatens me with video clips of me pretending to be John Travolta. Overall, it was one of the greatest days of my life, and I couldn't have been happier to marry Gada and felt blessed to have our families come together. Some of the greatest challenges, however, lay ahead.

In line with traditional Islam, Gada had not dated before marrying me. Neither one of us had any real experience with intimate relationships, much less marriage, and this meant that we had quite a bit to learn in our first year of marriage. For one thing, we were both used to having quite a bit of personal space. Marriage changed all that. I think for many newly married couples, the first year is a lot like "playing house." You're still getting used to each other, personal habits and the like. For a couple that was brand-new to the world of male-female adult relationships, this adjustment period really did take some time.

There was no doubt about our basic compatibility and love for each other, but even with all that in our favor, we still had to get to know each other all over again. It's one thing to be engaged, quite another to actually be under the same roof. Ultimately, this brought us much closer together, and, of course, it helped to always keep in mind the imam's words about mutual respect and cherishing each other. All of this, however, becomes much more challenging when one has to live with the other's dirty socks and whether one squeezes the toothpaste tube from the bottom. The fact that we also prayed together helped put all of that other stuff into perspective.

The blessings continued to grow. I finished my Navy commitment and we moved to Phoenix so I could join my father in practice when his partner, Kenneth Desser, retired from private practice, and I took over his patients. Dr. Desser's confidence in my taking over his primary care practice of over thirty years was humbling. My father's pride at my years in the Navy was exceeded only by his pride at his closest friend's writing to his patients of the trust he had in me as a physician taking over his practice and joining my father. Gada would enroll in graduate school to obtain her doctorate of pharmacy. Three years later, in January 2002, she would give birth to our first child, Zachariah, and then graduate. I would be blessed with my own private practice. A dream American life was coming together for us, personally and professionally, in the last year of the twentieth and the beginning of the twenty-first century. At that point, I couldn't even imagine the shadow that 9/11 would eventually cast, and how it would ultimately change my life. For the time being, I was consumed with God's miracles: the miracle of my first son's birth and the miracle of healing revealed to me daily in my practice of medicine.

Being present at my son's birth reminded me in many ways why I became a doctor as well as how intimately Islam is tied to much of my philosophy of medicine. Seeing him born reminded me all over again of God's Grace and Majesty and at the same time of the knowledge that has been passed on through the ages in the medical field to make the miracle of birth and life almost a routine thing. My father and grandfather both used to remind me that the Qur'an tells its followers to pursue knowledge wherever it may be found, and the early centuries of Islam bore out this admonition in very remarkable ways in relation to medicine.

Much has been written about Islamic contributions to medicine—of how, for instance, while the Dark Ages went on between the seventh and thirteenth centuries in Europe, Arab and Islamic contributions to science and technology were at their height.

Books have been written about Islamic and Muslim contributions to medicine. The great Arab chemist Jabir Ibn-Hayan discovered sulfuric and nitric acids. Also during this time, Arab and Islamic civilization contributed much to advancing the state of hospitals, including improving hygienic standards, having separate wards for those with infectious diseases, maintaining proper records for patients, and spurring great pharmaceutical innovations. There were also significant Arab Islamic discoveries and innovations in the fields of ophthalmology, anesthesia, cardiovascular diseases, and obstetrics, and the noted scholarly and technical contributions of physicians such as Al-Razi (Razes), Al-Zahrawi, Ibn-Sina (Avicenna), and Ibn-Rushd (Averroes), who not only greatly contributed to medicine, with his insights on practical treatment, but was also a philosopher noted for his insightful and controversial interpretations of Aristotle. Ali Ibn-Isa (Jesu Haly) in particular was known for his contributions to the field of ophthalmology and wrote the classic text, *Tathkirat Al-Kahhalin* (*A Note for the Oculists*), which is the oldest book in its original language on diseases of the eye.

The Qur'an and the spirit of Islam itself encourage the study of the sciences as a window into understanding God's creations. The Prophet Muhammad is thought to have exhorted Muslims to "seek knowledge even if it is in China," which means one should be willing to go to any lengths and distance to learn about God's creations. There is also a well-known saying of the Prophet Muhammad, "There is no disease that God has created, except that He also has created its remedy" (Bukhari, 7.582). It is up to men and women of science to find these cures, but the idea is stated quite clearly that knowledge is the pathway to such progress. During Europe's Dark Ages, Muslim physicians wrote much about medical philosophy and ethics, including such thinkers as al-Razi, who emphasized the continuous education of the physician, and Ibn-Sina, whose tenth-century treatise, *The Canon of Medicine*, was used as an essential reference book in European medical schools right up to the seventeenth century. These facts and rich history are important to me as a Muslim, though they certainly do not blind me to the grim realities of our current challenges within the interpretation of our faith today. But Bernard Lewis said it best in a few passages from the introduction to his essential book, *What Went Wrong* (Oxford University Press, 2002):

> There is indeed good reason for questioning and concern, even for anger. For many centuries the world of Islam was in the forefront of human civilization and achievement. In the Muslims' own perception, Islam itself was indeed coterminous with civilization, and beyond its borders there were only barbarians and infidels. This perception of self and other was enjoyed by most if not all other civilizations—Greece, Rome, India, China and one could add more recent examples. . . .
>
> In the centuries designated in European history as medieval, the Islamic claim was not without justification. . . .
>
> And then suddenly the relationship changed. Even before the Renaissance, Europeans were beginning to make significant progress in the civilized arts. With the advent of New Learning, they advanced by leaps and bounds, leaving the scientific and technological and eventually the cultural heritage of the Islamic world far behind them.

Both the successes and the failures of Muslims in their history can and should call for a broad analysis of our theology within the context of the times we lived. What aspects of our theology and culture fostered free learning and academics at times in the history of Muslims, and what aspects suppressed it at others? Many thinkers have addressed this issue—a struggle borne out in my own life and dedication to liberty.

As a Muslim physician, I can cite four essential principles that have guided me in my daily practice: knowledge, humility, compassion, and ethics. It is not always possible for me to save a patient, but it is extremely important that I bring all the knowledge possible to any given case, and at the same time be cognizant of my own limits. There are cases I must refer to other specialists, or where I must stretch the limits of my own knowledge. I can think of nothing more toxic to the practice of medicine than arrogance, which blinds one to one's own limitations and to knowledge one has yet to gain. Yes, it's true that my chosen field has its fair share of arrogant doctors, but I truly believe the very best practicing physicians are characterized by their desire to learn more (and put it into practice) and their ability to keep their talent in perspective.

For me, humility has a deep spiritual basis, for the Qur'an and my faith have taught me that God is ultimately responsible for one's gifts and that it is incumbent upon us to develop them. I believe that God will ultimately judge every one of us not for our accomplishments but for how hard we tried to maximize the impact of the gifts and challenges he gave us while we were alive.

I also believe that humility is very important in the doctor-patient relationship. If I am not sufficiently sensitive and open to my patient's needs, it is more likely that poor-quality treatment can occur. When I put my own ego aside, and allow God to work through me as He does all of His creations, so that real healing can occur, the patient receives the greatest treatment benefits. As a physician I view my role simply as that of a consultant, not a paternal director of health. Autonomous patients come to me of their own free will in a trusting covenant of doctor and patient, not to abrogate their free will but to gain personal insight and recommendations from their own physician about what steps they can take to improve their health. My goal is always to have the patient trust me, to feel sufficiently comfortable to confide in me, and from such a relationship, it is much easier to get to the core issues of an illness. For instance, to merely bark at a patient that his heart problems are largely related to poor diet and lack of exercise doesn't really do anything to set the person on the right path. However, if a true bond of trust has been developed, my experience has been that the patient is much more likely to follow my advice.

This, of course, is where compassion is also so important. Islam has taught me to genuinely love and care for my patients. My sense has always been that God is watching my every act and that compassion is exercised not only out of respect for the patients but for myself and God's favor. I consider it paramount that patients not only receive the benefit of all my education and knowledge, but also understand in a deep way that their health and well-being are greatly important to me.

I must give credit once again to my father for his example. He never said to me that it was important to care about your patients and to show it, but he demonstrated that by his actions. The deep love that he felt for them and that they felt for him was every bit as important as the latest innovations he had learned in cardiology and nuclear medicine, his chosen specialties.

At the core of my identity as a physician has been the feeling that I am doing the right thing. While much of the difference between right and wrong most of us learn in our childhood, the ability to reason toward a sense of what is right while understanding why everything else is wrong, or perhaps not "as right," is essential to the practice of medicine. My interest in, and often obsession with, biomedical ethics began long before medical school and continued as a lifelong area of study, activism, and leadership for me in my practice. In medical school and in my residency training I took every opportunity to study, research, and write about medical ethics. And since then, I have spent countless hours staffing and leading ethics committees in every medical community in which I've practiced. Bioethics to me was at the core of what it meant to be a physician; understanding and teaching it gave me a sense of gratification that not only was I practicing medicine, but I was helping resolve the toughest cases in our community when other physicians and their health-care team would reach an impasse. To this day, the bioethics consultations and teaching I do bring me some of the greatest gratification in my work.

I truly believe it is a privilege for me to be able to practice medicine, a gift given to me by God, and to that extent all of my patients are also God's gifts to me. It is they who have allowed me to learn my profession, who every day teach me that there is always more to learn, and nothing is more rewarding than to be part of another person's healing process.

The fact that I chose to be a primary care physician also has much to do with my Islamic faith. While it is true that I could have probably made much more as a surgeon or in other subspecialties of internal medicine as a proceduralist of some sort, primary care to this day gives me an unparalleled holistic appreciation for the patient. I not only know the scope of the patients' medical problems, but also develop an appreciation for their psychological challenges, since nearly every one of their maladies begins with a contact or evaluation in my office. All of this gives me a deeper understanding of God's creations, and even more opportunities to be a part of the healing process.

Primary care also gives me the chance to really get to know my patients over a long span of time, because most often they are with me for years, unlike the patients of a surgeon, who typically has a short-term relationship with the patient based on removing a circumscribed problem. I wanted to be able to have long-term relationships with my patients, and primary care was the best way to do that.

While the spirit of my faith has definitely influenced me greatly, I have also benefited greatly from Western teachers and the Western philosophy of medicine I learned in my training. One of the most influential people for me has been the great Dr. William Osler (1849–1919), who was one of the founders of Johns Hopkins University and the father of internal medicine. His book, *The Principles and Practice of Medicine*, is one of our specialty's foundational bibles, as it has been for millions of other physicians around the world. Osler's contributions are far too many to name here, but he gave the world the full-time, sleep-in residency, and emphasized hands-on care for medical students, introducing them to the patient ward very early on as an essential part of their education. It was Osler who said, "If you listen carefully to the patient, they will tell you the diagnosis." I found Osler's emphasis on the importance of a patient's history to be at the core of the nexus between intellectual medicine and the doctor-patient relationship. This essential wisdom has guided my medical career from the very beginning.

The Principles and Practice of Medicine was published in many editions up until 2001. Osler was humble in his own way in giving due credit to Avicenna for his great influence through the years, recognizing him as "the author of the most famous medical textbook ever written." He pointed out that Avicenna's *Canon* remained "a medical bible for a longer time than any other work."

This, of course, is proof to me about how East and West can work together to inspire each other and push medical progress forward. The foundation of my faith, and all it has taught me about compassion, humility, ethics, and seeking knowledge, as well as the long legacy of Islamic and Western contributions to medicine, have combined to give me all the tools I need not only to treat my patients, but with the Grace of God, to help heal them as well.

I also realize that what has become a narrow way of thinking among so many Muslims worldwide has caused us to lose many of the attributes that used to guide Muslim families and communities throughout history. In my own protected life in Wisconsin, and then the Navy, I was able to maintain an idyllic perception of my own faith and culture and its compatibility with the West. This idealism later gave way to a pragmatic grip on the reality, which is a crisis of recent history, leadership, and liberal scholarship among Muslims.

My journey as a physician has also been helped by the fact that I live in the most medically progressive country in the world, always on the cutting edge of technical and treatment innovations. While it is a challenge sometimes to keep up with the rapidly changing field of medicine, and at the same time to deal with the rapidly shrinking compensation many of us doctors are experiencing—another story in itself!—I feel thankful to God for the privilege to practice medicine in a country where competition and innovation push me to be the very best doctor I can be.

By the end of the 1990s, I had everything I could ask for: a beautiful and intelligent wife who shares my faith and my life, a career in medicine that was everything I dreamed it would be, and the start of a growing family. I could not have guessed that on a clear September day in New York in 2001, the world would change forever, and with it my life. I also could not have foreseen that my background as a physician, and my training in getting to the core causes of an illness, would help me as I later exposed the malignancy at the heart of this tragedy, the spiritual cancer known as Islamism.

PART II

AMERICA AND ISLAM AFTER 9/11

5

CHANGING THE PARADIGM

I so wish my grandfather and father had been alive to witness the long-overdue courage of Arabs across the Middle East who for the first time in generations began to stand up for their rights and their independence from their oppressors. Beginning in Tunisia and spreading to Egypt, Yemen, Bahrain, Libya, and Syria, to name the most significant uprisings, each country evolved in its own way, with the Syrian regime of Bashar Assad staying true to its reputation as the most repressive, barbaric regime of the Middle East, murdering, imprisoning, and torturing thousands upon thousands as they began their own revolution in March 2011. Many counted out Syria from the "Arab Spring" of 2011, saying that the level of repression from its minority-controlled Ba'athist Alawite Assad regime had a consolidation of power that made them immune to a popular uprising. The Assad regime and its military henchmen would again prove to be the most violent in the Middle East and were unconstrained by international pressures or morality. For Syrians, the dream of a spring was long smothered by a level of torture and terror unmatched anywhere else in the Middle East. They remained undaunted by month after month of an unending cycle of demonstrations across the towns of Syria followed by military repression, the murder of civilians, and the systematic military suffocation of communities whose suffering would only give rise to more demonstrations. The only question remaining was what kind of Syria and how many Syrians would be left when Assad finally made his exit. I can see how any attempts to shrug off the yoke of oppression may be looked upon as a "spring" after a long totalitarian winter. The reality, though, is that spring has hardly begun. Middle Eastern countries in general have been buried under a host of oppressive dictatorships for generations.

To "dig out," they will need a Marshall Plan of sorts by which we change the paradigm from throwing cash at our allies to actually investing in institutions (perhaps "pay as we go" joint programs) that help them build free societies based unapologetically on the ideas of liberty, freedom, and democracy rather than Islamism, socialism, or any autocratic systems. We must be careful not to facilitate a process that exchanges one oppressor for another, by, for example, moving from the secular fascism of Hosni Mubarak or Assad toward the theocratic supremacism of the Muslim Brotherhood groups and their Islamist allies. No one should ever be fooled by the bill of goods that Islamists often sell in order to get into power. While the power of the Islamist groups should not be underestimated, it is often overestimated. But as Middle Eastern countries climb out of their winter, the processes that will bring them closer to a real spring will be realized when they address the innumerable conflicts and incompatibilities that have emerged over the past centuries between the West and East. As the yoke of secular fascism is removed across the Arab world, it will begin to expose another long-festering incompatibility— that between the West (liberty) and Islamism (political Islam). The following table highlights some of the core ideological fault lines. While each of these fault lines deserves an in-depth discussion, the list by itself highlights a central narrative.

West (liberty) (Americanism)	vs.	Islamism (political Islam)
Individualism	vs.	Tribalism
Individual ideas	vs.	Collectivist thinking
Pluralism	vs.	Tolerance
Minority rights	vs.	Majority rights
Liberty	vs.	Democracy
Secularism and the "republic"	vs.	Theocracy
Democracy	vs.	Autocracy
Rule of law	vs.	Martial law
Government as protector of the individual	vs.	Government as protector of morality and God
Nationalism	vs.	Theocratic (Islamist) states
Reverence for religion	vs.	Reverence for past glory of religion and the desire to revive this glory
Truth	vs.	Corruption
Sanctity of life and humanitarianism	vs.	Dehumanization of life

Gender and racial equality	vs.	Misogyny and racism
Freedom of speech	vs.	Blasphemy laws
Freedom of choice	vs.	Apostasy laws
Cognitive reactions	vs.	Visceral reactions
Faith (relationship with God)	vs.	Religion (relationship as a community with God)
Constitutional law (derived from natural law)	vs.	Shariah law (derived solely from particular interpretations of the Qur'an and God's law)
Free markets and capitalism	vs.	Socialism

These conflicts will not resolve through elections, democracy, or a separation of powers. These conflicts need generational and institutional investment.

For so long we have compartmentalized the issues related to Islam as either domestic or foreign. We have even dealt with our policies toward each nation separately rather than by recognizing common themes. One of those common themes across the world, whether Nidal Hasan's massacre at Fort Hood or our legitimate fears of the Muslim Brotherhood takeover in Egypt, can be addressed only by defeating the ideas of political Islam within the Muslim consciousness with the universal ideas of liberty. What we do among American Muslims in this, the most open, free laboratory in the world, will carry over virally into the consciousness of Muslims around the world. These ideas are not new. There are Muslim thinkers who have advocated the separation of mosque and state. Most recently, for example, the work of Kyai Haji Abdurrahman Wahid, former president of Indonesia, is highlighted in the recently released English translation of the book *The Illusion of the Islamic State*. This book lays out, as is implied in its subtitle, "How an Alliance of Moderates Launched a Successful Jihad Against Radicalization and Terrorism in the World's Largest Muslim-Majority Country." They did that by exposing, as the title suggests, the fact that the "Islamic State" is an "Illusion," shaking the very theological foundations upon which such a state is built.

The Muslim ideas and thinkers devoted to modernity, reform, and liberty are out there; they just need our unwavering support, clarity, and perseverance. The United States just needs leadership in Washington that is willing to take sides in this battle only just beginning within the House of Islam between the advocates for liberty and those for Islamism. The U.S. government's relationships with Egypt, Syria, and Saudi Arabia define much of what is wrong with how we deal with the Middle East. In all three cases, the security interests of the United States are betrayed in many ways and yet we continue on the same course year after year. In addition, by supporting tyrannical, corrupt leaders in those countries, we have sent a message to the rest of the Middle East that while we say we support democracy, freedom, and human rights, our actions have at times revealed an agenda diametrically opposed to such things. The U.S. credibility problem among Arab nations cannot be overstated. It is a *huge* issue for millions upon millions of Arabs who see a great contradiction between what our country claims to stand for and the sorts of regimes we have supported around the world.

I am reminded of an American friend of mine who years ago made a trip to visit relatives in Argentina. Several of his cousins confronted him at the time and asked him, "Why is it that the United States, which claims to stand for freedom everywhere, has such a long history of backing up dictators in our part of the world, men who are responsible for thousands and thousands of deaths of ordinary citizens?" My friend had a response that shocked them, but nevertheless had the ring of truth. "Well," he said, "the problem is that we don't necessarily support freedom around the world, we support anticommunists, which is not exactly the same thing." This was in the late 1970s, when many countries in Latin America, including Argentina, were under the rule of right-wing military dictatorships. In several countries, including Chile, Argentina, and Uruguay, citizens would "disappear" in the middle of the night, abducted by the military, many of them never to be seen again. Citizens were often tortured as well. All this was done in the guise of keeping the country safe from communism, but the "cure" proved to be quite deadly, as the government dispensed with the normal process of justice and did whatever it wanted whenever it wanted. There are some conservatives who claim this ultimately kept U.S. interests protected and that therefore the means justified the ends. Such utilitarian thinking has done much to harm the image of the United States in the world. This is not said in order to encourage those who see the United States as being in the wrong no matter what we do, the "blame the U.S. first" crowd, as Jeanne Kirkpatrick called them. However, Ms. Kirkpatrick's famous speech lacked balance. There are cases where you can justifiably blame the United States for wrongheaded policy that has resulted in great damage to other nations. With the fall of the Soviet Union and the disappearance of the global Soviet threat of the Cold War, it is long overdue that we reboot the paradigm by which we calibrate our foreign policy in the world. Condoleezza Rice stated it best on June 20, 2005, at the American University in Cairo: "For sixty years, my country, the United States, pursued stability at the expense of democracy in this region, here in the Middle East—and we achieved neither. Now, we are taking a different course. We are supporting the democratic aspirations of all people." If American soft power is going to wield any more respect or influence now in the transformations across the Middle East, it will need to take steps to be recognized as a force for moral, ethical leadership and defense of advocates of liberty and universal freedom. As long as we are portrayed as a "weak horse" that vacillates in our principles, and whom we support is based upon the morally weak concept of the "lesser of two evils," we will have little influence upon their ideological battles.

South America is still in the process of trying to recover from years and years of extremely corrupt governments that left nations bankrupt and owing quantum debt. Can the United States be blamed for the status of these nations? Of course not. However, we cannot look away from our part in supporting such governments, and in lending them billions of dollars, even when we knew the likelihood of getting paid back was next to none and that they were likely to use the money to oppress their masses. As a result, such nations are essentially owned by the United States and other nations, which, of course, creates enormous hardships and resentment for ordinary citizens, as their economies teeter constantly on the edge of disaster. Many South Americans suspect that the United States had an ulterior motive when it made these loans and that they were made in bad faith, with the knowledge that once the debtor nations defaulted, it would give the United States economic leverage over these countries. Whether that is true or not, it certainly set a terrible precedent.

The idea that we could keep communism at bay by supporting

the worst sort of tinhorn dictators actually worsened the problem we wished to solve. Such oppressive and corrupt leaders pushed many people more to the left, with the idea that anything was better than the current government. And as we will see with the Middle East, our misguided policies over the last sixty years or so have actually pushed some of their citizenry in the direction of Islamism. The emerging power of Islamist movements in Tunisia, Egypt, and Libya proved that.

In the Middle East, we have continued our habit of supporting bad leaders. Saudi Arabia, for instance, whom we call an ally, has a long history of imbuing its children with the most virulent anti-Christian, anti-Semitic, anti-U.S., and anti-Israel messages. This actually takes place in educational settings, where along with their ABCs and math tables, children are taught that Christians and Jews are "unclean," that violence against Jews in particular is often justified because they are considered "enemies" of Islam, and that Israel is an abomination that should be destroyed. It is not by chance that most (fifteen of nineteen) of the 9/11 hijackers were from Saudi Arabia. The Wahhabist mind-set that rules the legal system in that nation has turned it into one of the most intolerant nations on earth, a country replete with oil money and modern technology, but from a moral perspective stuck in a premodern time in an inhuman, medieval legal system.

After 9/11, the Saudis were supposed to address the poisonous rhetoric being doled out in their schools, pressured, of course, to do so by the United States. Our Presidential United States Commission on International Religious Freedom (USCIRF) identified Saudi Arabia as a country of particular concern with regard to religious freedom. They helped expose the virulent nature of Saudi government texts used at a Saudi Embassy–run school in Northern Virginia, the Islamic Saudi Academy (ISA). This was especially relevant since it was operating on our soil and laid claim to a valedictorian, Ahmed Omar Abu Ali, who was later convicted in Saudi Arabia and given a life sentence for joining Al Qaeda and plotting to kill President George W. Bush. There is little evidence that the Saudis have changed their ideologies. Their corrections of texts amounted to whiting out a few "bad passages," but this text, as poisonous in its way as *Mein Kampf*, could not be changed with whiteout.

If anything, the United States has continued to pursue the same sort of policy with Saudi Arabia post-9/11, despite the religious fundamentalist mind-set that contributed to the formation of Al Qaeda and permeates the highest levels of the Saudi government. All of this is done by us because we need their oil and their strategic positioning in the area (against Iran). As far as U.S. security is concerned, we are willing, even after 9/11, to turn a blind eye to reality, even if it means that the Saudis will surely turn out more radicals, some of whom may eventually stage terrorist attacks on the United States.

The House of Saud and their domestic allies and radicals, the Wahhabists, of course, know this. Their oil money buys a lot of complicity and many other things, including professorships at places like Harvard or Georgetown University. Their millions of dollars in contributions to such universities have made it possible for them to fund Middle East Studies programs in which Islamist professors or their sympathizers are free to set the agenda they want, one that is typically anti–United States, anti-Israel, and often anti-Semitic. Such researchers as Daniel Pipes have spent many years uncovering the skewed agendas such professors offer, but largely to no avail, as far as universities' changing their policies with respect to such programs. This points to the need for more awareness among the general public and college administrators of how the Islamists work.

Americans at large don't seem to realize that radical Islam has a more subtle form, a propaganda arm that is determined to reach as far into the United States as possible, and that is making steady progress every year in anesthetizing Americans to the insidious threat of political Islam. In relation to Saudi Arabia alone, our reliance on their oil has created a monster of outrageous proportions. It's not just that we need their oil to help meet our energy needs, but that all the billions of dollars that this oil has given the Saudis have allowed them the wherewithal to support Islamist groups right here in the United States and across the world. Some have said in relation to Islamist terrorism that every time we fill up our gas tanks, part of the money goes to support such groups, which, of course, is true if one traces the roots of Islamism back to those countries, and if one considers how madrassas and Islamist mosques and schools have provided the ideological framework for Islamist movements, both "peaceful" (that is, propagandistic) and militant.

Saudi Arabia is a prime example of how an autocratic monarchy (despots) makes deals with the other devil—the Islamist theocrats. The royal family allowed the Wahhabis to control the legal system of Saudi Arabia in exchange for their own control of the government, military, and the economy (oil). Many Middle Eastern thugocracies are maintained with a similar relationship between what are often secular fascists in power and radical Islamists who are at times imprisoned and at other times fueled in order to maintain a bogeyman that the "secular" government can threaten the population with, along the lines of "Without us, they would be next to rule you." During the so-called Arab Spring, Qaddafi before his ultimate demise threatened his people that if he left, Al Qaeda would take over. Mubarak did the same in Egypt before his departure, letting Islamists out of jails and warning the population that the Muslim Brotherhood might soon take over. Mubarak's regime, however, did much to encourage a mind-set similar to the Muslim Brotherhood's. So-called secular Egyptian television would show the deeply anti-Semitic movie *Protocols of the Elders of Zion* during every holy month of Ramadan in order to indoctrinate the population into the groupthink of Islamism and anti-Semitism. The regime was secular but willingly fueled radical Islamism. After Mubarak's departure, the Islamist and Salafist gains in elections proved his self-fulfilling prophecy of legitimate concerns about Islamist takeover. But the Islamist ideologies were prevalent not as a sign of Egypt or Tunisia's future but rather deep-seated by-products of the previous generations of tyranny.

Any discussion about changing Middle Eastern paradigms must include the paramount issue of the Saudi oil lobby. The case for alternative sources of energy could not be more pressing. Without a need for their oil, we can "kick the bums out," as the fans used to shout at the Brooklyn Dodgers on bad days. But in this case, it will be for real. Saudi-supported groups in the United States would wither and die. Islamist professors would have to find real jobs, and even the U.S. madrassas, as well as certain mosques, would have a hard time staying afloat. As Deep Throat said to one of the young reporters in *All the President's Men*, "Follow the money." More to the point, dry up the source of the money and one may find that a large section of Islamism will simply disappear.

In comparison to Saudi Arabia, the problems the United States has with Egypt seem fairly straightforward. Egypt receives billions of dollars in aid from the United States every year, which was one of the conditions of signing the peace treaty with Israel all those years ago. In one way, of course, such a situation has worked very well: there has not been a war between Israel and Egypt since that time. However, if one looks closer, there are some very big problems. Mubarak was forced to step down after just a few weeks of millions of Egyptians protesting in the streets. The military stood down and Egypt entered an unforeseen period of transition. But that transition is not going to be easy, since the soil tilled in Egypt by Mubarak, his National Democratic Party (NDP), and the military and intelligence services created a society beleaguered by illiteracy, unemployment, corruption, anti-Semitism, and Islamism. Mubarak's newspapers were filled with anti-U.S. and anti-Israel rhetoric. The band of thugs who ran Egypt preferred to get the nation focused on blaming outsiders for their problems in order to divert their attention from their own condition. This attitude, of course, presumes that all Egyptians are incapable of seeing the obvious, bigger picture: that the United States was giving billions to their dictator and his fellow thugs that allowed him to stash away, by some reports, over $70 billion for his retirement. He will not be seeing those billions, instead seeing the inside of a cage during his trial by an Egyptian court that began in August 2011, but the role of the United States remains etched in the memories of Egyptians. Once again, we claim to support freedom and democracy in the Middle East, but here is a clear case of supporting a corrupt thug who made sure year after year that Egyptians did not have the rights and freedoms, or economic opportunities, for that matter, that they could have had in a true democracy. And what is our reason for supporting such a state of affairs? Supposedly because he kept the radical religious elements at bay, or at least out of the seat of power. Sound familiar? Wasn't this why we said we supported right-wing dictatorships in South America, with the idea that doing so kept the communists out? We have history repeating itself, and once again most Americans look the other way.

At the same time, some may ask, "Why should I care? My government sends money to all sorts of countries it probably shouldn't, and there's not much, if anything, I can do about it." Well, the truth is, there is something all of us can do to stop it, but the reason one should care is very simple. The longer any population, whether Egyptians, Saudis, or Syrians, suffers under such a regime, the more likely it is that religious fanatics can appeal to certain parts of the populace. As mentioned earlier, one of those who fell under the spell of the fanatics was Mohammed Atta. He simply found the situation in his country unbearably hopeless, and while he had an advanced degree from an esteemed German university, he felt there was no place for him in what he considered the corrupt wasteland of his country. This is not said in any way to justify or excuse what Atta did on 9/11. Even if he had had to do it from outside Egypt, Atta could have mounted a peaceful movement for true democracy and human rights in his country. The odds were stacked much higher against Gandhi when he did the same in India many years before, and he eventually succeeded.

Still, it is important to understand that violent radicals simply do not develop in a vacuum. In South America, the tug-of-war between the disparate socioeconomic strata in various countries, the minority of "haves" versus "have nots," created the extremes of conflict between left-wing and right-wing groups, and eventually led to the right, once in power in the 1970s, doing away with any sort of rights for those it considered enemies of the state. The Shah of Iran's failure to deal with human rights in his country eventually helped usher in the Islamist regime of Ayatollah Khomeini (who actually offered even fewer rights to his people, just like Castro after Batista, but so it goes with extreme political movements).

I do not believe in isolationism, and in fact such a mind-set is sure to lead us into failure against our threats. We live in a global economy with nuclear-empowered nations that, left to their own devices, without a check and on-the-ground competition from the United States, could quickly create even more imminent threats that could spin out of control. But if engagement is based on the precept that "our enemy's enemy is our friend," we cannot then expect to have credibility around the world as a moral nation. What I'd like to propose is something very radical indeed, a solution whose roots go all the way back to our own origins as a country: Let's actually support leaders and institutions around the world, even if they are relatively unknown, that embrace liberty and human rights, not just those that support our so-called interests. We must make a more holistic assessment of what effect our support for corrupt thugs will have in the long term upon our interests. How can our collective conscience countenance support for despots who treat their people like slaves? Our support does not need to be binary—either friend or foe. There should be an open discourse about the moral strings attached to our support and exactly what our feelings are about a nation's violation of human rights principles. We should have the president and the State Department make regular assessments, grading other nations diplomatically from A through F on their alignment with principles of freedom, liberty, and human rights. We may have to engage all of them for short-term problems, but we can also make it clear that while a Saudi Arabia may be an ally for a number of reasons, its own society is a D- or an F when it comes to universal human rights and freedom, and we will work to help them become an A, laying out those specific policies and principles that divide them from liberty and universal human rights.

There are those who say that in the Arab countries, it is not likely that democracy will ever work, that the countries are so tribal in nature that dictators and theocrats will probably continue to rule for the foreseeable future. But how do we know that? When have we ever really supported pro–human rights and pro-liberty leaders in the Middle East to give them even a chance at success (excluding Israel)? Even in the 2011 Arab Spring, over and over we came very late to supporting the heroic actions of the freedom activists.

Some may rightly point to Afghanistan and Iraq and say that those are recent examples of a change in policy, but while the corruption and "moodiness" against us in Afghanistan remain stupefying, and Iraq may turn out to be a success story as they become more and more independent. But the advocates of liberty are certainly still struggling against Islamists and corruption. What might the Middle East look like if Arab countries could create the sort of democracy and opportunities that Israel has created for its people? There are those who say that the problem is that the Arab countries are still finding their way after so many years under the yoke of colonialism. While it is true that many countries in the Middle East did not break free from European colonizers until after World War II, the fact is that Israel did not even come into being until 1948. From the very start, Israel was a true democracy and embraced human rights. Some may say that is because of all the European and American influence in Israel, that it was a country formed by Westerners in the Middle East, but still, however one explains it, Israel remains the lone beacon of true freedom and democracy in the region.

What, then, if anything, can be done in a country like Egypt that is going through a great transition? We do need to continue to send them aid. But it needs to be in the form of investments with measurable results, not blind handouts. What about the idea of leadership that is anti-Islamist and pro-liberty and pro-democracy? What about the idea that instead of creating all-powerful dynasties, leaders should be accountable to their citizens? Can't all our billions of dollars in aid come with some of those strings attached? Do we really believe that a military dictatorship, even if Mubarak is gone, is still the answer just to keep the radicals at bay? Or is the smarter way to keep radicals at bay to defeat them in an open battle of ideas in a free Egyptian society?

After Cairo's revolution, I can only pray that this is a revolution that will not only oust Mubarak's ilk, but usher in an era of true liberty and prosperity for Egypt. My concern is that what could stop all of that in its tracks is the Muslim Brotherhood—the global expansionist dreams of political Islam and its founders, Sayyid Qutb and Hassan al-Banna. My hope and all the signs are that the younger Egyptian generation is not as a majority driven by Islamism, but by a sincere desire for freedom and human rights and economic independence. Whether they can organize to override the Islamist designs of the Brotherhood has yet to be seen. Groups like the Brotherhood thrived in the political nuclear winter of Mubarak. The liberal democrats have a lot of time to make up, institutions to build, and ideas to spread. We must openly take their side and help them, not turn away blindly or help their oppressors.

The demonstrators in Syria, my family's motherland, showed in 2011 just what kind of a hellish regime controlled their lives and just what sorts of risks they were willing to take for real freedom. If there was one nation in the Middle East whose removal of its strongman would be in America's and Israel's immediate interest, it is Syria. Bashar Assad's cozy relationship with Hezbollah, Hamas, and Iran have long made his regime a major liability for American security. Assad's regime allowed many Al Qaeda operatives who killed Iraqis and Americans in Iraq to operate freely in Syria. Lebanon has remained chaotic because of Assad's henchmen and their thuggery. The Assads long held power through the outright brutalization of the Syrian people, which has created a global Syrian culture of fear. The pathologies within Syria after nearly half a century of rule by one of the worst fascist regimes in humanity are multidimensional. There are more Syrians living outside Syria than inside because so many have fled the brutality of the regime. And even though many of them now live in freedom after leaving their motherland, many are still afraid to speak out against Assad because of the long tentacles of the Syrian government. Any public comments or activities against the domestic and foreign interests of the Assad regime by any Syrians around the world may place our close or even distant family members in danger of reprisals, including imprisonment and torture. Assad always knew full well the impact that any global effort to isolate his government could have on his longevity.

One cannot overstate the degree of coercive influence that has for over forty years frightened Syrians around the world into submission. One can see in the inhuman brutality the Syrian people were subjected to during their 2011 revolution that the Assad regime views its citizens as slaves. While I have never even been to Syria, because of my own family history, that fear was conveyed to me by the grim reality of having family within Syria's walls. So I remained relatively silent. As an American to this day I still cannot fathom that fear, but I realize it exists. But in the memory of my grandfather I had to finally speak out, and in 2011 a group of us Syrian Americans with conscience formed a national group, Save Syria Now!, and began speaking out at every opportunity about the injustices and brutality of Bashar Assad and his thugs. Assad learned from his father, Hafez. The culture of fear created by the Assads among Syrians domestically and abroad was unspeakable.

The unbelievable courage exemplified by the freedom activists on the streets of Syria in 2011 spilled over to all of us Syrian Americans with a conscience in the United States. It drove many of us for the first time to set aside family fear of reprisals and do what we could to get the voices of the demonstrators heard. Their plight needed to be seen by all, and the Obama administration needed to do something. Silence and inaction were no longer an option for many Syrian Americans. Syria is a diverse nation, with a 75 percent Sunni population and a large Kurdish and Christian population, in addition to Alawites, Druze, and others. Many courageous opposition groups evolved inside and outside Syria. Unfortunately, the Syrian National Council, which gathered initially in Turkey, garnering the premature support of the Obama administration, was inordinately influenced by Syrian Islamists. For this reason many of us of Syrian origin helped drive the formation and empowerment of an alternative, far more diverse opposition coalition not influenced by Islamists—the Syrian Democratic Coalition (SDC). We formed the SDC with a clear mission and pledge that all of our members signed promising a vision for Syria that was pluralistic, non-Islamist, and based in liberty and minority rights. But traction for any opposition coalition is often impossible in the tyrannical environment that they seek to replace. It will be a protracted process with many obstacles. The evolution out of oppression will be difficult, if not an abject failure, without leaders in the West able to take the side of liberal democrats over Islamists. If there is a single Arab nation where the Muslim Brotherhood and Islamists have little chance of takeover, it is Syria. Yet they have shown considerable influence simply due to their organization. As a crossroads nation in the Middle East with modest oil revenue, it has a very strong mercantile tradition and culture. Educationally, it also had a strong history before the devastation that the Assads wrought on the country.

The courage of Syrians taught me more than anything in recent memory the lengths to which people of conscience will go to win back their freedoms and their dignity. I know if my grandfather were alive he would tell me that while my work against political Islam and for liberty-based reform can pose security threats and exact a high price, it pales in comparison to the courage of Syrians who died in the streets in the Syrian revolution that began in 2011 with the hope of giving other Syrians and future generations freedom, much as our Founding Fathers did in the United States.

When it comes to other predominantly Muslim countries throughout the Middle East as well as elsewhere, some standards should apply. We have a choice as a country. We can continue to prop up corrupt, oppressive leaders, or we can take a chapter out of our own better history and learn from that. After World War II, General Eisenhower said that the way we could know if we had been truly victorious in defeating the Nazis would be whether in fifty years Germany was free and prosperous. It's been over fifty years since then, and Germany is a united democratic nation that is a model of freedom and prosperity. Our efforts on behalf of the Japanese and the South Koreans were similarly successful. The proof is there that when we want to, we can help re-create the successful American "experiment" in freedom, democracy, and prosperity in other lands. This, in fact, is the America that is loved throughout the world, the one that has used its strength and know-how to help change other nations for the better. Just as Islamism must become a thing of the past, the other America, the one that supports secular tyrants whose oppressive regimes have unintentionally helped the cause of the theocrats, also needs to be relegated to the dustbin. We can help advocate a third pathway toward liberty within Muslim-majority nations.

At the same time, there are certain standards that should be applied by Muslims both inside and outside the United States to support and guide the U.S. government in steering a course that will be beneficial not just to U.S.–Middle East relations but to the world at large. These standards should include:

1. An Islamic narrative that does not constrain universal human principles.

2. Muslim leaders who support the separation of mosque and state, even as they take stands on social or political issues.

3. The affirmation of an egalitarian approach to faith beyond the constraints of simple tolerance. Tolerance implies superiority, while pluralism implies equality.

4. Recognition that if government enacts the literal laws of God rather than natural or human law, then government becomes God and abrogates religion and the personal nature of the relationship with God.

5. Separation of mosque and state, to include the abrogation of all blasphemy and apostasy laws.

6. Empowerment of women's liberation and advocacy for equality, which is currently absent in many Muslim-majority, misogynistic cultures.

7. *Ijtihad,* negating the need for Muslims active in politics today to bring theology into the political debate. Nowhere in the Qur'an does God tell Muslims to mix politics and religion or instruct by what document governments should be guided.

8. Creation of movements and organizations that are specifically opposed to such radical or terrorism-supporting groups as Al Qaeda, Hamas, Hezbollah, Jamaat al-Islamiya, and Al-Muhajiroun by name, rather than simply being against undefined, generic notions of terrorism.

9. Public identification without apologetics of government leaders and power brokers of Muslim-majority countries who are dictators, despots, or Islamists, and

are, as such, antiliberty and antipluralism. Muslims enjoying freedom in the West are just now beginning to help fuel mass movements to liberate their motherlands from dictatorship and theocracy. Now we need to help and empower only those who want to move these societies toward secular liberal democracies founded on individual liberties for all based in natural law.

10. Establishment of classical liberal Muslim institutions and think tanks to articulate, disseminate, and educate concerning the above principles. The idea that individual liberty and freedom and Muslim theology need not be mutually exclusive must be taught to Muslim youth. Our Muslim Liberty Project at the American Islamic Forum for Democracy is dedicated to this end.

When we have truly taken the time and the effort to reshape how we deal with the Middle East and Muslim nations in general, we will find that once again America can change the world for the better. In this case, it could be that a modernizing Islamic reformist movement both within and outside the United States will give government the push it needs to change the nature of U.S.–Middle East relations.

6

ARAB RESPONSES TO 9/11

In his recent book, *Blood Revenge: Family Honor, Mediation and Outcasting,* Joseph Ginat talks about four issues that he considers core to Arab tribalism: blood revenge, mediation, outcasting, and "honor" murder. Ginat makes the point that revenge and "honor" murder are not actually supported by the Qur'an and offers plenty of quotations to back up this claim. Others, such as Robert Spencer, have argued the opposite: that the Qur'an offers plenty of verses that call for revenge and "honor" murder. They make the points argued by militant Wahhabists who believe in an extreme version of Islamism. In a future chapter, we will specifically examine some of the most common Qur'anic quotations that are offered as proof by some that "honor" killings are sanctioned by the Prophet Muhammad, something that I believe is largely the result of misinterpretation and bad or intentional mistranslation from the original Arabic, but for now I think it will help to take a closer look at some other aspects of Arab tribalism related to social and political traditions. To truly understand the lack of public outrage of many in the Arab and Muslim American community when it came to 9/11, it is crucial to understand how Arab tribalism affected such a phenomenon and how it continues to affect this community up to the present day, despite the fact that there are now many second- and third-generation Arab Americans.

One must first begin to understand that Arab culture is one of the oldest in the world. Hammurabic law—"an eye for an eye"—still predominates in many Arab countries, so that punishments that are particularly barbaric to the West, such as cutting off the hand of a robber and stoning adulterers, continue in such nations as Saudi Arabia and Iran. Along with such ancient laws, what the tribe thinks is more important than individual opinion. While in the United States, a son or daughter may behave publicly in ways that are quite controversial and simply say they are being themselves, in ancient cultures the idea is that whatever a son or daughter does reflects directly on the entire family or tribe. For the tribe, anyone who behaves in a dishonorable way is considered a direct threat to the tribe's survival, and if the family does not address the individual's dishonor, they themselves risk being cut off from the tribe. In ancient times, this literally meant the family could perish, as they would be forced to face the elements alone. In modern times, the consequences are typically a bit more blurred, and often largely psychological, but the threat of being cut off by the community still carries enormous weight.

Beyond the idea of dishonor, the tendency to overly conform to certain ways of behaving as well as certain political ideologies is very widespread in Arab culture. The Islamists have taken advantage of this cultural trend toward rigid conformity to spread their ideas about political Islam throughout the Middle East, knowing quite well that Arab "groupthink" would allow it to catch fire in certain quarters where people were inclined to both religious fundamentalism and political activism, and once that was the case, could prove to be a very powerful force against reform. The Muslim Brotherhood is one painfully clear example of that: very clear, straightforward ideas about Islamist supremacy that have spread their way beyond Egypt and throughout the Muslim consciousness across the world. Their idea is to unite Muslims as a "tribe" in a campaign of worldwide domination, often using the suggestion of gross victimization of Muslims; what is truly frightening is how rigidly their adherents embrace this ideology, with every bit as much fervor as a committed Stalinist or Nazi in the last century. The whole idea of a link between the Israeli-Palestinian crisis and the threat to the West of terrorism is false. Any link is a deception. Islamist terror is inspired by Islamism, not by any specific geopolitical conflict of the day. Islamists use such geopolitical conflicts as the Israeli-Palestinian conflict, Iraq, and Afghanistan to collectivize Muslims in a Machiavellian way against a common external enemy (America, Israel, Christians, the Jews . . .). If somehow the Israeli-Palestinian crisis were solved today, tomorrow Islamists would find another diversionary rallying crisis to fuel the platform of political Islam.

One must keep in mind that the idea of "rugged individualism" is very much an American phenomenon, and that while machismo is on display throughout the Arab world, even the most "macho" Arab dictators, such as Saddam Hussein, are not exempt from the influence of tribalism. For instance, while Hussein rose to power at a time in Arab history when secular nationalism was very much in vogue, as the years went on, there was more and more distrust of the corruption of secular governments. The Iranian Islamic revolution that brought Khomeini to power also led many in Arab countries to wonder if a theocratic government might not be the solution to their ills. So what did Hussein do? He began to wear traditional Arab garb and was seen to pray in public. Was he really a genuinely devout Muslim? Of course not. His extremely lavish, corrupt lifestyle and murderous regime were proof that was not the case.

Hafez Assad did the same as the Islamists (the Muslim Brotherhood) gained influence in Syria. Assad beat his citizens into submission through murder, imprisonment, torture, and abuse.

The pathologies within Syria after nearly a half century of rule by one of the worst fascist regimes in humanity are multidimensional. The culture of fear is deep and pervasive. The free speech of Syrian expatriates remained largely muted by the long tentacles of the Syrian government.

It is well-known within the Syrian expatriate network that the Assad regime has countless global sympathizers and agents who either directly or indirectly provide information to Damascus on any and all activities of Syrians who live abroad. In exchange for this information they may get a number of benefits, from being told that their families will be "left alone" to receiving financial benefits from the Syrian security apparatus. At times this information will lead to the detaining and torture of other Syrians domestically in order to obtain more information about antiregime activities. The information thus obtained is used to create psychological countermeasures both in Syria and outside in order to prevent any type of movement against the interests of the Assad regime.

Hafez Assad was not to be messed with, and eventually, after decades, the people of Syria became quite passive, fearful, and submissive to the regime. Repeatedly, Assad's henchmen would make public examples of anyone who spoke out against the regime, as witness the massacre in Hama in 1982 of more than forty thousand Syrians, including women and children, in just a few weeks. Hama became the standard by which Syrians measured the lengths to which their oppressors would go to silence them. In the Syrian uprising of the spring of 2011, the people of Dara'a, Homs, Banias, and other towns across Syria began to feel "Hama Rules," as Tom Friedman described them after the Hama massacre. But 2011 was different. They could not leave the street because they knew the fate that awaited them if they did. There was a crack in the yoke of oppression and a change in the tide of tribalism that fed off fear and groupthink.

In terms of how tribalism plays out on the familial and societal levels, one needs to continue to keep in mind that having a different opinion or lifestyle in certain Arab countries can get you killed. The sort of political satire that plays well in many Western countries is not acceptable in most Arab countries. In Jordan or in Saudi Arabia, for example, one can be arrested for simply talking negatively about the royal family. We're not talking threats, but simply being in disagreement with their regime, and publicly saying critical things, what is generally recognized as free speech in America. In a tribal culture, where disrespect of the chief is unacceptable, it can cost you dearly.

Egypt's Anwar Sadat was a much more dramatic example of a "tribal leader" who would break ranks with the tribe. Mind you, Sadat was always an autocrat who dealt with his political enemies swiftly and by less than democratic principles. But one could not help but respect the leadership he showed in his approach toward Israel and Prime Minister Begin. For decades, blind hatred of Jews, Israel, and the United States had been the norm in many Arab countries, including Egypt. Sadat toed that line for some time, but in what was a life-changing moment for him that also changed history, he decided that he wanted to pursue peace with Israel via the United States. If many in the Arab world at the time wondered about his sincerity, and perhaps thought that he was simply laying a trap for the Israelis and the United States, they were soon proven wrong. Sadat was completely sincere, and being driven in part by his own Islamic faith, did everything possible to make a peace deal possible. It's true that Sadat did not tolerate dissent, and was a despot in his own way. At the same time, he was completely ahead of his time in reaching out to the Israelis and Americans to make peace.

It was a tremendous risk, and eventually he paid the ultimate price for being a peacemaker with his life, assassinated by agents of the Muslim Brotherhood. Trust me when I tell you that there were many in the Arab world who were happy when he was killed. I can remember Arab Americans who said to me that he deserved to die for making peace with the "enemy." The man was a visionary, one of the most forward-thinking Arab leaders in the last hundred years, and yet there were many Arabs who could not have cared less about the progress he made on behalf of peace between the Egyptians and the Israelis. For them, he had betrayed the tribe, the entire Arab world at large, and such disrespect to them was worthy of death.

A domestic example of this tribalism and how so-called leading American Arab organizations are compromised and often corrupted was reported by Jennifer Rubin of the *Washington Post* in June 2011. Malek Jandali, a Syrian American classical pianist and composer who often played with the Atlanta Symphony Orchestra, was set to be honored by the American-Arab Anti-Discrimination Committee (ADC) at their annual dinner. But the piece he chose to play had lyrics that stated, "I am my homeland, and my homeland is me. The fire in my heart burns with love for you! Oh my homeland, when will I see you free? . . . When the land is watered with the blood of martyrs and the brave, and all people shout: Freedom to mankind!" The president of the ADC, Safa Rifka, who had a long-standing relationship with Assad's man in D.C, the Syrian ambassador to Washington, insisted that Jandali change his song choice. Jandali, a brilliant musician, never before an activist, refused, and he was disinvited. When the media pressed the ADC, they responded that it was "not their policy to promote any particular side of a dispute." That is, as long as it does not involve the United States or Israel. For this stance, Jandali's parents, living in Homs, Syria, were beaten by military thugs in September 2011, and after they fled to the United States, their home was broken into and ransacked. The relative silence, if not facilitation provided by the ADC on American soil, speaks volumes to the corruption of Arab tribalism.

On a less dramatic note, we can look at something rather eccentric, though not a crime, like eloping. In Western culture it is something that happens often enough. There may be disapproval or even eye-rolling, but as a general rule it doesn't result in one's being kicked out of one's family. Not so in Arab culture. While arranged marriages are not as common as they once were in the Middle East, parents are still very much involved in their children's weddings, and at the very least, the families of both the bride and groom get to know each other in advance of the ceremony, and sons and daughters are expected to marry people from "good" families. This, of course, goes on in the West as well, but if a son or daughter goes against the parents' wishes and marries someone simply because he or she loves that person, regardless of the family's societal status, it may cause tension in the family, but the parents eventually accept their child's decision.

Here, in my experience in the Arab American community in the United States, such understanding is not typically the case. There is still much traditionalism when it comes to marriage, and if one marries someone the family does not approve of, or who is not of the same religion, this tends to be a much bigger deal than for those more assimilated into the American mainstream. My parents, for instance, embraced Western values of democracy and human rights long before they ever emigrated to America, and once they got here quickly developed a very deep love for this land. But if my sisters or I had eloped and gotten married in Las Vegas, it would have been a source of deep family shame. The idea of protecting the honor of one's daughters runs very deep in Arab culture, pathologically more so than for the sons, and is inextricably linked to overall family honor—and we were no exception to that rule.

* * *

Despite the advantage of free speech in America, there are definitely tribal-based reasons why not all Arab Americans take advantage of it, even when it comes to an event as tragic as 9/11, which affected all Muslim and Arab Americans in one way or another. I honestly believe there are many Arab Americans who wanted to speak out against the terrorists but didn't, out of fear of the reactions of others in the Arab American community, as well as how it might have affected family members who still live in the Middle East. I say this because I personally know Arab and Muslim Americans who did not speak out for just that reason, who passionately felt the tragedy of 9/11 and at the same time were concerned about being censured or worse by others in the Arab American community who might accuse them of being too sympathetic to a country that has supported Israel in its wars with various Arab countries. Beyond that, those who still have family in the Middle East are keenly aware that in the global village in which we now live due to the Internet, what is said in New York or Los Angeles or Phoenix can easily be heard or read in Cairo or Damascus the same day.

While it is not outrageous to believe that the despotic regimes in the Middle East actually scan such statements made by Arab Americans in America—there is proof they do—and that potentially such statements could negatively affect a person's relatives in such a country, my experience has been that most Arab and Muslim Americans who don't speak out are really more afraid of reactions closer to home.

My own mother, as keenly intelligent, warm, loving, compassionate, and independent as she is, is still very consumed with Arab rules of etiquette here in the Arab American community, so that what you say, and whom you say it to, and whom you invite to a dinner and don't, and so forth, take on monumental importance. Her social and tribal priorities are a reflection of the priorities of the rest of her Arabic social circles. She has always waged her own battles on those points that led her at times to the limits of her own moral outrage, and they were often the same as mine. Her and similarly my wife's engagement of the greater Arab and Muslim American social network ("ABS—the Arabic Broadcasting System") put them in a position to be the primary targets of fallout from my reform work. Refusing to engage me in my ideas publicly or even personally, many in the local community instead opted for more passive-aggressive social pressure to try to marginalize me and my family and in effect get me to stop shaking the trees. In many ways that pressure had more impact than any substantive public debates ever could have, and that is exactly why they employed it. Simply for questioning the imams and countering political Islam and its Muslim Brotherhood legacy organizations, our families would confront a social pressure and marginalization locally and across the nation that defies explanation, other than as simply a subconscious form of psychological countermeasures known in the military as "psyops." More important than individualism, diversity, and critical thinking is the homogeneity of the social clique, the tribe. Shake the trees too hard, especially where the neighbors and the nation can see and hear the debate, stand back for the fallout, even if you are speaking the truth or at least raising the questions no one else is raising.

So, when one extends that analysis to Arab American reactions to 9/11, what one has to keep in mind is that stepping out and making public statements that go contrary to much of accepted American Muslim beliefs about U.S.–Middle East relations—and actually holding Muslims to account for the sort of culture that helped form the mind-set of the 9/11 hijackers—is a very big deal indeed. I quickly found out just how deep Arab tribalism goes when I formed AIFD and took on some of those widely accepted political belief systems. Some incidents in particular are worth recounting.

For instance, when I organized the "Standing with Muslims Against Terrorism" rally in Phoenix in 2004, there were local Arab Muslims who promised their support and then for a variety of reasons withdrew it in advance of the rally. In some cases, I found out that they did so because they were afraid of how they might be perceived by other Muslims in the community and of the potential backlash. Again, Arab tribalism comes to Phoenix, and in this case, the prospect of others' disapproval outweighed what they knew to be morally right. In other cases, both tribalism and politics came to play a part. Some who had agreed to support the rally withdrew their support when I refused to address the Israeli-Palestinian issue, or to let other speakers do so. I was unequivocally against that, and for good reason. How could we expect anyone in the community to take us seriously if, on the one hand, we claimed to renounce terrorism, but on the other, appeared to make that conditional, based on Israel's need to change policy related to the West Bank? That made no sense to me and still doesn't. The saving grace was that there were in fact hundreds of local Muslims, among them some of our closest friends, who did brave the social pressure and join us in the nation's first Muslim rally against terrorism. But only hundreds showed up, when at any given citywide prayer service in Phoenix, five to ten thousand Muslims show up.

This pressure was also another clear case of people who let tribalism and politics dictate their actions, instead of what they knew to be morally right. At first, they were all for the rally, but then, as they encountered some initial backlash in the community, even in advance of the rally, they backed off and played the game of moral equivalency. No, I told them, you cannot say there is no real difference between a country that defends itself and a homicide bomber who kills innocent men, women, and children on a bus. You cannot say that directly, or indirectly, because however you phrase it, I told them, you're wrong, and I will not have the rally somehow made irrelevant by such absurd, unfair statements and apologetics born out of moral weakness. I stood my ground, and they, as expected, chose not to participate.

In addition to this, the hate speech against my work flowed into Muslim homes in Phoenix. As was mentioned in the introduction, the *Muslim Voice* published a half-page cartoon against me portraying me as a dog at the end of a leash held by the staff of *The Arizona Republic*—corrupt propaganda fit for Hamas or the despotism of President Hafez Assad of Syria. Even when anti-Islamists are devout and orthodox and heavily involved in mosques and local worship they will spread the libel that we are "ignorant," "nonpracticing," or "not part of *The Muslim Community*," as if it were one community that determined who was or was not a part of it. Never mind my children's regular attendance at weekend school or our attendance at mosque fund-raisers, dinners, Ramadan gatherings, and Friday prayers. The truth did not matter when lies could be used to malign the greatest threat to their existence—a conservative American Muslim voice for reform against Islamism from within our Muslim communities and consciousness. Again, this is a real case of tribalism, in which someone who breaks ranks with the status quo is somehow perceived as a lapdog for powerful interests, since nothing else could explain why I actually support Israel's right to exist, or why I have a deep love for my country and believe in its right to defend itself. Just the same, if my fight against Islamism and the most negative aspects of Arab tribalism provokes this sort of reaction as well as similar disapproval from CAIR and other Islamist organizations, then I know I am really doing my job! I experienced a more insidious Arabic psyop right before my testimony to Congress on Muslim radicalization for the House Committee on Homeland Security led by Chairman Peter King (R-NY) on March 10, 2011. I received it the evening before the testimony of what would become the most controversial hearing since 9/11. A socially prominent spouse of a leading Muslim in the local Phoenix Arabic Islamist establishment sent me an illustrative and pointed email on the evening of March 9, 2011. She opened by telling me that she was writing to me on the day before I was to publicly give my "views on Islamic matters." She affectionately called me "our dear brother" and then began the guilt trip and her channeling of God:

> *Since you were born and raised in this country, you know that generalization about people is totally wrong, and more so when we are wrong, and worse yet, if we did that without checking with the people that we are representing [emphasis hers]. Our dear and respected brother, several times your views were not welcomed by the majority of the Muslim community, if not all. . . . We will not gain earthly matter if we upset Allah. . . . Please please, our dear brother, remember that, when you are speaking to the world. It is not right to go on public television, radio, and or newspaper, and tag Muslims with some unfitting names. . . . Anytime, anyone speaks ill about Muslims, someone gets killed right here in the United States of America, whether he or she is a Muslim or Seikh. Do you really like to see that happening in this very country. Allah will not reward such move. Surely that is not what Allah's Vicegerent would do. Look at the Muslims around you. How on earth, do you feel right to speak ill about them? . . . We certainly don't need a good friend of ours to say something hurtful, not right, and or ill about any Muslim in public and in a country that is not fully aware*

how good many Muslims are. . . . Since you have some kind of
ground in the media here, you are going to be questioned by the
higher authority even more than a regular person.

She closed by invoking an even greater guilt with a pious reminder that I "be careful of every word" I say. She reminded me
that I should be mindful that my actions in this life will shape my
next and she prayed that God support my good intention—an ad-
monishment reserved for deeply spiritual and religious Muslims.
She ended, *"Allah bless you"* (name withheld).

Never mind the actual substance of my testimony to Congress
the next day. Never mind her Muslim responsibility. She was
intimidating me with the suggestion that my openness might be
responsible for hate crimes against Muslims and God will see
this and hold me accountable! If this midnight-hour guilt trip on
March 9, 2011, from a close family friend isn't oppressive tribal
psyops, I don't know what is. Of all the twisted logic in her note,
the most interesting thing about this email is that while criticizing me for being anti-Muslim, she is also demonstrably appealing
to me as a devout Muslim with a strong belief in God, actually
paradoxically acknowledging that this person honestly realizes
that Islam and God are very important to me.

One of my relatives once said that if nine people agree on
something, and one person doesn't, well, then, that one person
must be wrong. Without intending to, I believe he very accurately
defined the essence of tribalism. I, on the other hand, believe that
it is that one person with a contrary opinion who can be responsible for real progress. Galileo ring a bell? What if Einstein had
decided that he could not be smarter than Newton? Just a few
years ago, most people would not have believed it would be possible to post rally videos onto the Internet from our cell phones.

145

However, the visionaries among us saw things differently and made it come to pass.

For that matter, who would have even believed back in the 1990s that an African American would be elected president of the United States in the early part of the twenty-first century? I would bet you that Barack Obama believed it could be so, as much as others around him might have ridiculed him if he had spoken his dream aloud at that point.

When it comes to Arab tribalism, I believe we have a long, difficult battle ahead of us, but at the same time if those of us of conscience step forward, and are willing to pay the price—whatever that may be—to question the status quo, then I believe that eventually we may see a world in the Middle East and in the Arab American or Muslim American community at large where differences of opinion are encouraged, instead of snuffed out.

7

AMERICAN RESPONSES TO FORT HOOD

I believe that everyone who cares about the future of the media in this country should read *Bias: A CBS Insider Exposes How the Mainstream Media Distort the News*, a book written by Bernie Goldberg a few years back. Goldberg spent twenty-eight years at CBS and progressively began to see a trend at his news station (he worked for Dan Rather) and others of a liberal bias in their news reports. For instance, one of the stories that Goldberg talks about is how back in the 1980s the media, in lockstep with each other, began to report that the AIDS epidemic that had just begun would soon be extremely widespread in the heterosexual community. At the time, the disease was primarily confined in the United States to male homosexuals and IV drug users. The prediction that the disease would soon be widespread throughout the general population of the United States, like a modern Black Plague, was presented to the American public as though it was fact, though if one looked closer there did not appear to be hard research to back up this claim. There was a reason for that. There was *no* hard research, but merely the opinions of AIDS activist groups who speculated that the disease would soon decimate Americans regardless of sexual orientation.

The groups' mission was to get more attention focused on the problem of AIDS, which they justly felt was being ignored by a lot of Americans, including influential politicians, many of whom looked at it as a disease that affected only gays and drug addicts, and therefore seemed unconcerned about doing anything to help the afflicted. These groups wanted more focus on treatment and prevention, and if they had to bend the truth to make that happen—by making the possibility of a widespread epidemic seem like unquestionable fact—then so be it. The problem is that the media went with the story without bothering to question it. This, of course, was a major problem, since there was not even the pretense of objectivity. When Goldberg questioned reporters and producers about this, their responses were fairly uniform: Perhaps the story was not based on fact, but it was for a good cause. What did it matter, they seemed to say, that the story was based on speculation if in the long run more people got helped?

The problem with this kind of thinking is that no matter how good the cause, objective thinking gets tossed aside. Was it noble to want to help minorities with a terminal illness who were being marginalized in many quarters? Of course. Was it okay to stretch the truth toward that end? No.

The problem is that these biased scenarios continue to play out in the mainstream media over and over again, and the Fort Hood massacre was no exception. The media's PC whitewash brigade came out in full force, and as we shall see, without intending to, many of them encouraged the sort of victimology mind-set that is at the core of Islamist thinking and violence.

As soon as I heard that an American Muslim who was also an Army psychiatrist committed these horrific killings, I got an awful feeling in my stomach. My God, I thought, here is someone with a background very much like mine, and he has turned on his fellow soldiers and killed them in cold blood. The parallels were stark for me, to say the least. It's not that I didn't think that Islamists gone militant were capable of something like this, it's more that when it actually happened, I felt shocked just the same. Intellectually knowing something can happen and then seeing it happen in real life are two very different things. Knowing that this radical Islamist walked the halls of many of the same military hospitals and training centers that I did as a U.S. Navy medical resident and officer hit closer to home for me than any other attack.

I knew right away that the media were likely to be in touch with me about this story, and sure enough, the phone started to ring with requests for interviews—a number of CNN shows, various national radio shows, including William Bennett and Laura Ingraham, as well as such newspapers as the *Dallas Morning News*. Some frequent questions were: How could this happen? As a Muslim, can you explain it? What is it that separates someone like yourself from Major Nidal Hasan, since both of you are Muslims who served in the armed services? Usually followed by, Were you harassed when you were in the service?

From the very first interview, I made it clear that I believed that this was a militant Islamist terrorist act, that all the proof was there, from his shouting out *"Allahu Akbar!"* as he began shooting, to his affiliation with the radical, homegrown American jihadist Imam Anwar Al-Awlaki in Yemen, to his anti-American statements to other officers, including telling a group of them at what was supposed to be a medical psychiatric lecture that there are Muslims who believe that non-Muslims are destined for hell and among other things should have hot oil poured down their throats. Is this, in fact, what Hasan himself believed? This should have been the question military authorities asked. Why was he talking about such things at what was supposed to be a medical lecture? In my Navy days, had I done such a thing, my superiors would have been perfectly within their rights to inquire about my motivation and determine whether I had been compromised by an ideology. So how was it, I wondered, that Hasan's superiors somehow overlooked what would appear to be some telltale signs of possible disloyalty or worse within their ranks? The only answer that I had was that so-called political correctness had taken precedence over common sense and the most basic security precautions that should have been taken.

As for how Hasan turned into an Islamist terrorist, I made it clear that in the current environment, it is not that hard to do. I told several interviewers that there are plenty of radical mosques right here in this country and, more accurately, many mosques that preach an Islamism that is more often than not nonviolent but is a necessary precursor of the Islamist extremism that influenced Hasan. As more information came out about Hasan and Imam Al-Awlaki, the media continued to seem bizarrely nonplussed by the fact that the jihadist imam who was directing him had been the imam at mosques in Denver and San Diego, and at Dar Al-Hijra, one of the largest mosques in the country, in Northern Virginia. I recalled how the Islamist imam I had interviewed for the position of imam at Bethesda Naval Hospital in the mid-nineties had demonstrated a separatism classical for entrenched political Islam. So it did not surprise me that Imam Al-Awlaki, who was sliding down the slope of radicalization himself before he'd become a radicalizer, had found a home there right around the time of 9/11 (2001 and 2002). In fact he led an Islamic prayer service at the Pentagon. Two of the 9/11 hijackers can be traced back to his teaching. He defended the Taliban in an online chat for the *Washington Post* after 9/11 and told *National Geographic* that Israel was responsible for 9/11. If one is inclined toward radicalism, the teachers are there and more than willing to take on new pupils. Hasan's evil acts should open our eyes to the ideologies being disseminated on our soil that send Muslims down the slippery slope of radicalization, making them susceptible to violent jihadists like Awlaki.

While many of the interviews went well, I noticed many of the news reports seemed to tiptoe over Hasan's Muslim background and its relevance to his violent actions. They often loved having me on because the host and their producers felt that my bio and loyalty to the United States quickly and effectively dispelled the stereotypes created by Hasan's murderous rampage. However, when I went beyond the surface and openly discussed the need for America to dissect and expose the nonviolent Islamist precursor ideologies (political Islam) that fueled Major Hasan for years, it fell upon deaf ears. Few wanted to have anything to do with Hasan's theo-political radicalization. This even included the Pentagon brass, which put together an eighty-four-page after-action report that not once discussed Islam, Islamism, jihad, or any theo-political stimuli of Hasan's. It didn't even mention his name. Some wanted to emphasize that he must have been psychologically traumatized to do what he did and rejected out of hand the idea that religious ideology might have played a part. Others felt he must have been harassed, effectively making his motivation similar to that of the Columbine shooters: picked on to the point where a mental break resulted. But that, of course, is an overly simple read of what happened at Columbine, and at the same time it does not seem to explain Hasan, since there appeared to be no real evidence that he had been harassed about his religion or ethnicity. With some reporters, it seemed as though they had more empathy for Hasan and his religion than for his victims.

Behind many of these reports was the unspoken idea that it was this country's fault or the Army's, anybody's responsibility but Hasan's. While I believe totally in our need to respect cultural, ethnic, and religious differences, and that this is part of the core of what makes America great, we do no one any favors when we deny reality and we enable pathology. At the same time, I'm not suggesting a rush to judgment. But when an Army psychiatrist gives away his Qur'an to a neighbor the night before the shoot-ings and says he's going to do God's work, when he begins to openly criticize the U.S. military's strategy in the Middle East—bringing into question his overall loyalty to his country as a member of the Army—and when his business card lists him as SoA, a "Soldier of Allah," and he shouts *"Allahu Akbar!"* before he opens fire on his fellow soldiers, when all of these pieces of the puzzle have come together, then it is outright irresponsibility for a journalist to gloss over those salient facts.

The height of absurdity for me was when Chris Matthews asked me in reference to Hasan's emailing back and forth with a radical sheikh in Yemen, "Is it a crime to call Al Qaeda?" At the time, I was in such a state of disbelief that he could actually pose such a question that I was not able to say what I really wanted to, which was "You *can't* be serious! Of course, it's a crime to call Al Qaeda if you're a member of the Army, since we are, in fact, at war with this terrorist group. And as President Bush said once upon a time in reference to the American civilian population, 'If you're calling Al Qaeda, we want to know about it.'" The clip with Mat-thews asking this was run over and over again on Fox News as an example of PC correctness gone amok.

There were also the predictable media appearances of members of CAIR and other Islamist groups, who made it a point to em-phasize their own diagnosis that Hasan was mentally ill, that no one should view his actions as having anything to do with Islam. Interviewing Nihad Awad, CAIR's national executive director, Chris Matthews asked him if Hasan should have been given conscientious objector (CO) status, thus preventing the rampage. Such lines of thought are foolish and dangerously deny the deep-seated theo-political ideology that threatens us. CO status would not only have been an affront to every Muslim who serves hon-orably in our armed services, but it would also have stigmatized all of us patriotic Muslims. Do they have the right to make such ridiculous statements? Of course. This is America and they are guaranteed freedom of speech. But to see the press, almost without exception, roll over for them again and again, and never really question such a position in face of the facts, was absolutely chilling for me. What it means is that ten years after 9/11, the media still don't get it, that there is a dangerous force in the world called Islamism that has caused the deaths of millions of people through the years, and that in this case was the main cause behind the murder of thirteen soldiers by one of their own. At times like these, it feels to me that it's 1938 again and that there are lone voices in the wilderness, like Churchill's, trying to convince their compatriots that this man called Hitler is deadly serious about world domination and that Britain must take action before it's too late. In the here and now, the forces of Islamism have shown us over and over again how serious they are about their goal of Islamic world domination, that they are willing to pay the ultimate price in what they deem to be the service of God, and yet over and over again, we have those in the media tell us that there's no such thing as Islamism, that we need not trouble ourselves with all the homegrown plots, that they obviously were not that serious, and so on. Over ten years ago, if someone had said that men armed only with box cutters would be able to hijack four planes, destroy our tallest buildings, and attack the Pentagon, most people probably would have said that such a thing could happen only in the movies. Well, it happened in real life, and the mind-set behind that sort of action is still very much alive out there, in many different Islamist groups that want to destroy the West as we know it, by whatever means necessary, and impose their interpretations of shariah law wherever they can. In some cases, they simply want to destroy us—period. For the sake of our children and our children's children, the very least we owe them is to take the fight seriously, and do what must be done, not only to prevent another 9/11 but to stop another Hasan before it's too late.

As I watched the memorial service on November 10 for the victims of the November 5, 2009, Fort Hood massacre, I was overcome by emotion, especially during the roll call. Those fallen servicemen and women were part of the very U.S. military I used to care for as a Navy doctor. Words cannot express the depth to which the evil actions of Major Nidal Malik Hasan hit me. I had proudly dedicated a good portion of my life to serving as a physician and a lieutenant commander in the U.S. Navy. Since 9/11, I have been equally dedicated to defeating the ideology of political Islam that fuels our enemies. Yet again, despite years of work and dedication, I found myself utterly impotent. I found myself also feeling a deeper chagrin for yet another monster produced by Islamist ideology.

Rationally, I knew this horrible act did not happen because of anything I did or did not do related to my work trying to defeat Islamism. But I found myself helplessly listening to President Barack Obama mourn for our nation as it began to grieve over more senseless deaths at the hands of a radical Islamist. This time, this Muslim fascist did not come from abroad but was a domestic, homegrown enemy. He was—until the day his fellow soldiers died at his hands—wearing our American uniform, having sworn a false oath to uphold the Constitution and protect his nation and our citizens "against all enemies foreign and domestic." He not only trampled all over his officer's oath but in a matter of seconds became an icon of this nation's greatest enemy of the twenty-first century.

What hit me harder than any other moment in recent memory was when I realized that at the core of an analysis of the differences between my own psyche and that of Dr. Hasan is a central, soulful understanding of Americanism, liberty, our global enemy, the real source of radicalization, and the underlying battle for the soul of Islam.

No longer can anyone blame education, as Dr. Hasan had an M.D. and an MPH. No longer can anyone blame economics. Dr. Hasan was a well-to-do major in the U.S. Army. No longer can anyone blame immigration or assimilation. Hasan was American born and had what from all accounts was a relatively normal childhood growing up in Alexandria, Virginia, the son of Palestinian Jordanian immigrants, graduating from Virginia Tech on an ROTC scholarship, and then graduating from USUHS (Uniformed Services University of the Health Sciences) School of Medicine.

The parallels for me as the son of Syrian immigrants, who served proudly in the U.S. Navy, and who received my medical degree on a military scholarship, were overwhelming. I thought back to Neenah, Wisconsin, how happy I was there, and how blessed I was by all the friendships I made in my life through school and especially in the military. But then, after you peel away the similarities of the professional and cultural layers of Hasan's life and mine, you are left with one profound, existential, and all-encompassing difference between Major Hasan and myself, the former Lieutenant Commander Jasser. At the core of my soul, at the source of my conscious and subconscious existence, is an unyielding dedication to the liberty and freedom that this nation gives me. My faith, my Islam, taught me that I must give back to every relationship I have, whether it is my relationship with God, with family, with my communities, my patients, or with my nation. That is in essence *why* I joined the military. I joined to give back to a nation with which I have always been in love. The deepest responsibility for that which you love is to give back to it. The Marine Corps motto of *Semper Fidelis* (*Always Faithful*) and dedicated to "God, Country, Corps" epitomized who I was as a naval officer. I was the boy my parents raised. Hasan was the polar opposite.

It's time to have a public national conversation about that boy Hasan's parents raised. They must have felt pride in their son, who had graduated from the only military medical school in the country and had fulfilled an American dream that so many in the Middle East share. But if that was the case, then pride obviously was not enough to counter the toxic ideas that filled his head. Blaming psychiatric disease just does not pass muster here. This individual may have been reprimanded, as most in the armed services are at one point or another, but his psyche survived a military medical school and training program, and he was promoted to major. As a fellow physician, I find it exceedingly difficult to believe that he was an "impaired physician." His primary malady appears to be a very Islamist one, which involves the core belief in Islam's inherent supremacy over the United States and the Western world in general.

In a case like this, we must finally ask the hard questions. From what ideology did Hasan's ideas come? Did he learn them from his parents? Are such American Muslim children learning obsessive entitlement (as victims) or are they focused on individual responsibility? Are they learning poisonous conspiracy theories about America, Israel, and the West (political Islam), or are they learning liberty, reason, balance, nationalism, and patriotism? For such parents, would their version of the Marine motto be "Islam, ummah, Country, Corps?"

Do they refer to their motherlands of Syria, Jordan, Egypt, or Pakistan as "home," or is America their home? Are they publicly critical of the autocracies, theocracies, and monarchies of the Middle East? Or do they equate them with the United States? Do they teach their children to speak out and question Muslim authority, question imams, question tribalism, question aspects of shariah, question their parents (with respect), and question any aspect of religious practice or doctrine that conflicts with modernity, morality, and universal equality?

My sense, having had much experience with the pathology and paralysis of Muslim tribalism, is that Dr. Hasan's murderous spree was the direct result of an Islamist ideology obsessed with Israel, obsessed with global victimology and conspiracy theories that increasingly blame America and Israel for all problems in the Middle East. Without a strong understanding and appreciation of the beauty of American liberty, our Constitution, and our citizenry, and fed a steady diet of anti-West, anti-Israel ideology, such an American-born Muslim can actually begin to feel totally apart from the country of his birth. It can begin in the family, be fostered by the politico-religious literature and media, solidify in the political mosque, and exponentially amplify on the web via cyberjihad.

One example among many is the malignant input of such global media as *Al Jazeera*. American Muslims who are brainwashed to believe the American military is immoral through and through (as embodied in stories like that of the Abu Ghraib prison crimes) typically ignore the millions of other stories of lives saved through the liberation of Muslims from such oppressors as Saddam Hussein and Mullah Omar. *Al Jazeera* is a perfect example of the poison of political Islam that infiltrates the minds of Muslims. It is a primary media venue of the global Muslim Brotherhood and the radical Sheikh Yusuf al-Qaradawi. It has an intense and insidious anti-American outlook and is driven by an Islamist agenda. Islamist groups in America such as CAIR only amplify this mantra that the American soldier is in the Middle East participating in a "war against Islam" rather than a war for Muslim liberation. Combine this prototypical Islamist outlook with an American Muslim military officer who slides down a slippery slope of radicalization and seeks theological advice from the likes of a Wahhabi cleric (Sheikh Al-Awlaki in Yemen) and we can begin to understand what happened to Dr. Hasan.

Sadly, our nation has yet to seriously engage in the global war of ideas against this Islamist propaganda and the thousands of other "Islamist media outlets" that influence millions of Muslims, especially within our borders. We must confront and counter the forces of political Islam found both in foreign media and in venues right here in the United States, or it is likely that such biased sources of information will help create other Major Hasans. I discussed this in my public commentary on the realities of the ideologies of the flying imams from Phoenix. For example, during a Friday sermon in April 2004, Imam Ahmed Shqeirat, a leading Phoenix-area cleric of the Islamic Community Center of Tempe, displayed an image, which CAIR had distributed nationally, of an American soldier in Iraq with two young Iraqi boys. In the photo, the soldier held a sign saying, "Lcpl Boudreaux killed my dad, then he knocked up my sister." Never mind that the photo was probably doctored. When I confronted him about the poisonous nature of his sermon, he could not explain how such a photo related to Islamic theology or spirituality. He had no insight into the impact such a toxic message about our military would have in radicalizing vulnerable Muslim youth against our nation on a given Friday afternoon.

My family, in contrast to Major Hasan and Islamist movements, taught me that our Islam was not political Islam. Our Islam taught us to be dedicated internally and outwardly to our local communities and our nation, just as fervently as those of other faiths. This quid pro quo of life, this responsibility and accountability without any sense of entitlement is, in fact, part of the common ground of values that Islam and America share. I was blessed to learn this from my parents, who passed on their own patriotism to me early on. After they escaped from Syria and sought political freedom in the United States, they quickly shed any Syrian nationalism for loyalty to their adopted nation, which gave them freedoms that their motherland never did. They taught me that it was the abandonment of military service by the middle and upper classes in Syria, Iraq, Egypt, and Libya, and in other Middle Eastern countries, that contributed to destroying their societies, as the military then became overrun by corruption, thugs, and those who valued power above all else. This was the direct opposite of the American experience, where pluralism and the devotion of all segments of American society to our military help keep this nation strong. It was for this reason in large part that I joined the U.S. Navy.

My family and I could have never guessed that the poison of Middle Eastern tribalism, corruption, and Islamism would follow us here to America. Dr. Hasan gave away his soul to the militant version of a theo-political ideology (Islamism) that created an irreparable chasm between his oath to this nation and his faith, which became consumed by the supremacist world vision of a violent strain of political Islam—Wahhabism.

My hope is that once we extract any information we need from Hasan about his radicalization and contacts, and once he is found guilty, he receive the death penalty. If I may set aside my Hippocratic oath for just a few seconds, let me be the first to sign up to be one of those who carry out the ultimate punishment for this man. While I know that is not how we carry out capital punishment in the United States, this is part of how I feel in the aftermath of this massacre. There would be no greater symbol of how wrong Dr. Hasan was in his "theology," that he could not go to war against Muslims, than for him to find himself dead at the hands of loyal, patriotic American Muslims enacting the will of the American military court.

In conflicts of the soul, neither Homeland Security, the FBI, nor the DOD will ever make any inroads whatsoever into the treatment of this profound pathology. As successful as their programs have been, they have in reality only been a whack-a-mole program. The only real treatment that has any hope for humanity against the plague of political Islam is a complete reformation of the mind-set within the Muslim consciousness that forever separates mosque from state and frees Muslims to identify from our soul with America. American Christendom ultimately taught its faithful to "render unto Caesar what is Caesar's, and to God what is God's" after 1776 and then 1789. It then came to better understand it through the Civil War and then the civil rights movements of the twentieth century. Muslim reformists and leaders need to publicly affirm the death of the Islamic state and the need to end the Islamist drive to install shariah law in government. Any compromise will only lead us further along the slippery slope down which otherwise normal Muslims in the West and throughout the world fall as they revert to a combustible conflict within their soul.

Will Dr. Hasan's horrible example somehow wake up Muslims to the realization that it is time to uncompromisingly extinguish this conflict within the souls of our coreligionists? The "ummah" as a faith-based *nation* must be sent to the dustbin of history and relegated to spiritual and theological matters only. Many Muslims are saying this. Asra Nomani, writing for the *Daily Beast*, stated, "It's critical that we ditch the concept of the 'ummah' with a capital 'U' and recognize that we are an 'ummah' with a small 'u' meaning our religious identity doesn't have to supersede other loyalties and identities." The Qur'an must not be used as a constitution for government. In fact, there is nothing in the Qur'an that dictates such an interpretation. Clerics, imams, and ulemaa (Islamic scholars) must no longer be advisors on public legalisms in government. Our laws as Muslims must be based in reason alone. Most important, allegiance to God and Islam must have nothing but positive impact upon our primary allegiance to this nation.

This allegiance can no longer be assumed but must be discussed openly and theologically by American Muslim experts and leaders. It was reported that Hasan reached out to a civilian imam. We need to know what that imam would have told Hasan if he had hinted at confusion about his faith and the Army when he spoke to him. Even a lukewarm response from that imam (a leading national imam on ISNA's board) and others poses a grave danger to our nation. And why didn't Major Hasan seek solace in a military chaplain? In any just war declared by our commander-in-chief, according to the Islam I know, certainly Muslims can be morally and theologically justified in killing other Muslims. For example, we are not in Afghanistan and Iraq to fight "Muslims" but rather to liberate the citizenry of those states (who happen to be majority Muslim) from authoritarian regimes that fuel global terror.

Let's make one thing clear. If Muslims like Dr. Hasan ask for conscientious objector (CO) status it is because they are political Islamists. It is *not* because they are spiritual Muslims or follow the faith of Islam, at least not the Islam I know. Muslims have been fighting wars against other Muslims from the beginnings of the faith. Those who think he should have been given CO status are accepting the Islamist propaganda that this was a war against Muslims.

Sadly, the problem is quite pervasive. In 2011, the assistant deputy secretary of the Army granted U.S. Army Private Naser Abdo CO status and recommended his dismissal from the service. Abdo had joined the Army infantry in August 2009, only to demand in June 2010 that he be granted CO status, falsely claiming that his faith and military service were incompatible.

He was found in possession of weapons and explosive materials and went AWOL, fleeing indictment for possession of child pornography. Investigators say he told them he planned to attack the military. As he was led out of a federal courtroom, he shouted, "Nidal Hasan Fort Hood 2009!" Like Major Hasan, Abdo also did not become a militant overnight. Radicalization is a natural evolution for an individual consumed by the Islamist narrative. The Army's approval of his CO status will wreak untold damage on the perception of Muslims in the military, because it implicitly validates Islamism as a belief system and the potential of an insidious disloyalty from every Muslim. It saddened me to see the silence from so many American Muslim organizations that should have been outraged at Abdo's exploitation of Islam for his Islamist agenda against our military. Yet from the highest levels on down, the theological underpinnings of Islamist radicalization remain ignored by military officials who fear appearing to discriminate against Muslim soldiers. The systemic denial is only getting worse. In December 2011, the House and Senate Homeland Security committees held the first-of-its-kind joint hearing on the growing threat to our military from radical Islamists. Darius Long, the father of Army private William Andrew Long, who was shot and killed at a U.S. Army recruitment center in Little Rock, testified, "My faith in government is diminished. It invents euphemisms. . . . Little Rock is a 'drive-by' and Fort Hood is just 'workplace violence.' The truth is denied." Abdulhakim Mujahid Muhammad, aka Carlos Leon Bledsoe, who cited American actions in the Middle East for his motive, was sentenced to life in prison without parole. Our nation, and especially we Muslims, cannot counter an ideology that no one has the courage to name.

Theologically, it is time for Muslims to confront the entire concept of the Islamic state and address the fact that it is a totalitarian view of society in direct conflict with allegiance to the

United States. Jamal Badawi, a darling of ISNA and a prominent theologian on websites sympathetic to the Muslim Brotherhood like Islamonline, has written extensively, in the process exposing his American Islamist line on *loyalty*. On April 26, 2006, he stated in reference to the crime of apostasy under an Islamic state, "Apostasy is a capital crime as it threatens the integrity and stability of the Muslim community and state." Note, while Badawi may dismiss this discussion as only in "Muslim majority states," that fact reveals his hypocrisy. His promotion of the Islamic state, as a Canadian, is a threat to the West, pure and simple. Thus, as he describes it, the Islamic state and Islam as a faith are basically one and the same and are dependent upon a supremacist legal system that allows government to maintain its own interests above that of the individual. This is entirely incompatible with the oath of American citizenship and the oath of a military officer. Badawi actually cites radical Brotherhood Sheikh al-Qaradawi as "eloquent" and points readers to al-Qaradawi's barbaric defense of apostasy laws, wherein al-Qaradawi states, "As for hadith specifying the death penalty for apostates, they have been proven to be authentic. Besides, they were put into effect by the Companions in the era of the Rightly-Guided caliphs." ISNA and Badawi cannot deny that this feeds into the separatist mind-set of the likes of Dr. Hasan. If Major Hasan believed America was in a war against Muslims and their Islamic state, he had to religiously act against the secular American state, or he would be disloyal to Islam and its state. Imam al-Qaradawi goes even further in discussing murdering apostates and punishing blasphemers. He states:

Some early Muslim scholars are of the opinion that the following verse refers to how to deal with apostates. The punishment of those who wage war against Allah and His

messenger, and strive with might and main for mischief
through the land is execution- (Al Ma'idah 5:33). We have
referred to Ibn Taymiyah's opinion to the effect that waging
war against Allah and His messenger by speaking openly
against them is more dangerous to Islam than physically
attacking its followers and that moral mischief in the land is
more hazardous than physical mischief.

The rest of this commentary by Yusuf al-Qaradawi on apostasy, which was endorsed by Badawi, reads like a theocratic, supremacist manifesto of the Islamic state for Islamists and the Muslim Brotherhood. As for future Hasans and Abdos, Dr. Badawi's and Sheikh Qaradawi's opinions on treason against Islam remain tacitly supported by the silence of such American Islamist organizations as ISNA, MPAC (Muslim Public Affairs Council), and CAIR, and to my own chagrin are virtually *unopposed* by any measurable clerical movement within Islam in the West.

Let's now look further at domestic Islamist commentary. In the United States, legal Islam seems to be led by the Assembly of Muslim Jurists of America (AMJA). This "esteemed" so-called American organization, with profound Saudi influence and multiple imams cross-pollinated with ISNA and mosques across the United States, revealingly had on its home page in 2009 a rather seditious repudiation of the Pledge of Allegiance and a plethora of other legal defenses for the Islamic state against the Western secular state. The conclusion of their white paper stated, "The basic conflict between the declaration of faith and testimony that there is no god except Allah and that Muhammad, peace be upon him, is the Messenger of Allah, and the declaration and pledge of Allegiance of the USA is irreconcilable." Dr. Hasan could have just decided on his own to violently fulfill that message for the

Islamic state and against the secular state for which he could not pledge allegiance or fight. Salah Al-Sawy from AMJA concluded in a 2008 online fatwa, "As for optionally obtaining citizenship of a non-Muslim country it is definitely prohibited without a doubt, moreover it could be a form of apostasy." Incredibly, in a fatwa from AMJA in April 2006, Sheikh Mohammed Al-Haj Aly, who is an attending pediatrician at Albert Lea Medical Center of the Mayo Health System in Albert Lea, Minnesota, makes it rather clear that apostasy is a crime, according to his American juristic interpretation of Islam. He states:

> *As for the shari'ah ruling, it is the punishment of killing for the man with the grand Four Fiqh Shari'ah scholars, and the same with the woman with the major Shari'ah scholars, and she is jailed with Al-Hanafiyyah scholars, as the prophet, prayers and peace of Allah be upon him, said: "Whoever a Muslim changes his/her religion, kill him/her", and his saying: "A Muslim's blood, who testifies that there is no god except Allah and that I am the Messenger of Allah, is not made permissible except by three reasons: the life for the life; the married adulterer and the that who abandons his/her religion."*

These Islamic pronouncements about the mandate to kill apostates and the only reason to kill a Muslim (born out of treason against Islam) run hand in hand with the conflict within Islamists of giving loyalty to America and refusing to pledge allegiance. It is insulting to me as an American Muslim that this organization calls itself American. This is only the tip of the iceberg. CAIR, MPAC, and ISNA can protest the unfairness of the way in which they are painted on the issue of apostasy and loyalty to an American legal system versus shariah all they want. But they cannot deny the separatism this teaches and the slippery slope provided for future Dr. Hasans. And they are disgustingly silent with regard to any attempt to publicly counter the impact of fatwas like so many out of AMJA and even ISNA itself, as I experienced firsthand at that ill-fated convention I attended in the mid-1990s.

With these treasonous slippery slopes ignored and yet plain for all to see, created by American Islamist groups like ISNA and AMJA, is it any wonder that lost, anti-American individuals like Major Hasan fall freely into a barbaric, fascist version of our faith?

I must, we must, believe that Hasan's Islam is much different from my Islam and the Islam of most patriotic American Muslims. My coreligionists and I have our work cut out for us. We must work to widen the gap between those two Islams as much as possible, as far as possible, and as obviously as possible.

To add insult to injury, the Pentagon brass put out an after-action report on the massacre. I read and re-read their eighty-four-page report and never found the following statement that should have been there: "On November 5, 2009, the United States Army was viciously attacked from within by an ideologue bent on pursuing an agenda of Islamist extremism. This ideologue fell under the separatist influence of political Islam while serving as an officer. It is incumbent upon our force to begin to understand this theo-political ideology that threatens our soldiers internally and externally." Those critical lines are completely missing from the Pentagon's report. In fact, the words "jihad," "Islam," and "Islamism" never appear. In fact, even the barbarian's name, Nidal Hasan, is not in the report, oddly titled "Protecting the Force: Lessons from Fort Hood." For the life of me I don't understand how they can envision force protection without having the intestinal fortitude to identify the fueling ideologies. Instead, the report seemed to blame junior officers who did not report Hasan's behavior. It seems wholly unjust in a culture so pathologically politically correct to hold his fellow physicians accountable to a politically correct system that even the brass at the Pentagon could not rise above in the report.

As a former chief resident at Bethesda Naval Hospital, I can also speak to the inadequacies in the counterterrorism, counter-radicalism, and insurgency training of commanders such as those being held to blame for Hasan's promotion and movement up the chain of command. Studying theo-political internal threats is simply not part of the training of any military physician. Hasan's superiors are medical professionals trained to evaluate his ability as a physician and a psychiatrist. As we have all heard, his commanders were seriously concerned about his actions and the role his faith played in his everyday interactions with patients. Had they brought those concerns to his review process, they would have been vilified as Islamophobes. Even if Hasan's superiors had appropriately identified his behavior, a military discharge is light-years down the path of administrative counseling and punishment he would have received. Which begs the question, would a demoted Hasan have been any less a threat? At a January 15, 2010, press conference, Secretary of Defense Robert Gates himself confirmed this state of affairs: "Current policies on prohibited activities provide neither the authority nor the tools for commanders and supervisors to intervene when DOD personnel [are] at risk of personal radicalization."

A few years ago after a lecture I gave to deploying military officers, I had a conversation with an Army colonel who does quite a bit of force training. He had an interaction with one of the active-duty military imams that concerned him, but because of political correctness he had nowhere to go with his concern. So he bounced it off me. He described to me how he had asked an active-duty imam what he would say to a soldier who came to him asking if it was against "our faith" to fight against Muslims. The imam replied that he would tell the soldier, "I am not qualified to answer the question." The imam felt that the question was asking for an official fatwa, a legal "religious opinion or ruling." The colonel was dumbfounded and pressed the imam further, asking him, "Then who is qualified if not you and who would you send the soldier to for an answer?" The imam replied that he would refer the soldier to the Islamic Society of North America (ISNA), which is the outsourced certifying agency of Muslim chaplains in the U.S. military. Unfortunately, ISNA is also a political Islamist organization that has been overly critical of the U.S. wars in Afghanistan and Iraq. It is also the same organization whose speaker, Siraj Wahhaj, offended me in the nineties when I saw him tell his audience to replace the Constitution with the Qur'an.

ISNA glorified Imam Zaid Shakir's response for the Zaytuna Institute to the Fort Hood massacre as supposedly a shining example of moderation for their entire membership. In fact, I was rather offended by Shakir's very first paragraph, which demonstrated his and thus ISNA's disdain for our military. Shakir opens his pathetic response by saying, "There is no legitimate reason for their deaths, just as I firmly believe there is no legitimate reason for the deaths of the hundreds of thousands of Iraqi and Afghani civilians who have perished as a result of those two conflicts. Even though I disagree with the continued prosecution of those wars, and even though I believe that the U.S. war machine is the single greatest threat to world peace, I must commend the top military brass at Fort Hood and President Obama for encouraging restraint and for refusing to attribute the crime allegedly perpetrated by Major Nidal Malik Hasan to Islam." This is the organization that an active-duty imam uses for guidance?

It is ridiculous that our military would be "outsourcing" spiritual guidance for our force members. It is insane that they would use ISNA when it is part of the problem. ISNA's roots can be traced back to many of the founding tenets of the Muslim Brotherhood. It refuses to recognize the separatist influence of Islamist ideology. The imam's use of ISNA is akin to the Trojans bringing the Greeks' horse inside the walls of Troy. Our military should never farm such deeply essential counseling out. As to the answer the imam should have given, he should have told the colonel that he would counsel the Muslim military member that not only does his oath to this country and the military take precedence over any other oath, but the concept of the ummah (as Islamic nation) is dead and no longer relevant or competing for his allegiance from a spiritual perspective. There have been many wars fought between Muslims, and this war is not a war against Muslims or Islam, but rather one to free the Iraqi and Afghan populations from their despots. If our active-duty Muslim imams cannot confer such advice upon our Muslim soldiers they are a significant liability to our force protection.

Until our nation sets aside political correctness and becomes more comfortable discussing the seditious pronouncements of many Islamist leaders and the dangerous nexus between Islam and Islamism in the Muslim consciousness, those differences will be difficult to see. Ultimately, as Muslims begin to actually separate mosque and state, political Islam will be marginalized and the Islamic state's separatist influence will disappear.

If this deep-seated problem is ever going to be solved, the solution is going to have to come from within the House of Islam, from within our own Islamic souls and a consciousness born out of a genuine love for American freedom and liberty.

8

THE THREAT OF HOMEGROWN ISLAMIC RADICALISM

There has been much talk in recent years about the threat of homegrown Islamic radicalism in the United States. Beyond Fort Hood, there was in 2010 the issue of "Jihad Jane" (as the press dubbed her), who sought to provide material support to Al Qaeda, and Faisal Shahzad's failed attempt to detonate explosives in Times Square, and many more in the years since 9/11. They include the following thwarted attacks by Muslims born in the United States or who are naturalized citizens:

- May 2002, Jose Padilla: American citizen accused of seeking a radioactive-laced "dirty bomb" to use in an attack against America. Padilla was convicted of conspiracy in August 2007.

- September 2002, Lackawanna Six: American citizens of Yemeni origin convicted of supporting Al Qaeda after attending a jihadist camp in Pakistan. Five of six were from Lackawanna, New York.

- May 2003, Iyman Faris: American citizen charged with plotting to use blowtorches to collapse the Brooklyn Bridge.

- June 2003, Virginia Jihad Network: Eleven men from Alexandria, Virginia, trained for jihad against American soldiers, convicted of violating the Neutrality Act, conspiracy.

- August 2004, Dhiren Barot: Indian-born leader of terror cell plotted bombings of financial centers.

- August 2004, James Elshafay and Shahawar Matin Siraj: Sought to plant bomb at New York's Penn Station during the Republican National Convention.

- August 2004, Yassin Aref and Mohammed Hossain: Plotted to assassinate a Pakistani diplomat on American soil.

- June 2005, father and son Umer Hayat and Hamid Hayat: Son convicted of attending terrorist training camp in Pakistan; father convicted of customs violation.

- August 2005, Kevin James, Levar Haley Washington, Gregory Vernon Patterson, and Hammad Riaz Samana: Los Angeles homegrown terrorists who plotted to attack National Guard, LAX, two synagogues, and Israeli consulate.

- December 2005, Michael Reynolds: Plotted to blow up natural gas refinery in Wyoming, the Transcontinental Pipeline, and a refinery in New Jersey. Reynolds was sentenced to thirty years in prison.

- February 2006, Mohammad Zaki Amawi, Marwan Othman El-Hindi, and Zand Wassim Mazloum: Accused of providing material support to terrorists, making bombs for use in Iraq.

- April 2006, Syed Haris Ahmed and Ehsanul Islam Sadequee: Cased and videotaped the Capitol and World Bank for a terrorist organization.

- June 2006, Narseal Batiste, Patrick Abraham, Stanley Grant Phanor, Naudimar Herrera, Burson Augustin, Lyglenson Lemorin, and Rotschild Augustine: Dubbed the "Liberty City Seven" and accused of plotting to blow up the Sears Tower, five were ultimately convicted on terrorism charges. Lemorin and Herrera were acquitted.

- July 2006, Assem Hammoud: Accused of plotting to bomb New York City train tunnels.

- August 2006, Liquid Explosives Plot: Thwarted plot to explode ten airliners over the United States.

- May 2007, Fort Dix Plot: Six men accused of plotting to attack Fort Dix Army base in New Jersey. The plan included attacking and killing soldiers using assault rifles and grenades.

- June 2007, JFK Plot: Four men accused of plotting to blow up fuel arteries that run through residential neighborhoods around JFK Airport in New York.

- 2009, Najibullah Zazi and associates: Traveled to Pakistan and received training from Al Qaeda before returning to the United States and plotting to use a weapon of mass destruction to blow up commuter trains.

- Late 2009, a group of five young American men from Northern Virginia: Traveled to Pakistan, where they were detained and sentenced to ten years in prison on terrorism-related charges.

- July 2010, Virginia native Zachary Chesser: Arrested by the FBI while attempting to travel to Somalia, where he intended to join the terrorist organization al Shabaab as a foreign fighter.

- Since 2006, more than twelve U.S. citizens have been killed in Somalia while fighting for al Shabaab.

- Farooque Ahmed, thirty-five, of Ashburn, Virginia: Sentenced in 2011 to twenty-three years in prison, followed by fifty years of supervised release, after pleading guilty to charges stemming from his attempts to assist others in 2010 whom he believed to be members of Al Qaeda in planning bombings at Metrorail stations in the Washington, D.C., area.

Despite this, much of the mainstream press appeared committed to downplaying the threat of homegrown Islamic radicalism, which for me raised serious concerns about just how far we can go with our so-called political correctness. If it were neo-Nazis who had planned such seditious, violent actions, or some other far-right political group, would the media tend to downplay what they were doing? Based on what I've observed through the years, I would have to say they would give quite a bit of attention to any such far-right groups, including religious ones, if they were of any given background except Muslim. This to me is an absolutely outrageous state of affairs. As an American Muslim, I don't expect to be treated any differently because of my religion, and if some of my fellow Muslims are showing a pattern of radicalism within the country—however small that percentage may be—it needs to be addressed in the media, through law enforcement, and, of course, in our American Muslim communities. I don't need to hear from the "talking heads" in the media that only a very small percentage of the American Muslim community is radicalized, and an even smaller number are likely to commit violent acts. For that matter, Muslims who belong to Al Qaeda are a very small percentage of Muslims worldwide, but it takes only a small number of fanatics to wreak havoc in the world. Such a dismissal also belies any comprehension that these radicals emanate from a far more prevalent and insidious ideology that is separatist at its core: political Islam.

By comparison, one could say that most people who drive are not drunk or under the influence of drugs. That, however, is small comfort to someone who has been in an accident with a drunk driver, or worse still, lost a loved one to someone under the influence. Should we not address the problem of drunk driving because it is only a small percentage of people who drive while impaired? Anyone who suggested such a thing would not be taken seriously. And yet, when a clear pattern of radicalization reveals itself in the American Muslim community, including planned acts of terrorism, it is downplayed by many in the media as being "overblown."

Islamism is a theo-political movement dedicated to advancing a supremacist version of Islamic law, or shariah. Islamists believe that an Islamic state is the ideal form of governance. Regardless of which sect of Islam their interpretation of the shariah comes from, Islamists reject all aspects of individual liberty, including universal freedom of expression and freedom of religion and equal access to government leadership by all citizens. They do not believe that every individual merits equal protection before the law. Islamists want their version of Islam to dominate all aspects of human existence, including politics, social interactions, economics, and spiritual life. They actively persecute non-Muslims and those Muslims who disagree with their views. Until we identify Islamism as the problem, rather than the nebulous "violent extremism," we will make no inroads into counterterrorism.

So it should be no surprise that the media largely portrayed Americans' reactions to two recent events as examples of Islamophobia. These were the plans for what was dubbed the "Ground Zero Mosque" in the summer of 2010 and Representative Peter King's (R-NY) House Committee on Homeland Security hearings on "The Extent of Radicalization in the American Muslim Community and the Community's Response" in March 2011.

As you know from earlier chapters, I have been involved in my share of mosque-building controversies, going all the way back to my early years in Wisconsin. However, the Ground Zero Mosque was the first time I was ever opposed to the building of an Islamic center with a mosque. The media attention to this, one of the top news stories of 2010, unfairly polarized American positions as either anti-Islam and anti-Muslim (those against the mosque) or blindly pro-Muslim and oblivious to the fact that any Muslim could be a terrorist or sympathize with ideas that radicalize (those for the mosque). Quite steadily, over 73 percent of the American public was against the mosque, believing they had a "right" to build it but it was not the "right" thing to do. Those who know me were not surprised that a devout Muslim could be opposed to the building of a mosque. However, the issues in this case were clear from the start. For one, Imam Faisal Abdul Rauf, the developer Sherif El-Gamal, and others involved in the initial plans for building this mosque and its dysfunctional public rollout seemed to be less concerned with the feelings of those who lost loved ones on 9/11 than they were with their need to make a statement about what Islam represents. I addressed all of these issues in an opinion piece in the *Wall Street Journal* on September 10, 2010. Part of what I had to say was the following:

Imam Rauf and his supporters are clearly more interested in making a political statement in relation to Islam than in the mosque's potential for causing community division and pain to those who lost loved ones on 9/11. That division is already bitterly obvious.

As someone who has been involved in building mosques around the country, and who has dealt with his fair share of unjustified opposition, I ask of Imam Rauf and all his supporters, "Where is your sense of fairness and common decency?" In relation to Ground Zero, I am an American first, a Muslim second, just as I would be at Concord, Gettysburg, Normandy Beach, Pearl Harbor or any other battlefield where my fellow countrymen lost their lives.

A little further on, I addressed the fact that Rauf was willing to see Muslim Brotherhood leaders and members as moderates:

In your book, *What's Right With Islam*, you cite the [Muslim] Brotherhood's radical longtime spiritual leader Imam Yusuf Qaradawi as a "moderate." Reformist American Muslims are not afraid to name Mr. Qaradawi and his ilk as radical. We Muslims should first separate mosque and state before lecturing Americans about church and state.

I also found the idea of an Islamic center so close to Ground Zero to be very insensitive to those who lost loved ones on 9/11. I would not have been opposed to the idea of building a modest-sized mosque in the Ground Zero neighborhood. In fact, there is already a small mosque nearer to Ground Zero than the controversial project was, and I have no issue with that, and can't think of anyone who does. But as I stated in the opinion piece:

> There are certainly those who are prejudiced against Muslims and who are against mosques being built anywhere, and even a few who wish to burn the Qur'an. But most voices in this case have been very clear that for every American freedom of religion is a right, but that it is not right to make one's religion a global political statement with a towering Islamic edifice that casts a shadow over the memorials of Ground Zero.

Such a lack of humility goes against what Islam teaches. In fact, even the name that Rauf and his associates were using for this Islamic center initially, before changing it to Park 51, is quite revealing of their real intent: the Cordoba House. The very name harks back to the Islamic conquest of Spain and the huge mosque that was built in the area of Cordoba. Why refer to such history unless it is relevant to one's overall philosophy? I don't understand why anyone would want to bring up that period in Islamic history, when Muslim conquerors made their way throughout Europe, any more than I can understand why someone would want to refer in a glorious way to the Christians' role in the Crusades. In fact, when President George W. Bush once made reference to the hunt for Bin Laden and his ilk as a "crusade," the media had a field day with his statement. He never used that term again because it was open to being misinterpreted as some sort of Christian suprema- cist reference. Yet when Rauf and his group talk about the Cor- doba House, the media for the most part had nothing to say about it. I concluded my piece by saying:

> Islamists in "moderate" disguise are still Islamists. In their own more subtle ways, the WTC mosque organizers end up serving the same aims of the separatist and supremacist wings of political Islam. In this epic struggle of the 21st century, we cannot afford to ignore the continuum between nonviolent political Islam and the militancy it ultimately fuels among the jihadists.

I got plenty of reaction to this piece as well as to the various in- terviews I did about the issue. In one case, I debated Reza Aslan, the author of *No God but God* and other books. I have respect for Reza's talent as a writer and for his dedication to studying Islamic history, but he and I are miles apart when it comes to the conclusions we have drawn about radicalism among Muslims. He has written that he believes that the "Muslim Reformation" has already happened. I don't understand how anyone can look at the stonings of women that still take place in Iran, the corporal and "*hudud*" punishments performed routinely in Saudi Arabia and Pakistan and many other areas of the world where shariah is interpreted in the most narrow, fundamentalist way, and not see that overall reform is still a long way off. Any supposed scholar of Islam who tells Americans that the Muslim Reformation has already happened is either in deep denial or is actually a cog in the wheel of the global Islamist project that practices dissimulation, deception, and denial. Reformation implies compatibility with modernity. Reformation intimates a resolution of the conflicts we have discussed between Western democracies and Islamist ideologies. No such resolution has occurred. If it had, terrorism, a symptom of that conflict, would be on the wane. The groups with which Aslan aligns himself, such as MPAC and ISNA, are notoriously silent about the need for reform toward the separation of mosque and state and the defeat of the ideas of the Muslim Brotherhood. No surprise, since those groups are part of the American Muslim Brotherhood legacy group network.

In relation to my opposition to the Ground Zero Mosque and emphasis on concerns about how a project worth over $150 million could be funded domestically, Reza described himself as "speechless," and then, of course, went on to prove that he wasn't by commenting at length about why there was no problem with building a fifteen-story Islamic center so close to Ground Zero. He did not seem to be able to understand why such an imposing and extravagant structure would offend those who lost loved ones on 9/11, or how this could in any way be perceived to be an Islamist approach. Not to mention that if the structure received any foreign funds from Muslim-majority nations or Islamists, it would send a clear message of conquest from the ruins of war, a point made eloquently by genuine moderate Muslim scholar Fouad Ajami on the Bill Bennett radio show. At first, I wondered if this was some sort of manipulative stance Aslan was taking, because I was at a loss as to how someone could not see this as a simple case where we must be Americans first, Muslims second and consider the memories of those lost on 9/11. I stressed that if Muslims like Rauf were actually concerned with building understanding in the community, why not build an American center devoted predominantly to counterterrorism issues addressing the problem of Islamist radicalization instead of an Islamic center? Aslan is proof that Islamism is the province not only of those schooled in narrow-minded madrassas, but also of those who are intellectually gifted and have studied at some of the best Western universities. The advocates for Islamism are numerous, and each has his own agenda. Aslan's is between him and God. His refusal to engage in a substantive discourse about Islamism, its association with radicalization, and its funding streams is typical of pseudointellectual Islamists who provide cover for the global theo-political movement of Islamism.

My family and I had defended our mosques against public obstacles in Wisconsin and then in Arizona. In fact, the mosque leadership in Scottsdale, Arizona, had asked me to speak publicly on their behalf in their defense against growing opposition before the city's Development Review Board in November 2001. We ultimately were approved. But just as we were committed to building the mosque in Scottsdale because it was a clear-cut case of religious freedom needing to win out over government interference, I will remain opposed to the Ground Zero Mosque because it is important that common decency and reverence for all those Americans killed on 9/11 should triumph over the narrow aims of Islamists disguised as "moderates."

One may ask how the Ground Zero Mosque controversy relates to homegrown radicalization. While the lines of connection may not be readily apparent, if one looks closer it becomes easier to see that the willingness of someone like Imam Rauf to defend a Muslim Brotherhood member as a "moderate" is part of a much bigger problem. Rauf never objected to all the support he received from the Muslim Brotherhood legacy group coalitions on behalf of his center. The Islamist groups became surrogates for Imam Rauf and his wife, Daisy Khan, and the controversial developer, Sherif El-Gamal. In fact, as the attention to the project exploded and Rauf finally returned to the States from abroad, he ended up being removed as the imam to the project, marginalized to the board. He then saved face by stating that he was starting a global Cordoba Initiative that was going to consume his time and take him out of New York City. His first stop included a keynote address at a Detroit meeting of ISNA that also featured none other than Siraj Wahhaj—hardly a moderate. You will recall how I had publicly repudiated Wahhaj after his proposed intention to replace the U.S. Constitution with the Qur'an. The so-called moderate Imam Abdul Rauf seemed to have no problem sharing the stage with Wahhaj. Rauf, an author of several books on Islam and America, could certainly not claim ignorance as a defense against his dissimulation with leading Islamists. What was so unique and profound about the national discussion of the Ground Zero Mosque, later called "Park 51," was that for the first time the discussion of the "Muslim" issue did not come on the heels of some horrific incident or terror threat. It came after a clash of symbolisms became unroofed. It was as if a national scab had been peeled away. Over 73 percent of Americans did not agree with the construction of the center despite the vast majority of Americans never having an issue with Muslims or with mosques in their neighborhoods. Certainly, I believe a majority of American Muslims followed those opinions of the American public. In essence, this issue brought to bear the division within our Muslim communities between those who believe our families are here to bring Islam to the West and those who are here to learn about freedom and liberty and bring those ideas into a modernization of our interpretation of Islam—more simply, the division between revivalists and reformists.

So the Ground Zero Mosque issue was closely related to

the causes of radicalization. One does not become radicalized overnight. There is a change of consciousness involved for most people, the need to be able to see things through an Islamist prism. In fact, without the ideological framework and infrastructure there could be no terrorists, Muslim or otherwise. The savvier Islamists have become experts at using the very freedoms they are given in the West against the very ones whose free and open systems they want to Islamize. One of the easiest ways to do that is to accuse critics of being "Islamophobes," which is what Aslan essentially called me on CNN. One of the most essential characteristics of the Islamist is an insistence that Muslims are being victimized by non-Muslims around the world. Rauf and his group used this narrative extensively throughout the Ground Zero Mosque controversy, with the idea that anyone against it must be against Islam and all Muslims. Taken to its logical extreme, such a mind-set of victimization can eventually lead to a willingness to commit violent acts in the name of God. In fact, Rauf had the temerity to tell Larry King on CNN that even if he became convinced that moving the mosque was the right thing to do, he felt that doing so would pose a national security risk because radical Muslims around the world would act out against an American public that appeared to be anti-Islam. So much for moral courage! And so much for our American policy never to negotiate with terrorists. This is not to blame Rauf for someone like Nidal Hasan, but the toxic condition of Islamism comes in several different stages. Most illnesses, for that matter, come in various stages of seriousness, which is why cancer, for instance, is described as Stage 1, 2, and so on. The bigger problem, of course, is those who do not acknowledge that there is a problem. This is exactly what happened in certain quarters when it came to Representative King's hearings on the problem of homegrown Muslim radicalization in America.

* * *

From the moment Representative King, chairman of the House Committee on Homeland Security, announced his intention to hold hearings on the simple question of radicalization among American Muslims and the Muslim community's response, the PC media charge began. Comedian Jon Stewart went so far as to compare King to Senator Joseph McCarthy and branded the hearings a "witch hunt." He was not alone. The reflexive tilt of the media and liberal politicians in general was to assume that these hearings were wrong, and they geared their reports accordingly, in typical fashion rounding up the "usual suspects" for "expert" commentary, representatives from CAIR and other groups obsessed with victimization and grievances. Representative King announces he's going to look into radicalization among American Muslims, at the core of which is an Islamist mind-set, and whom do the media choose to interview? Islamist apologist groups like the Muslim Brotherhood legacy groups, who went into full tilt about the targeting of Muslims and how victimized they were. The committee spent months interviewing Muslim and non-Muslim experts on radicalization and decided to go with an all-Muslim panel to provide testimony on radicalization. After a number of interviews, I was formally asked to testify. As the media pressed to know who was on the witness list, my name was the first released to the public, many weeks before the March 10, 2011, hearings. The media onslaught was amazing. For the first time since Fort Hood, mainstream media were reaching out to me and AIFD for our view on counter-radicalization. I received attention from NPR, the *Washington Post*, and CNN, having worked very hard for years to get our nonpartisan American Muslim message of reform, counter-radicalization, and liberty beyond conservative media. It seemed almost universally true that the preconceived notions of liberals about my position as presented to them by Islamist propagandists were abandoned once they realized the genuine and apolitical position of tough love with which I approached the treatment of radicalization. As we got closer to the hearings and the vitriol against Representative King exploded, the blindly partisan left media, such as Media Matters, the *Nation*, and other surrogates, chose to treat me as they would a partisan conservative rather than an observant Muslim reformer seeking the nonpartisan truth about the root cause of Muslim radicalization within our communities and what we should be doing about it.

Perhaps King's purposes might have been better served by holding hearings on "Denial of the Problem of Islamism in America." This is no less a problem than radicalization among American Muslims, perhaps in the long run an even greater one. How can you solve a problem when you can't even admit there is one?

I was very honored to be called to testify, but I knew from the very start, before I ever spoke a word at the hearings, that I would probably be branded an "Uncle Tom Muslim." An offensive Facebook page of the same name about me would appear on the day of my testimony before Congress. A former executive director for CAIR-Columbus, Babak Darvish, even publicly endorsed the hate page and tried to drive Net traffic to it.

Such insults and worse soon followed, but I looked at all that as proof that the message of AIFD was getting through. If they did not see me as a threat to the well-established order of Islamism and PC blindness, they would have no reason to attack me.

Just the same, there is a certain hard, cold reality to taking a position that is greatly unpopular to the Islamists and the PC brigade (interesting how those two forces seem to work together in their own strange way). There is the simple fact of physical safety, and the realization that there are people who could assault or kill you for taking a position contrary to theirs. Representative King himself received death threats, and concern for my own safety impelled me for the first time to hire private security staff to accompany me to the hearings. All of this struck me as a very odd form of progress for AIFD and myself. A few years back I had struggled to get attendance at our local Muslim Rally Against Terrorism, and now I was testifying before Congress, bodyguards in tow. A friend once said to me, "The ultimate proof of the power of your message is when you will need bodyguards." True, I guess, but a sad commentary on the challenge of dissent from the Islamist party line. Interestingly, the day of the hearings was filled with every media outlet. I had never participated in anything quite like it. I spoke to a broad range of media all the way from *Al Jazeera* to CNN to Fox News to the *New York Post* and *The Washington Post*. The hearings were covered live by C-Span and, based upon the volume of feedback I received, widely watched. The post-testimony press conference led by Chairman King was covered live by many outlets.

One of the things I emphasized in my testimony was that the problem we face is threefold: first, the Islamist mind-set, which at its logical extreme leads to terrorism; second, those non-Muslims who believe that at its core the problem is Islam, that it is a violent religion and leads to acts of terrorism; and third, those, Muslim and non-Muslim alike, who believe there is no such thing as Islamism and that any criticism of Islam amounts to Islamophobia. How, I asked, with all these extreme views, is one supposed to get at the core of the hearings: the problem of radicalization among American Muslims? There is an urgent need, I said, to simply acknowledge there is a problem. That has to be the starting point, and from there Muslims must decide among ourselves that, while antiterror policies and programs on behalf of the government both here and abroad may address some of the immediate threats, without a fundamental overhaul of the Islamist mind-set no real progress will be made and we will be chasing radical Islamists for generations to come. It was sad that I even had to remind a number of members and reporters that while Homeland Security had kept us safe, the number of cells and threats against our homeland have only increased since 9/11, and that according to the Investigative Project on Terrorism the two years before the hearings had seen the arrests of over 226 Americans on terror charges by the Department of Justice, 186 of whom were Muslim. For a faith group that constitutes less than 2 percent of the population to produce over 80 percent of the terror arrests points to a major problem in my book.

Another core area I focused on was the need for Muslims to honestly, openly, and humbly cooperate with hearings like Representative King's and with law enforcement in general. I understood that every Muslim I knew would report to authorities anyone who threatened an act of violence, but cooperation goes far beyond that. It includes positive messages about the FBI, our military, and DHS. It includes a culture of countering the separatist ideology of Islamism and the ideas that fuel radicalization. To that end, I talked about how CAIR and a group of Muslim attorneys called Muslim Advocates had admonished American Muslims not to speak to the FBI without an attorney, which does not foster a philosophy of cooperation. In fact, CAIR Michigan had a video message telling its membership to report any questionable activities at mosques and elsewhere to CAIR, which would then be entrusted with taking it to the FBI. So a civil rights organization would decide whether reports were actionable, criminal, or discriminatory—a Muslim civil rights group with which the FBI formally broke off all communication in 2008 due to its relationship and sympathy with Hamas. Its constant victimization routine against the FBI and targeting of informants created a message to Muslims that they should cooperate only as a last resort. The groups speak about partnership with law enforcement, but the vast majority of their bandwidth is consumed with antigovernment propaganda—hardly the foundation of any real ideological counterterrorism work. Instead they feed the distrust of Muslims and the fear that has increased among Americans since 9/11 with the continued efforts of Muslims to perpetrate terrorist acts against the United States.

I also spoke about how in the midst of all this, American Muslims who are both devout and patriotic find themselves caught in the middle of all these contentious forces. It is still up to us as American Muslims to speak out against the problem of radicalization among the faithful, to point out that this is a problem that hurts everyone, including Islam. We Muslims are the only ones with the knowledge and understanding to begin the reforms necessary to counter the root causes of radical Islamism. It is a Muslim problem that needs a Muslim solution. The common rationale offered up, that radicalization is only a problem among a small percentage, and that violence is an even smaller problem, just does not cut it when we look toward honest and effective solutions. It was always a weak excuse, and seems even weaker in light of the continuing problem of radicalization among American Muslims, including a persistent pattern of planned (but mostly failed) terrorist acts.

I spoke at length about Nidal Hasan, and how much concern his story gave me, since we had similar narratives. So where, I asked, was the line drawn? How did Hasan become radicalized? Within his story are many clues about what needs to be done for counter-radicalization programs. Hasan's radicalization was not something that happened overnight, but was on a continuum. It started with a change in thinking, with someone who perhaps was leading a very ordinary life beginning a shift in which his primary identity becomes that of a Muslim. The New York Police Department's Report on Radicalization laid it out as a four-step process:

Stage 1: Preradicalization
Stage 2: Self-identification
Stage 3: Indoctrination
Stage 4: Jihadization

External events may conspire to lead such a person to believe that the West is engaged in a war on Islam, and that it is his duty as a Muslim to defend the faith. Such external events could include financial stress, loss of a job, or divorce, which could lead one to begin to reconsider the purpose of one's life. One could begin to focus more on one's religion, and as part of that process begin to attend a mosque that espouses a brand of political Islam that encourages a mind-set of victimization and hatred of the West as being engaged in a war against Muslims. Combine this shift in identity with perhaps a steady diet of anti-West diatribes at the mosque and other outlets and one can find oneself, without being completely aware of it, headed toward jihadization. The poet Goethe perhaps put it best by saying that with a few degrees' shift in one's character one becomes capable of the most unspeakable things. The only way to counter radicalization is to inoculate Muslims against the separatism of political Islam with the ideas of liberty. However, as the NYPD's report makes clear, this four-stage process is not an inevitable path, and that once someone heads in that direction, there is a way back. One may begin the process, but then have a change of heart when it comes to committing violent acts. One may renounce extremism altogether or become one of those recruiters of jihadists who don't actually engage in violent acts but instead become an essential part of the indoctrination process.

The problem, I stressed to those present, is the failure of Americans at large, including much of the political system, to realize that this is taking place, that radicalism remains a real and present danger, and that we American Muslims must be held to account for not doing enough to address it. To counter the Islamist narrative, it is not enough to say in private as a Muslim that one is against it. Just as the Islamists remain an extremely well-funded and powerful force that comes in various forms—as so-called moderate organizations that claim to care only about protecting Muslims' rights, or as outright Islamist doctrinaires, or as violent extremists—those of us who believe in the separation of mosque and state and are opposed to Islamist radicalism must be just as persistent and vocal in our opposition. Even if our voices are few, if we persist we will be heard eventually. I see my own testimony at the hearings as proof of that. AIFD is barely nine years old, a mere child in the world of nonprofits, but our message continues to be heard more and more around the country and around the world. In a country in which freedom of speech and assembly are real rights, I can offer my views and let those who value them welcome me, and those who don't shun me. Still, my freedom to chart my own course on these issues, as an American and a Muslim, remains very real.

After my official testimony, with the room packed and quite warm and throngs more waiting in the hallway, with every major media outlet represented, nearly every member of the committee was present and for almost four hours we were interrogated. Nothing spikes the interest of congressmen and -women like a media frenzy. So they were each anxious to use their five minutes to the fullest. Many questions were probing and appropriate. But some laid bare the profound obstacles our nation faces as we sit back impotent against the ideology of Islamism. Congresswoman Jackie Speier (D-CA) used her time to ask the following:

SPEIER:

While I think these anecdotes are interesting, I don't believe these are experts. And I would suggest that if we're really going to be complete in this hearing, we should also be investigating the Army of God and their website in which they openly praise Christian terrorists as part of an effort to look at homegrown terrorism in this country.

Let me start by first asking Dr. Jasser if you believe the majority of mosques in this country are actively recruiting terrorists.

JASSER:

That's not what I said, ma'am.

SPEIER:

I'm just asking you that question.

JASSER:

No, I do not believe the majority of mosques are actively recruiting terrorists.

SPEIER:

Do you believe you have expertise to be speaking?

JASSER:

It's interesting. That's the question that the theocrats ask me all the time, so it seems like you're asking me the same thing. My love of my faith, my demonstrable experience in dealing with this issue of reform, of knowledge of not only my scripture and my practice of faith, but the Constitution I think positions me pretty well to deal with it and be part of the solution. I'm not sure who else you'd like to solve this problem, but I think it's only Muslims that can do [it]. And it would be sort of like asking at the time of the American Revolution that you want to have testimony about the Church of England's threat to America and you would only listen to the priests. And, you know, that would be wrong, because it was the lay community that ultimately—the intellectual lay community that understood their faith, that brought about the reform and the change against the establishment. So—so I hope you don't look upon expertise as something that gets handed down from the clerics, most of whom are part of the problem.

SPEIER:
No, but I'm a practicing Roman Catholic. I go to church every single Sunday. I'm a lector in my parish. And I'm no more prepared to speak about the pedophilia in the Catholic Church because I am a practicing Roman Catholic. And I think we do need to have experts come here to testify on homegrown terrorism in this country. And while I appreciate the anecdotes of those who have spoken, I don't think that they are necessarily very enlightening.

It was surreal to me that because I was called to testify by Chairman Peter King (R-NY), so many of the Democrats looked at me and attacked me as a partisan "conservative" rather than see me through the lens of the subject matter of these hearings—how do we counter American Muslim radicalization? This partisan paralysis and the way in which Representative Speier parroted the talking points of major Islamist organizations in America spoke volumes to one of the primary obstacles to reform—the inability of so many political leaders in America to see beyond the political bickering and encourage Muslims devoted to reform to actually come together to diagnose and treat the problem.

The overall response to my few minutes of testimony was amazingly positive. I got my share of hate mail, to be sure, but we also had over fifty Muslims sign up that afternoon to become members of AIFD. Both Muslims and non-Muslims showed their support. Sadly, it seemed in the following weeks that the vast majority of Muslim responses against my testimony came from those who had neither heard nor read my full testimony. Most Muslims who listened to my opening statement and over three and a half hours of questioning from members of Congress on the committee were exceedingly positive.

A great exception to such support was the Islamist groups and their apologists. Chief among them was Representative Keith Ellison, the first Muslim member of Congress. Chairman King graciously gave him an opportunity to testify as a member of Congress. He turned his few minutes of opportunity for testimony into his own melodrama. He received a great deal of media attention for his bizarrely tearful testimony at the hearings about an American Muslim first responder who died on 9/11 (and initially was mistaken as a possible terrorist suspect) but was later recognized as a hero in the language of the Patriot Act. True to Ellison's character, rather than attack me in his testimony or to the media, he proceeded to viciously attack me and AIFD two days later in the comfort of a large Muslim gathering in Detroit. The Islamist media in attendance (*Arab American News*) conveniently ignored his hateful rant against us at the Islamic Association of Greater Detroit in a function sponsored by the MSA of the University of Michigan–Dearborn. Answering a direct question from a Muslim about my testimony, he tried to dismiss AIFD as an irrelevant organization by saying that our "supporters could all fit in one phone booth," and that I had taken my cues from Ayaan Hirsi Ali, that she figured out how to make money by criticizing Islam, and that I must have figured out how to do the same. I'm not sure what planet Ellison is living on, but the last time I checked, Ms. Ali had risked her life to make a film that criticized Islamist practices that marginalize and degrade women. As many know, her collaborator on that project, Theo van Gogh (a nephew of the famous painter), was killed by an Islamist, shot several times in broad daylight, and left with a note pinned to his chest that Ali was next. She was in protective custody in the Netherlands for quite some time before she decided to come to the United States. My understanding is that much of the money she makes from her speeches and writings goes to cover the intense security coverage that she still must employ. She risked her life to speak her mind, and her life remains in danger, and yet Ellison has the audacity to imply she did this simply to make money. I may disagree with Ayaan about the essence of Islam, the faith that I love, but we are each a product of our environments. Ellison's attack on her and me exposed his real intellectual corruption. I was a practicing physician long before I was head of a nonprofit organization. While I practice internal medicine and don't make the kind of money that subspecialists or surgeons make, my earnings as a doctor dwarf what I make with AIFD. I suspect that Ellison is quite aware of the falseness of his arguments and accusations, and that his intent is simply to be a provocateur. What a testimony to his "un-Islamic" character to openly indict my motivations, or "*niya*" (intentions), as pious Muslims call them, behind my back. How pathetic and unbecoming for a sitting congressman.

It is certainly a way to ingratiate himself with the Islamist organizations that appear to be a bedrock of his support. It is no secret, for example, that Ellison has no problem supporting the Saudi royal regime, that far from having anything critical to say about a nation that gave us Wahhabism and continues to be a hotbed of Islamic radicalization, he supports doing business with Saudi Arabia. In relation to cooperative business ventures between his home state of Minnesota and Saudi Arabia, he had this to say in a recent issue of *Arab News*: "Saudi Arabia and the U.S. have a lot in common. They have common interests and aspirations. Both can support each other to grow and to build on the excellent relationship that has existed all this while." Wow. We have much in common with the Saudis? It's called oil, and because of our reliance on it, we have found ourselves for several decades as virtual economic prisoners of this repressive regime. But you will not find a critical word from Ellison about any of that. You will not find a critical word from Ellison regarding CAIR or ISNA or other such groups that have received direct support from the Saudis. On the contrary, he continued his relationship with CAIR, speaking for them at a number of fund-raisers long after the FBI severed its ties with the group. In the same article from *Arab News* (a Saudi-owned newspaper), Ellison went on to say, "When President Obama was to give his historic Cairo speech and address the Muslims of the world, his first stop was Saudi Arabia before he headed to Egypt. That just shows our President understands the history and importance of the relationship with Saudi Arabia and understands how important it is to convey respect to King Abdullah, so our relationship is improving." Convey *respect* to King Abdullah? That's important for our president to do? When President George W. Bush walked hand in hand with the Saudis, the mainstream liberal press had a field day criticizing that (and rightly so), but when it comes to President Obama, somehow the right thing is to "convey respect" to the king? Yes, let's convey respect to a king who is responsible for abysmal treatment of women in the name of Islam, who severely punishes any sort of dissent, and who continues the barbaric practice of public beheadings and severing limbs in the name of God.

Perhaps it is time for reporters of courage and conscience to take a much closer look at who funds Keith Ellison and whose interests he actually represents. Then we can clearly know who is doing what for the money, and who is actually motivated by a need to speak out against the injustice and violence and blindness of Islamist supremacist groups.

To that end, coincidentally, in the summer of 2010 we launched the Muslim Liberty Project, which happened to be coming to fruition only a few weeks after the hearings in March 2011. There could not have been a better time for AIFD to formally launch a movement meant to counter the Islamist radicals.

The idea for the Muslim Liberty Project grew naturally out of my attempts to show how the embrace of country and Islam need not be mutually exclusive. The idea arose from a sense that if political Islam is the problem, what ideas can we give Muslims that will allow them to continue to love their faith, love God, and love the American legal system and culture without having to resort to Islamism? Having noticed that it was basically impossible to change an Islamist who was over forty to a non-Islamist, we changed our focus to the education and empowerment of Muslim youth and young adults for liberty and against Islamism. If we inoculate them with the ideas of liberty and freedom they can never be taken over by the supremacism of political Islam. Once we began to circulate the idea, it began to take on a life of its own. Our idea was simple: let's get young American Muslims together to discuss these ideas with a professional facilitator. Before we knew it, we had interest from all over the country. We thought it made sense to get these people together and thought that there might be someone in the community who might support such a get-together. Sure enough, a very generous supporter offered to fund just such a gathering, thinking that it was a crucial step forward not just for American Muslims, but for America itself, with the idea that ultimately it must be Muslims themselves who solve the problem of Islamism.

We had an essay contest in which hundreds of young American Muslims around the country addressed the issue of balancing faith and love of country. We asked Muslims between the ages of fifteen and thirty to submit essay answers to four major questions covering shariah, the separation of mosque and state, whether it was permitted to question imams and scholars, and whether the American system of governance was better than or inferior to the Islamic state. I was not at all sure what kinds of reactions we would get and was absolutely amazed to find so many young people who implicitly understood this need for balance and how we must be counter voices and offer alternatives to the forces of Islamism. It was actually somewhat difficult to pick the winners, those who would be flown out to Phoenix all expenses paid for our first group meeting of the Muslim Liberty Project. We brought in over twenty-five American Muslim youths and mentors from twelve states.

The three days we spent together gave me hope that a new day may indeed be dawning in the Muslim world. Unlike Reza Aslan, I don't believe a Muslim Reformation or Enlightenment has taken place yet, but based on what happened in Phoenix from March 25 to March 27, 2011, I believe it can. We had young Muslims born and raised in this country, and others who were recent arrivals from countries such as Pakistan, Iraq, and Iran, but they all shared a common vision that love of country and of faith are entirely possible, that it is possible to love the U.S.

Constitution and the Qur'an, and at the same time to keep both in perspective in relation to wider society. They all agreed that the ideas of liberty and its deeper understanding have yet to take root in most of the leadership of the mosque-based Muslim communities that they have experienced. But these youths came away with a revolutionary idea for American Muslims, one I believe has its roots in the time of the Prophet Muhammad: that being Muslim and the practice of our faith do not have to be mosque-centric. Yes, the mosque is certainly a place for worship, prayer, holidays, charity, and community, but it does not have to be the center of the community, let alone control the Muslim identity.

By the end of our three days together, we had a plan in place to bring our message to the world, via local action as well as social media outlets, and with the overall idea that our voices would be heard, that instead of the same revivalist static message coming from groups like CAIR (and their supporters, such as Keith Ellison), we could offer an alternative reformist message of embracing our faith, but not at the expense of compromising or rejecting the fundamental principles of liberty upon which the United States is based. All of us had varying ideas on how this could be accomplished—some were more inclined to writing opinion pieces, others planned to speak out at their mosque, or university, and so on—but with one overall idea: uniting in defense of our country and our faith. They started a social media platform, conference calls, town halls, and plans for future conferences to grow their movement.

As if by divine intervention, at the same time, the American Islamic Leadership Coalition (AILC) exploded upon the American scene in March 2011 as a group of diverse American Muslim organizations that provided a distinct alternative to the Muslim Brotherhood legacy groups that have dominated our communities. I had spearheaded the formation of AILC at the suggestion and empowerment of Congresswoman Sue Myrick (R-NC) and her brilliant national security expert, Andy Polk, with the advice and leadership of Walid Phares, a fellow at the Foundation for the Defense of Democracies. They understood the need for American Muslims to lead the struggle against Islamists and hosted a formative meeting in September 2010 on the Hill with a few American Muslim leaders who shared one thing—a desire to counter the agenda of the Muslim Brotherhood and their fellow Islamists. We grew from five members at our launch in 2010 to now over twenty members in a matter of weeks after my testimony for Chairman King's committee. The gelling together into the AILC of the diverse anti-Islamist work of so many courageous individuals like Manda Zand Ervin, Zainab Al-Suwaij, Tarek Fatah, Farzana Hasan, C. Holland Taylor, Tawfik Hamid, Abdirizak Bihi, Jamal Hasan, Hasan Mahmud, Jalal Zuberi, and Arif Humayun, to name a few, quickly became a signature initiative of our American Islamic Forum for Democracy much like the younger Muslim Liberty Project. Since then, among a host of other joint statements, AILC in 2011 published a comprehensive response to the Obama administration's empty counterterrorism strategy and put out statements in support of state protections against any unconstitutional interpretations of shariah law. The AILC was now a prominent sign to all those Islamist apologists and naysayers that critique of Islamism is not critique of Islam, and that contrary to the sarcasm of Congressman Ellison, our phone booth was bigger than they ever cared to imagine.

If someone had told me a few years back when I started AIFD that I would be surrounded by young American Muslims as well as a diverse coalition of over twenty American Muslim leaders in the AILC, determined to stand against the Islamists and speak up for both their country and Islam, I would have been hard-pressed to believe it. At times through the years, I've felt overwhelmed in the struggle just to find a few fellow Muslims on the same page with me, and wondered if the ideas that AIFD represents would remain just that, ideas supported by the lip service of many but without any translation into action. The Muslim Liberty Project and the broader American Islamic Leadership Coalition are proof to me that that is definitely not the case.

9

ENGAGING CONGRESSMAN ELLISON
AND THE ISLAMISTS

My history with Congressman Keith Ellison (D-MN) goes back long before the hearings on Muslim radicalization. On October 1, 2009, I was asked by Representative Trent Franks (R-AZ) to speak on Capitol Hill to members of Congress and their staffs regarding the threat of political Islam and its influence upon radical Islam. The basic theme of my talk was that Islamist terror cannot be defeated without addressing political Islam. I pointed out just one month before the Fort Hood massacre that we were failing miserably to counter the ideology that fuels Muslim radicalization. The proof: Despite a new dovish Obama administration that promised to leave Afghanistan and Iraq to take away the "Islamist narrative" that America is invading their nations, Muslim radicalization and terror cells were increasing exponentially. And yet when the NYPD put out its seminal report, "Radicalization in the West: the Homegrown Threat," MPAC and CAIR came out vociferously against it, stating, "The study of violent extremism should decouple religion from terror to safeguard civil liberties on free speech and equal protection grounds as a matter of strong public policy." Rather than demonize the NYPD's great work, these groups should have admitted that it was work Muslims should have been doing. If the root cause of Muslim radicalization is Islamism (political Islam), what good is any effort at counterterrorism that decouples any suggestion of theology, no matter how separatist, from terror? How can law enforcement effectively pursue counterterrorism in our country without recognition that political Islam and its narrative is the core ideology that, at its extreme, drives the mind-set of the violent extremists carrying out the attacks? Most Muslim groups in D.C. were Islamist-driven, using their bandwidth for diversionary tactics and anesthetizing Americans to the real threat—their own theo-political ideology as Muslim Brotherhood legacy groups.

A key player, and an honorary leader, among the American Islamist groups was Representative Keith Ellison. Soon after assuming office in January 2007, he began going around the country raising money for CAIR, headlining its fund-raisers from Chicago to Detroit to Phoenix to L.A. despite the fact that many of his colleagues in Congress had recently called for it to be investigated because of concern regarding ties to such terrorist groups as Hamas. Congressman Trent Franks and other members of our Arizona delegation tried to engage Mr. Ellison publicly for a discussion while he was in Phoenix raising money for CAIR in September 2009. But he dodged the meeting, claiming scheduling problems. We protested his visit and advocacy for CAIR-AZ while he was in town. But with my pending briefing in October on the Hill, he could no longer dodge us and agreed to join me at the dais for what was supposed to be a give-and-take on Islam, Islamism, CAIR, Islamist groups, and what our national strategy should be.

The event was open to the public and was hosted by Representative Trent Franks, chair of the House Religious Freedom Caucus. It was also attended by a number of other members of Congress, including John Shadegg (R-AZ), Frank Wolf (R-VA), Mac Thornberry (R-TX), and Henry Waxman (D-CA), as well as Representative Ellison.

In my comments, I made it clear that the recent spike in homegrown Islamist terrorist threats was clear proof that the problem has not gone away. In addition, I emphasized that the majority of these homegrown threats did not come from terrorists affiliated with Al Qaeda but were a sign of a deeper ideological pool. One of the reasons that I mentioned this was that the Obama administration had recently decided to basically rename the War on Terror the War on Al Qaeda, or more specifically an Overseas Contingency Operation (OCO), as if it is just this one group or tactic that is the problem. The truth, of course, is that it is Islamism that is the problem, and that is a force represented by many different groups, Al Qaeda, of course, being one of the most well-known. We later would see that as with a hydra, even removing the head of Bin Laden, as SEAL Team Six valiantly did on May 1, 2011, while symbolically a victory, did very little to affect the spread of Al Qaeda cells and activity among their global offshoots.

Bin Laden, true to his roots as the son of a billionaire entrepreneur and with a business education himself, aimed for Al Qaeda to have a substantial global presence. He used modern technology—the Internet, videos, satellite phones, and so on—like the CEO of a major corporation to spread his message around the world. He also formally declared war on the United States and on Americans at large, in one famous interview in 1998 saying that it was the duty of all God-fearing Muslims everywhere to kill Americans whenever and wherever they could find them. Most Americans did not take him seriously. Most Americans, in fact, did not even know who Bin Laden was before 9/11.

So the fact that he declared war on the United States and that his followers carried through with an act of war do make Al Qaeda different from most other Islamist terrorist groups, but the overall threat is the deeper, more pervasive Islamism. Acts of terrorism and groups like Al Qaeda are only one of its facets. Another aspect of Islamism is much less obvious to most Americans, and that involves a political arm devoted to supplanting secular law with seeds of shariah law. The point is not that the small Islamist minority could ever take over the United States, but rather that they pose as moderates as they seek to weaken our advocacy of liberty while Islamists take over Muslim-majority nations abroad and drown out other, genuinely moderate Muslim voices at home. Terrorism, for that matter, is a tactic of the militant Islamists, not the overall strategy, which involves a mission of worldwide Islamist domination.

For any true Islamist, the United States is the ultimate threat to their mission, as it represents everything they are against: freedom of religion, free markets, human rights, and secular-based law, as well as separation of church and state. It is significant that the fifty-seven Islamic states of the OIC (Organisation of Islamic Cooperation) did not sign the U.N. Declaration of Human Rights. They would sign only the Cairo Declaration of Human Rights in 1991, which was based on their interpretation of shariah law and an Islamocentric society. Their own declaration equated criticism of Islam with acts of sedition against the state and internationalized laws against blasphemy. None of the American Islamist groups, including the Muslim Brotherhood legacy groups, have taken a public position condemning these countries for their offensive positions in favor of the Cairo Declaration rather than the U.N. Declaration of Human Rights. The differences in the two declarations can be used as a teaching tool for the difference between the principles of Islamist societies and those of Western secular societies. Those who believe that Islamic democracies— where democracy simply means "elections" and some separation of powers—can be successful ignore the complete failures of Islamist nations and systems. Most important, because of their desire for global hegemony under Islamic states and absorption into the "neo-caliphate" of the OIC, they would never view Western democracies as their allies. Or, as Khomeini used to put it, you have the "little Satan," which to him was Israel, and "the big Satan," which for him was the United States, without which he did not think that Israel could exist, and which he considered the embodiment of Western decadence.

In my talk on Capitol Hill on October 1, I tried to bring several of these points into focus, and to make it clear that one must look at Islamism as a beast with many heads. If a homegrown jihadist here in the United States can plan his own terrorist attack independent of any group, then Islamism is much more widespread than one might like to think.

Then I shifted focus somewhat and talked about Muslim Brotherhood legacy groups in the United States, such as MAS (Muslim American Society), ISNA, MPAC, and CAIR. I mentioned CAIR's ties to Hamas, which the FBI acknowledged. I pointed out its obvious ideological foundation related to political Islam and its pretense that the entire American Muslim population approved its own theo-political agenda. I openly questioned why Representative Ellison would want to attend fund-raisers for CAIR in Phoenix and across the nation even after the FBI had formally disassociated itself from CAIR after the Holy Land Foundation trial. I spoke about the fact that many of his colleagues in Congress have recently asked to have CAIR investigated, based on its ties to Hamas. Representative Frank Wolf gave an entire congressional floor speech on his numerous concerns about CAIR in 2008. I found it odd, to say the least, that Ellison saw no conflict in his continued support of CAIR despite these glaring facts. Then I returned to my main point, which was that it is only Muslims, in the long run, who can defeat Islamism, because this is a problem within the faith's ideologies, and one that must be overcome through the continuing efforts of reformers who continue to expose radicals' betrayal of our faith and our country and at the same time push for worldwide reform against the more antiquated, medieval aspects of shariah law. In short, I made the point that Islam must come intellectually fully into the modern age, and that to do so, Muslims worldwide must embrace concepts of liberty and human rights, which by their very nature mean respecting others' beliefs, as well as the intrinsic need to separate church (or mosque) and state. I called upon leaders like Representative Ellison to no longer shirk their responsibilities and to lead the demand for reform against political Islam, rather than neglect and facilitate political Islam.

In relation to the Islamists, one of the things I pointed out was that so many Muslims live in denial that there are imams right here in the United States who advocate interpretations of shariah and Islam that are medieval. I pointed to leaders of the Assembly of Muslim Jurists of America (AMJA) and many of their anti-American rulings (fatwas). I discussed my concerns about Sheikh Hatem Mohammad Al-Haj's fatwa for the organization that, according to Islamic tradition under Islamic law, Muslims who leave Islam deserve the death penalty. Here they are, men who have been given more freedom to practice their faith than anywhere else in the world, and how do they exercise such a right? By endorsing a death sentence for apostates! Perhaps this is the ultimate case of showing the true colors of an Islamist. Even when given the opportunity to enjoy liberty and rights unknown in most of the world, they opt for the narrowest confines and interpretations of shariah law. God forbid they come to the United States to help absorb the ideas of freedom and liberty into their interpretations of Islam.

In the long run, I don't expect much more from such imams. If anything, they have shown that their ultimate loyalty is to their

base of power, which usually flows directly from Wahhabist petrodollars in Saudi Arabia. AMJA has many leading imams based
in the Kingdom despite being an "American" organization. And
what do American leaders like Ellison do? They ignore any suggestion that these imams are radical or deserving of criticism. I do
expect a very different standard of conduct from a U.S. congressman, which is why I was so shocked by Keith Ellison's reaction to
my comments about the problem of Islamism.

Ellison's remarks were brief, and could have been taken from
the basic Islamist playbook prepared by his friends at CAIR or
the MAS. The Muslim American Society provided accommoda-
tions for the congressman to attend his hajj in December 2008.
The MAS has long been felt to be the American central nervous
system of the Muslim Brotherhood, as discussed in a number of
reports, including an in-depth exposé from the *Chicago Tribune* in
September 2004, "A Rare Look at the Secretive Muslim Brotherhood." Instead of addressing the threat of Islamism or even acknowledging that it exists, Ellison turned the focus immediately
upon me. While he remained relatively calm, the substance of his
words betrayed his true intent. Ellison was basically out to portray
me as an "Uncle Tom" of sorts, actually having the gumption to
compare me to African Americans who try to curry favor with
whites by criticizing those problem members of their own race,
the street gangs, drug dealers, and so on, so that they can make
themselves look better. The implication was that I was doing the
same as an American Muslim, by emphasizing the radical elements of Islam, and not clearly seeing that all religions have their
extremists. And, of course, he also insinuated that perhaps there
was some sort of personal payoff for me for doing this, so perhaps
that way people wouldn't see me as one of *that* kind of Muslim,
the America-hating, terrorist kind. More to the point, he even
suggested that drawing this sort of negative attention to Islam

might actually result in a backlash against Muslims, that maybe even his own daughter, who wears the hijab, might be singled out for mistreatment. All this sound familiar? Remember when CAIR was implying that the television show *24* might create a backlash against Muslims because it actually portrayed Islamist terrorists on the show?

Ellison was also quick to defend CAIR, dismissing the fact that the organization was an unindicted coconspirator in the HLF trial by saying, as someone who had practiced law, that the fact that they were not indicted was what mattered. This, of course, is a clever way to avoid the obvious fact that if the legal system had considered CAIR to have no relevancy to HLF, it would not have been mentioned at all.

Is this the sort of man you want in the halls of power, someone who supports an organization that is doing nothing to help our nation against the threat of Islamism and is in fact obviously facilitating Islamism in the United States? Ellison will not even acknowledge that Islamism exists, and he deviously implies that reformers like me are nothing more than glorified "Uncle Toms." When specifically asked about my work and political Islam, he deceptively told the Muslim audience in Detroit on March 14, 2011, "I don't believe that my faith as a Muslim should be politicized. My faith is way bigger than politics. Right? So I don't agree with, but I don't even know what he's even talking about, quite frankly. I don't know what he means. No one ever demands that he define what he means." Even more important, is this someone who you think should have unfettered access to highly classified material that is crucial to our national security?

Instead of actually acknowledging the worldwide threat of Islamist terrorism, Ellison brought up Baruch Goldstein—the Israeli who machine-gunned and killed twenty-nine Muslims at prayer in Hebron—and talked about the fact that there have been Christians who blew up abortion clinics. I am not denying that there are extremist elements among Christians and Jews (as well as other groups) who have committed acts that can be labeled "terrorist." There is a big difference, however, between such isolated acts of terrorism and a widespread, organized movement that has caused the deaths of many thousands of people. One of my Christian friends once said to me, "Well, you know, we had the Inquisition." To which I said back to him, "Yes, that was hundreds of years ago. What modern Christian movement do you have that compares with Al Qaeda?" He had no answer for that because no such transnational Christian group currently exists, nor any Jewish group (or any other religious group, for that matter) that has devoted itself to worldwide terrorism and worked against the interest of Western democracies.

Such differences are important, because whatever problems and conflicts other religions may have, the malaise that is Islamism continues to be a worldwide threat and a force that undermines Islam as well. To diminish the threat of Islamist terrorism as Ellison did, by talking about Baruch Goldstein or the rare Christian who blows up an abortion clinic, is dangerously irresponsible. When I was offered the floor again, in one of my comments I made it clear that Ellison is suffering from denial in relation to the Islamist threat. Pretending a problem does not exist is a surefire way to make the problem worse. He conveniently made his drive-by attacks on me and vacated the room to his more interested colleagues and staff, claiming another engagement and again proving that Islamists care not about substantive engagement but about destroying their opponents in any way possible.

I must also ask, "Why is it that I am one of the very few voices questioning Representative Ellison on his defense of CAIR and his denial of the Islamist threat?" The truth is, if Muslims around the United States took it upon themselves to confront CAIR for its apologies for terrorist groups, for its tendency to cry "Islamophobe!" every time someone points out their Islamist practices, for taking on causes like the "flying imams," and for actually undermining Islam and American Muslims, if, I say, the voices of protest against them were loud enough, they would not have the power they have. It is once again the silence of the majority of Muslims that is proving to be our own undoing. It is the so far unaffiliated Muslim who must wake up.

In some ways, this situation reminds me of the way the Deep South used to be. White supremacists were responsible for laws that segregated blacks and gave preferential treatment to whites. Were the majority of southerners white supremacists or did the majority simply go along with what the white supremacists wanted as far as segregation laws? Did most white southerners approve of lynching blacks or did they simply turn their backs and pretend the problem did not exist? These are legitimate questions, but getting answers to them is not so easy. The reason is simple. Segregation laws were overturned, and for many southerners that part of their history became an embarrassment. So, instead of answering the question honestly, many might say today, "Oh, I never supported such a thing." But the better question might be "Did you ever actively oppose it?" Then watch them go silent. Or, as a patient of mine, who was stationed as a GI in Germany just after World War II, once said to me, "I could never find a German who actually admitted to supporting Hitler." He also could not find a single German who had actively opposed Hitler.

I see Ellison as a symptom of the problem, reflective of the widespread tendency of my fellow Muslims to cry "foul!" when no foul has been committed, who will, as Ellison did to me, talk about their worries about their "hijabi" daughters' being discriminated against, but do not appear the least bit concerned about Muslim honor killings that are taking place right here in the United States. If I had the chance to confront Ellison again, I might ask him, as I now ask Muslims who are reading this, "What are you doing to address the problem of radicalism in the mosques? Are you turning a deaf ear when they defame Jews and Christians and curse the very country that has given them the right to speak out?" I will give Ellison credit for one thing: he, at least, takes a stand, sadly one in defense of Islamists, which is more than you can say for all the silent voices out there in many American Muslim communities.

At the same time, I must also address those other silent voices out there—just as I did back in October 2009 on Capitol Hill—in the non-Muslim American community as well as in Congress. As much as I am concerned about the recent rash of homegrown Islamist terrorists, I am just as concerned about the overall lack of reaction in the American community in general. In Congress now, we have many members who seem to have an almost phobic resistance to linking the words "Muslim" and "terrorist," almost as if they take their cues from the mainstream media. Is there something I'm missing? If someone is committing acts of terror in the name of Allah, what other kind of terrorist is he, other than a Muslim? Is he a Baptist terrorist? A Methodist terrorist? Islamist terrorists do exist. It is especially relevant when the motivation arises from the global theo-political movement of Islamism. How are we ever going to deal with the issue if we can't even link the dots? There are those in Congress who are exceptions to this sort of "PC-think," including Senator Jon Kyl (R-AZ) and Senator Joseph Lieberman (I-CT) as well as representatives such as Trent Franks (R-AZ), Sue Myrick (R-NC), and Frank Wolf (R-VA). The problem is that they are not the majority.

All of this reminds me somewhat of England before World War II. Churchill was often the lone voice against Hitler, warning of the imminent threat and being ridiculed by many other members. What had happened? The English had fought World War I, and even though they won, they for the most part did not want to contemplate the possibility of another world war, one that would likely be even worse than the first one. So while England slept (as then Harvard student John F. Kennedy called his thesis, which later became a best-selling book), Hitler and his cronies continued to build their weapons and prepare for war. Sound familiar? It should. Iran is doing the same as we speak, as are many Islamist terrorist groups around the globe. While we argue about semantics—whether to call the War on Terror an "Overseas Contingency Operation" or "the War on Al Qaeda" and other such ridiculous things—the Islamists continue to prepare for war, on the battlefronts we call cities, as well as in various countries such as Afghanistan and Pakistan, and continue to mount their propaganda war via groups like CAIR and ISNA.

Since 9/11, New York City and now Homeland Security have promoted a citizen reporting program, which plastered on buses, trains, and subways the phrase "If You See Something, Say Something." This should apply not just to terrorist acts, but to the mounting propaganda war the Islamists have launched across the West. It's not just about the suspicious guy with the backpack, but about the propagandist who says that shariah law is no real threat to secular law, or the congressman who claims there is nothing wrong with his attending a fund-raising event for a group with terrorist ties.

As Americans, we need to be much more vigilant about the real nature of the Islamist threat. There are some madrassas (Islamic schools) right here in the United States that are teaching young, vulnerable students how to feel estranged from America, how to be anti-Semites, and in the worst cases, how to defeat those who don't think like them. We must not let it happen. We must take action to expose those who would undermine our freedom and national security by speaking out, shedding the light of day upon them by putting pressure on Congress to really acknowledge the threat and to act. For those of us who are American Muslims, our obligation to act is even greater, for this threatens not only our country but our faith as well. We must be in the vanguard, educating our fellow Americans to this continuing threat, and asking for their support in recognizing Islamism for what it is: a betrayal of Islam, and a threat to anyone who truly believes in liberty, principles of human rights, and democracy. We are the only ones who can solve this problem.

There is currently a "zero tolerance" policy in many workplaces regarding sexism and racism. So why not add Islamism to the list, as another form of discrimination that threatens us all? When a Christian preacher like Jerry Falwell made homophobic statements after 9/11—bizarrely blaming tolerance for homosexuals as somehow being related to what happened that day—he was justly called to task by many around the nation. We must do the same when it comes to Islamism. Universities such as Harvard, which so blithely take Wahhabi petrodollars and then in return have professors teach one-sided courses in Middle Eastern history that somehow conveniently blame Israel for all problems in that region, must also be called out on their collusion with the Islamists. Madrassas in the United States that teach children how to hate Christians, Jews, and the United States need to be called to account as well. We cannot continue to tiptoe around threats to our national security simply because someone may shout "Islamophobe," or, in my case, "Uncle Tom" or "Mossad agent" or the like.

As far as just how insane this so-called PC groupthink can get in reference to Muslims, and just how blind people can be to Islamists' aims, in an astonishing move, the Department of Justice decided to file suit in December 2010 against an Illinois school district in defense of a Muslim teacher based on an incredibly flimsy claim. The government claimed that the Berkeley district violated the civil rights of Safoorah Khan by not providing reasonable accommodation for her faith. In 2008, the math teacher asked for an unpaid three-week leave in order to perform her hajj, the pilgrimage to Mecca and a once-in-a-lifetime requirement in the Muslim faith. The district denied Khan's request twice because it did not meet the requirements specified by the union contract. Khan filed an unsuccessful EEOC (Equal Employment Opportunity Commission) complaint and then resigned because she felt the priority of her pilgrimage outweighed her contractual commitment to the district. Attorney General Eric Holder was entirely misguided. As a Muslim, I empathize with Khan's deep desire to complete her pilgrimage and pray for the day that I can do the same. However, this is a perfect example of the harm that federal government intrusion can do by giving Muslims special privileges for vacations that no one else can get. The special treatment demanded by Islamists in the name of freedom promotes a separatism that prevents the long-overdue reforms necessary to combat Islamism. The detachment of Muslim youth from our secular society and the fueling of an interpretation of Islam that is inflexible in regard to an egalitarian society such as ours are arguably the most important root cause of radicalization.

Khan's request would have stepped outside her contract and made Muslims a privileged class. The interpretation Khan's case demands speaks contrary to the very principles the government is trying to promote. The Justice Department, and now its choir of Islamist groups, has deceptively taken the position that Muslims such as Khan "should not have to choose between their religious practice and their livelihood." Contrarily, I believe that employers should not have to choose between the threat of intimidation from Islamists or the federal government and honoring the onerous demands of any single faith group or individual as a privileged class. The practice of Islam is central in my own life, but I have never demanded that others give me special consideration for that reason. My devotional Islam is between God and me, and I fear that any government intrusion ultimately fuels theocrats and their movements. Khan was not given what she wanted and made a personal decision to resign. It is exceedingly difficult to prove that "Islam" demanded that she perform her Hajj in December 2008. The faith asks only that once in her life she perform the pilgrimage. By refusing her leave of absence, the district did not force her to choose between faith and employment. We cannot continue to allow political correctness to send us down a path that promotes isolation versus assimilation and leaves liberty in a vacuum while Islamism thrives. The Framers wanted justice to be blind to faith to avoid creating special rights for a select few. Sadly, seemingly intimidated by the DOJ suit, the school district settled the case in October 2011, paying Ms. Khan seventy-five thousand dollars for her anguish, back pay, and legal fees. The district also agreed to provide Orwellian mandatory training in religious accommodation for all personnel. Which version of Islam will they teach as being the one with reasonable demands? The DOJ empowered an Islamist mind-set that demands special consideration, which is unacceptable in a society where all are equal before the law.

Here is the hope, though, the truly great thing about America that I have seen play out over and over again. We do not like bullies in this country. Once Americans at large truly begin to recognize Islamists for the bullies they are, for the thug mentality that lies behind their cries of victimhood, then Americans will turn against them (the them being Islamists, not Muslims) en masse, no longer carrying their water, and will not tolerate their attempts to undermine the liberty and human rights that are the hallmark of our country.

PART III
ISLAM AND ISLAMISM TODAY

10

DEFEATING POLITICAL ISLAM

If there is one book that people should read to truly understand Islamism, it is *Milestones* by Sayyid Qutb, one of the most prominent thought leaders of the Muslim Brotherhood and political Islam of the early to mid-twentieth century. While the roots of Islamism can be traced back hundreds of years, and Salafism and Wahhabism—with their mutual but varying ideas on "pure" Islam—can be considered as two of the primary sources of Islamism, the Muslim Brotherhood, and Qutb in particular, provided manifestos for this movement that are extremely influential right up to the present day.

In *Milestones* (written in 1964), Qutb often mentions *jahilyyah*, which he defines as the state of ignorance of the guidance of God. What is extremely significant about this is that in Qutb's view the entire Western world was riddled with *jahilyyah*. At the same time he considered most Muslims of his time to be suffering from such ignorance as well, due to what he considered to be watering down through the ages of "pure" Islam (in part because of Western influences but also due to what he considered Muslims tampering with the "purity" of Islam) so that it no longer existed.

Qutb saw it as his mission to revive such "pure" Islam, with its very strict interpretation of shariah law, and to never give an inch in terms of adopting or compromising with Western values, which he considered devoted to materialism, violence, and racism. Qutb did not form these views idly; he had lived in the United States for several years, and from such experience considered himself an authority on everything that was wrong with America and Western society.

In the first chapter of *Milestones,* titled "The Unique Qur'anic Generation," he lays out very clearly his mission:

> We must also free ourselves from the clutches of jahili society, jahili concepts, jahili traditions and jahili leadership. Our mission is not to compromise with the practices of jahili society, nor can we be loyal to it. Jahili society, because of its jahili characteristics, is not worthy to compromise with. Our aim is first to change ourselves so that we may later change society.
>
> Our foremost objective is to change the practices of this society. Our aim is to change the jahili system at its very roots—this system which is fundamentally at variance with Islam and which, with the help of force and oppression, is keeping us from living the sort of life which is demanded by our Creator.
>
> Our first step will be to raise ourselves above the jahili society and all its values and concepts. We will not change our own values and concepts either more or less to make a bargain with this jahili society. Never! We and it are on different roads, and if we take even one step in its company, we will lose our goal entirely and lose our way as well. *[Jahili here means ignorant and corrupt.]*

If this sort of rhetoric sounds familiar, it should. Bin Laden and other Islamists have been peppering their speeches with variations of it for years. For many young Muslims who live under corrupt, secular governments in countries where the future often looks hopeless, Qutb's words have particular resonance. While the discerning reader can easily spot the extremist rhetoric in Qutb's writings, and its inherent dangers, including a call for violent jihad in various sections of his work, a young person disenchanted with the dismal status quo in his country may, in fact, read it as truth and embrace the concept of a complete overhaul of society through "pure" Islam.

This is what makes *Milestones*, Qutb's seminal work, so dangerous. Because he was a gifted writer (and also wrote novels that helped elevate writers like Naguib Mahfouz—later winner of the Nobel Prize for literature—to prominence), he knew how to appeal to the reader's heart, mind, and soul. What Qutb sought was nothing less than a worldwide Muslim revolution, for he believed that was the only way man could save himself. Qutb used language that made him not only a political leader against dictatorship in Egypt but a religious leader whose works on the Qur'an were clearly from an individual who had a mastery of scripture and verse but read it through a supremacist lens that would feed the cancer of Islamism for a long time to come.

In Qutb's work, the vision of Islamist supremacy was crystallized with more clarity and purpose than it had ever been in the past. If existentialists like Sartre and Camus spoke to the ennui and anxiety prevalent in the Western world in the twentieth century, Qutb spoke to those Muslims in the Middle East and in other parts of the world who felt that their faith had somehow been stripped of its real meaning through progressive accommodation with what they saw as the corrupting influences of modern life. He also spoke to the revivalism many felt necessary for Islam against secularism. He, as did most Islamists, intentionally equated secular fascism with secular liberal democracy in the United States and Europe. As someone who endorsed the idea of worldwide Jewish financial and governmental conspiracies, and had no use for Christians or those of other religions, Qutb believed that it was the mission and purpose of Islam to cleanse the world of all those influences that prevented people from honoring their obligations to God.

It is important here to understand that Qutb genuinely believed that the West was out to undermine Islam and sought its destruction. His call to arms against the West and all corrupting influences was nothing more than what he saw as Muslims' God-given right to defend themselves against that which robbed them of their true faith. For Qutb, these were not just idle words, but ideas for which he was willing to, and eventually did, give his life. At first imprisoned for speaking out against the Egyptian government, he was hung in 1966, convicted of participating in a plot to kill President Gamal Abdel Nasser. While he was not actually proven to be the instigator or leader of the plot, it is important to note that it was his own book, *Milestones,* that sealed his fate, as passages of it were read aloud by the prosecution to show just how radical his thinking was. Qutb's ideas were an insidious fascism and supremacism that used an extreme interpretation of Islamic theology to insinuate itself into the minds of vulnerable Muslims. When met by Nasser's secular Arab nationalist fascism, he was made a martyr. Had the environment in Egypt been such that a genuine contest of ideas against the Islamism of the Muslim Brotherhood could have actually happened, rather than defeat through violent repression, they might not have flourished globally as victims, as they have to this day. This is not to say that the Muslim Brotherhood did not use violence and repression also, but as we see in the West, even in the supposedly equal playing field of a secular democracy, the ideas of the Brotherhood need to be confronted or they will fester and spread like a metastasizing cancer within Muslim communities.

For those who loved and followed Qutb, his execution made

him a *shaheed*, an Islamic martyr who died a hero's death, defending the faith with his life. The founder of the Muslim Brotherhood, Hassan al-Banna, was assassinated in 1949 after a member of the Brotherhood killed the then prime minister of Egypt. So Qutb's death followed in a tradition of perceived Islamic martyrdom for the Brotherhood's followers. This is significant for the modern day, as the overall influence of the Muslim Brotherhood on many terrorists groups such as Hamas, Al Qaeda, and Islamic Jihad (to name just a few) cannot be underestimated, nor can their call for martyrdom, if necessary, to further the cause of "pure" Islam. In his Pulitzer Prize–winning book, *The Looming Tower*, Lawrence Wright clearly draws the lines of connection between the Muslim Brotherhood, starting with al-Banna, moving up through Qutb, and through its influence on Bin Laden and his second-in-command, Ayman al-Zawahiri, and he describes the role such thinking played in the orchestration of the 9/11 attacks.

Al-Zawahiri joined the Muslim Brotherhood at age fourteen, and when his leader Qutb was executed, he made it his mission in life to fulfill Qutb's vision of a worldwide Islamic state. While still in his teens, he organized an underground cell devoted to overthrowing the Egyptian government and establishing an Islamic state. This group later merged with others to become Egyptian Islamic Jihad. Many years later, al-Zawahiri merged this group with Al Qaeda. So one can see the power Qutb's words had to motivate others to take up arms, and how his book *Milestones*, so little known in the Western world, can be directly implicated in the 9/11 attacks.

For the outsider who looks at the Islamist ambition to mount a worldwide revolution and considers it to be an outrageous proposition, consider a few facts. The Muslim Brotherhood started early in the twentieth century, and for quite some time its influence was largely confined to Egypt. In the last few decades, however, it has spread around the world as a primary influencer of too many terrorist groups to name here. *Milestones* continues to win converts to the cause, millions of them, which is exactly the sort of vision al-Banna and Qutb had for their group. Some of the leading Muslims in the United States will deceive Americans about Qutb's ideology. Mohammed Elibiary, appointed to Secretary Janet Napolitano's Department of Homeland Security Advisory Council (HSAC), and who purports to be an expert on "deradicalization," could not get himself to criticize Qutb in any effective way in an online interchange with Rod Dreher of the *Dallas Morning News*. Elibiary stated the following:

> Many Westerners who've read Qutb's and many others' work, see the potential for a strong spiritual rebirth that's truly ecumenical allowing all faiths practiced in America to enrich us and motivate us to serve God better by serving our fellow man more. At that point, America will have a spiritual product that's exportable and satisfactory to the spiritual marketplace's demand. So I'd recommend everyone read Qutb, but read him with an eye to improving America not just to be jealous with malice in our hearts.

One cannot change the stripes of a zebra. And despite all the dissimulation and intellectual jujitsu of Islamists like Elibiary who try to appear assimilated to Western secular liberal democratic ideals, eventually when called upon to criticize organizations and leaders by name, they will not be able to help uttering some form of apologetic. If anything, Islamism has grown more sophisticated over time, in terms of the methods employed to make inroads. Islamist apologists like Elibiary and a host of American Muslims with Islamist leanings have become quite influential in our government, and until we understand the root ideology that threatens us, we will make no inroads into counter-radicalization and the long, overdue Muslim reforms.

Terrorism is only one tactic of the Islamists. While al-Banna and Qutb believed in a head-on confrontation with the West, many of their followers have chosen more subtle and very often more effective means of ideological engagement, infiltration, and evangelism. The Islamist who detonates a bomb in a subway may temporarily accomplish the goal of having people live in fear, stimulating Western isolationism, and may even get a few people to listen to his political agenda. Think of Bin Laden in the days after 9/11 when he appeared on TV and gave the Americans ultimatums about what they must do to prevent another attack. Did we heed his demands? Of course not. If anything, they steeled the resolve of government and citizens to track down this cold-blooded killer and his followers. Bin Laden might say that was part of his goal as well, to get our military involved in Afghanistan and in Middle Eastern countries, so he could more easily bring the fight to us. Still, ultimately, what has happened is that we defeated Al Qaeda in Afghanistan and in Iraq and have them on the run in this country and all around the world. We got Osama Bin Laden and many others in the upper echelons of Al Qaeda. But sadly we have done little to counter the source ideology: political Islam.

Before 9/11, the terrorists may have considered the United States to be weak, corrupt, and decadent, with little will or discipline to defeat terrorism, but since then we have proved them wrong many times over. Yes, they knocked down our tallest buildings, attacked the Pentagon, and killed several thousand of our citizens. These are not small things. And yet, how much have they really gained? Have they dismantled our essential infrastructure, weakened our military, or even been able to successfully launch another attack within our borders since 9/11? The answer is no, no, and no again. This does not mean the threat has gone away, but simply that overall we are dealing with it quite effectively, at least on the terrorist front.

The problem is that it gets more complicated when we deal with Islamism's propaganda arm and groups like CAIR that claim to denounce Islamic terrorism—and yet basically never (other than a few times with reference to Al Qaeda) mention specific groups—and overall have learned to use our own country's liberties and rights against us. One of the primary ways that this plays out in American society is that Islamists use the victimization stance very effectively to complain that their rights are in danger, that they are discriminated against, most often in cases where it is simply not so.

Let's take a case in point. A few years ago, CAIR decided to take on the television show *24*, which deals with counterterrorism issues in a dramatic but fictionalized way. Some of the terrorists portrayed on the show were Arab Muslims. CAIR decided that this was racist, that it stereotyped Muslims as terrorists, and because of this, American Muslims might have to fear for their lives. I found this curious since I am an American Muslim and was also a fan of the show. Yes, it's true, they did show Islamist terrorists on the show. They also showed Arab Americans who were working for CTU (the counterterrorism unit) to defeat the terrorists. CAIR did not talk about that, but instead made it seem as if Americans who watched *24* were likely to go out and brutalize Muslim Americans. Was there any proof of this at all? Absolutely not. But they got an Associated Press reporter to take up their cause, and from the way he wrote the story, you would have thought that American Muslims around the country were shaking in their boots, and that because of the show, Americans were ready to attack them at any moment. The reporter did not bother to consider other Arab or American Muslims who might hold a different point of view and were not threatened by the show at all.

I made my views on this issue well-known, that I was a fan of the show, and even wrote an op-ed piece in the *National Review Online* that addressed the issue. I made it clear that as Muslims we need to stop whining that our rights are being violated when they're not and look at how we might protect our country from Islamist terrorists. I ended with a call for Muslims to form an American Muslim CTU. That view did not make me popular in certain Islamic quarters, but I stand by what I said then on this as a core issue that separates Muslims who are true to a humble Islam from the Islamists who are part of a global theo-political movement. The issue should not have been the show *24* but why the producers and writers of the show chose to have Islamist terrorists represented on it. When drug trafficking was tearing apart the city of Miami (among others) in the 1980s, were journalists racists because they revealed that many of the traffickers were Colombians? Of course not. It was the truth, plain and simple. In that same way, for *24* to show the primary terrorist threat to this country to be Islamist terrorist groups is fact, not fiction. But if groups like CAIR can convince the United States that showing Islamist terrorists in the context of a one-hour TV program is somehow "stereotyping" or "racist" or "anti-Islam," then perhaps they can distract people from the very real threat these groups and the underlying subtle ideology pose in the real world.

One of the easiest ways to spot Islamists is that every other word they utter is "Islamophobia." Many prominent counterterrorism experts are labeled Islamophobes repeatedly by groups like CAIR, MAS, and MPAC. In fact, in August 2011 the George Soros–funded Center for American Progress (CAP) issued a 132-page report titled *Fear, Inc.: The Roots of the Islamophobia Network in America.* Its objective was to supposedly "expose—and marginalize—the influence of the individuals and groups" that CAP claims are a part of an "Islamophobia network in America." This report purported to be an in-depth investigative analysis that connected the dots of a supposedly sinister antijihadist movement. But a glossy cover around 132 pages of political blog material does not make a report either journalistically or academically sound. The research would not be acceptable for a college term paper, let alone a report that was being billed as useful in-depth analysis. The report indicted me as a "validator" of this supposed Islamophobia network. CAP never even contacted me or our organization, AIFD. Instead it blindly libeled my work and regurgitated the unsubstantiated claims of American Islamists. In addition to broad liberal media coverage in the Unites States, the Iranian regime's Press TV featured the report on its home page as a major story highlighting the common cause of Islamists such as President Mahmoud Ahmedinijad and such organizations as CAP. Interestingly, Adam Savit noted in August 2011 at *Big Peace* that of the thirty news interviews CAIR provided in the first eight months of 2011 twenty-two were with Press TV, six with CNN, and two with Fox. The fact that this American Islamist group frequented a foreign radical Islamist propaganda arm of an avowed enemy of the United States in order to peddle the opinion that America is anti-Muslim and anti-Islam rather than decry the rampant human rights abuses in Iran itself speaks volumes to CAIR's agenda for Muslims.

The Islamists have found that merely calling someone an Islamophobe can be a powerful tool that the PC liberal crowd will respond to. Much of the mainstream liberal press, for instance, will rarely interview Steven Emerson, the exceptions generally being MSNBC and recently CBS. Is this because Emerson does not have useful information? On the contrary, Emerson for many years now has been considered such an invaluable source of information on various Islamist terrorist groups that government agencies have often sought him out to educate them and provide valuable background material for investigations.

However, because Emerson backs his assertions with volumes of facts, he has become a thorn in the side of groups like CAIR and MPAC. He has shown the clear links that common ideologies create between some of the so-called Islamic charity groups and terrorism groups like Hamas, and how they have been able to collect their money right under the noses of the U.S. government. So CAIR and other groups label him an Islamophobe, and various media outlets take the bait and essentially make him a nonperson, someone their journalists won't go near. Is this fair play, or the sort of objectivity that true journalism is supposed to stand for?

As a Muslim dedicated to reform, I find that my own media outlets are severely restricted. You would think there would be a great call to hear from Muslim reformers in the broad spectrum of American media, but that is not the case. The Associated Press, for instance, is a lot less likely to call upon my group, AIFD, for commentary, or other reformist groups like the Alliance of Iranian Women, or the American Islamic Congress, Lib for All, or the Center for Islamic Pluralism or any of our anti-Islamist (non–Muslim Brotherhood) groups in the American Islamic Leadership Coalition, and much more likely to call upon CAIR or MPAC or any of their Islamist colleagues. One would think that especially those on the left would want to demonstrate ideological diversity among Muslims and solicit non-Islamist opinions. Is the reason they do not do so because such Islamist front groups as CAIR, ISNA, MPAC, MAS, and the MSA truly represent the view of most Muslims? I truly don't believe so. However, they are much better funded than the reformist groups, and have a tendency to cry "wolf!" so loudly and so often that they make themselves hard to ignore. A media community deathly afraid of the "bigot" or "Islamophobe" label jumps at their command. Just search for a genuine mainstream media investigative report into those groups and their ideas and you will find very little. Why? Those groups just happen to conveniently represent a minority religious community that the media seem to feel is far too victimized for them to investigate any of these groups. Americans love the underdog, the victim, and the media simply exploit that fact and use Islamists to fit that victimization narrative for all Muslims. The reality is that many Muslims in the United States and globally strongly believe that those Islamist (Muslim Brotherhood legacy) groups actually represent a minority of Muslims in America and around the world. Still, much of the American media can be seen as complicit in these Islamist groups' agendas, simply due to the fact that they are not giving sufficient voice to other Muslim voices. They choose instead the lowest-hanging fruit—Islamist groups that have long ago come together to collectivize Muslims because they see Muslims only through a theopolitical lens as some kind of political party, not as a diverse faith group that separates religion and government.

Fox News, which is regularly accused by the mainstream media and Islamists of having a biased agenda, is actually one of the few media outlets that have proven themselves over and over again to be receptive to the message of Muslim reformers, myself included. Much of the liberal media seem to be fearful of us, those very voices calling Islamic radicalism to account, for "PC" reasons, meaning they fear that any criticism of Islamism will somehow be seen as a condemnation of Islam. What they refuse to acknowledge is that Muslim activists are divided into revivalists and reformists. The revivalists seek only to put a modern cloak around their central ideology of political Islam, while the reformists seek to bring modernity to their own personal interpretations of Islam through the separation of religion and state. The West needs to take the side of the reformers in this battle inside the

House of Islam. Does a white person who criticizes the idea of white supremacy or the idea of an Aryan race being superior to all others have a discriminatory agenda with his own race? Of course not. He or she is criticizing something that should be rejected by anyone with a grain of human decency. The same can be said for those of us who fear the way Islamism is undermining Islam and are concerned about its threat to the world. We love Islam, we love America, and we love the human race and wish to protect our faith, our country, and the world from a very destructive force. Do we not deserve the same fair hearing by the media as such groups as CAIR, ISNA, and other Islamists whose platform often conflicts with America's founding principles?

On Fox in May 2011, I was brought on to debate American policy toward Pakistan in the wake of the Bin Laden killing on their soil. In a discussion focused on foreign aid, Ahmed Rehab, the director of the Chicago office of CAIR, went immediately off topic and took the opportunity on national television to call me a "sock puppet of the right wing" and anti-Islam. After he was done with his ad hominem attacks, I retorted that there was nothing more pro-Muslim and pro-Islam than defeating the Islamist agenda and ideas of groups like CAIR. It is this very point that the mainstream media seem to conveniently ignore when they allow Islamist groups to be the predominant voice for American Muslims. They forget the ideological dynamics of Christian diversity that founded the United States of America. In Islam our battle also is from within, not outside.

Part of the problem, however, is that it is hard for average Americans to focus on the threat of Islamism because many don't even know the nature of the threat. We need to stop thinking that we're safe and sound in America just because we have not had a major attack within our borders since 9/11. The reality is that the homegrown Islamist terrorist threat continues to grow, as recently foiled plots reveal, and Al Qaeda and other groups still have their own operatives here. More to the point, though, we must realize that propaganda is just as powerful a weapon as a bomb, sometimes more so. No Nazis would have ever taken up arms to defend their cause if they didn't believe in it. In that sense, it all starts with a thought, a philosophy. *Milestones* inspired a fourteen-year-old Egyptian boy named Ayman al-Zawahiri to take up arms against his own government and devote his life to the creation of a worldwide Islamic state. He has not turned back since, despite coming from an upper-middle-class family in which a very comfortable existence could easily have been his lot.

Here in America, the Islamists continue to make inroads, even as at various levels they continue to be exposed. CAIR's connections to Hamas have been revealed, even more so recently in the Holy Land Foundation (HLF) trial, in which it was shown that so-called charity money—up to $12 million—was filtered through HLF and given to Hamas. It was shown that CAIR was formed from the Islamic Association for Palestine, which had common origins with HLF's Palestinian Committee, which in turn has clear connections to Hamas. In other words, when one follows the trail of the money, it is clear that all these groups are connected.

So how does CAIR respond to all of this? Do they admit to anything? Do they see any contradiction between their claim to be against terrorism and their clear sympathies and connections to a terrorist group? Do they join us in publicly countering Islamism and its incompatibility with Americanism? No, of course not. CAIR denies reality so often that I'm convinced they have begun to believe their own lies. There is a fundamental schism between basic American values of liberty and human rights and the totalitarian groupthink that is Islamism, a divide that is akin to the Grand Canyon, as is laid out clearly in the table at the beginning of Chapter 5.

True counter-Islamism requires a strategy for each one of the antagonisms shown in the table. Part of the problem, though, is that the average American is not aware of the Islamists' intent to undermine American democracy as we know it and replace it with such values as are listed in the table, and the average Muslim has as a rule not spoken out against this threat. These conflicts do not evaporate with immigration to the United States or even with assimilation. What is needed is genuine reform into modernity. As long as the narrative is just about violence, reform will never be realized. For the Americans who are aware of the Islamist threat, the lack of vocal Muslim criticism of Islamism often feeds the fear and the suspicion that perhaps all Muslims acquiesce in their goals.

And are they entirely wrong in such an assumption? Catholic friends of mine have often talked about sins of commission versus sins of omission. Is it not a sin of omission for Muslims of conscience not to speak out against the Islamists? How will Islamism ever be defeated if we as Muslims either refuse to recognize the Islamist threat, or do so only behind closed doors?

At the same time, one must be very well aware that anyone who wishes to take on the Islamists is dealing with a very powerful and underhanded force. With Islamists, unlike, say, communists or white supremacists, the battle can quickly become complicated, for "Islamist" is not even a term they use, but one that others have applied to them. Islamists may even claim to believe in equal rights for all, but their actions (and oftentimes their words) contradict them, and they still cling to the concept that those equal rights come not only from God but from Islam—a poison pill that always empowers theocrats. However, there are clearly defined ways that Americans can use to both identify Islamists and confront their antidemocratic, antiliberty mind-set and their desire for a worldwide Islamic state governed by shariah law.

One of the core questions to ask anyone you suspect is an

Islamist is, which should govern the United States, constitutional law or shariah law? If the person equivocates, and says that there is room for both systems of law within the United States, you're dealing with an Islamist. Obviously, if the person answers point-blank, "Shariah," that speaks for itself, but the Islamist is often not so direct anymore, since they have been called out by various writers and critics on this and held to account regarding Islamic law versus secular law. So, with the wilier Islamist, the idea is to present shariah as no real threat to U.S. constitutional law, merely a set of religious beliefs that Muslims privately practice, all of the edicts about barbaric punishments and unequal treatment of women notwithstanding. A Muslim like myself can stop an Islamist in his tracks by asking, what about the idea of reforming those aspects of shariah law—such as stonings, blasphemy, apostasy, sexism—so that it can more accurately reflect the present day? The typical response to such a question is that if shariah is reformed, then it is no longer shariah, and that this threatens the very existence of Islam. This, of course, negates the fact that reform has taken place within both Judaism and Christianity without either religion or their legal codes perishing. There were Catholics, for instance, who were opposed to the reforms of Vatican II, but despite this, the church did not disband, and congregants got used to new things, like hearing the mass in English instead of Latin. In fact, many of them preferred this, since they did not speak Latin.

Proceeding along the lines of confronting an Islamist, one might simply ask, what is your position regarding Al Qaeda, Hezbollah, Hamas, and so on? The Islamist is usually very good at condemning terrorism in a general way, but not so good when it comes to naming specific groups. In a case like this, if the person equivocates, and begins to describe these groups as politically based, and says that he might not agree with all their tactics, however—and the "however" here is very important because it signals where the person really stands—you must understand that U.S. foreign policy, and Israel, and so on. . . . I don't think I have to spell out the anti-U.S., anti-Israel litany, since they have done it ad nauseam through their CAIR, MPAC, MSA, and MAS groups and we have covered the matter in other chapters. The core issue is that Islamists will not directly attack these terrorist groups. Why not? Well, going back a few years, think of Sinn Fein versus the Irish Republican Army (IRA). Sinn Fein was (and is) the political arm of the IRA. As such, it was not within their purview to condemn the IRA's acts of terrorism. Eventually, Sinn Fein did actually negotiate a peace treaty with the British, effectively ending (at least for the last several years) IRA terrorism.

The difference with Islamist political front groups is that they do not appear to have any interest in seeking peace anytime in the near future. Think of Qutb's words about this: to never, never compromise with jahili forces. So the political front groups of the Islamists, such as CAIR, ISNA, or the MAS, are not likely to directly condemn the overtly violent Islamist groups, such as Hamas, because the truth is they have too much theo-politically in common but just may differ on tactics.

Another quick litmus test in discussions with Islamists is to ask them their position on Islamist theocracy in the Middle East. If they actually equivocate, try to soft-pedal the ascendant Islamism of the Muslim Brotherhood as "democratic," or even support the Islamist totalitarianism of such regimes as Saudi Arabia and Iran, it is a good bet that liberty is not something they're willing to defend, even though they live in the United States. Also, if they support the rule of Hamas in Gaza or of Hezbollah in Lebanon, because, they say, those groups are legitimate and have been elected, you're clearly dealing with Islamists. This so-called Arab Spring and its attendant discussion about the use of Islamist parties has revealed a great deal about core ideologies of American

Islamist groups. This is why the table in Chapter 5 clearly differentiates between democracy (mobocracy) and liberty. Yes, it's true, Hamas got elected to office in Gaza, which means that Islamism is alive and well there, that the concept of liberty for all, including Jews, Christians, and Muslims, has no meaning in that region.

In reference to American Muslims and their support of such regimes, this may seem like a very puzzling contradiction. Why live in the United States if what you really support is the quasi-theocracy of the Islamists of the Muslim Brotherhood in Egypt or Ennahda in Tunisia or the rule of terrorist groups, such as Hamas in Gaza and Hezbollah in Lebanon? The answer, as incredible as it may seem, is that for the true Islamist in the United States, the Constitution and all its attendant rights and laws are something they are merely using as a platform or as an opportunity as they seek to spread evangelical Islamism and create Islamist states around the world. Sound like a far-fetched ambition? Perhaps, but when one considers the inroads the Islamists have made in Europe in the last few years, it is not so incredible to think that they can do the same here in America. There are over eighty functioning quasi-shariah courts operating on British soil under the rubric of their arbitration systems. Sure, Muslims should have the freedom to engage in arbitration between their own parties; however, it is incumbent upon our governments to make sure that those arbitration courts do not promote systems and laws that keep Muslims unaccountable to the law of the land, which is based in "one law." Just ask many of the Muslim women who find themselves in those court systems and do not have the wherewithal to seek redress outside those separatist systems, which their husbands, fathers, or brothers coerce them through. Many of the Muslim women in Canada were able to avert the establishment of a shariah court system with help from the leadership of courageous and outspoken reformist groups like the Muslim Canadian

Congress. Yet, sadly, they did so only when the general Canadian population took heed of the concerns of larger non-Muslim Canadian feminist groups that finally protested shariah courts. This exemplifies the role that the majority in our population can play in helping reformists get our voices heard and respected. As a Muslim and a believer in liberty, I find it truly terrifying that organized institutional Islamism has followed our families here to the land of liberty and is establishing organizational footholds in the legal systems, educational systems, our mosques, and civil rights discussions. The poet Dylan Thomas once famously wrote, "Do not go gentle into that good night" and "Rage, rage, against the dying of the light." While in this case the poet addressed mortality, he could have just as easily been talking about the rights and privileges associated with liberty and the incredible foresight our forefathers had in separating church and state.

So when Somali Muslim cabdrivers at Minnesota airports refuse to transport passengers because they carry alcohol or pork products, or other Muslims insist upon taxpayer-funded footbaths at universities, or that public or private gyms become obliged to provide separate gym facilities for men and women because of their religious beliefs, one must realize that this is basically the public practice of shariah coming to America, however simple it may look to some. How one conducts one's personal life is one's own business, but when one seeks to change how commerce is conducted—which clearly states that there be no discrimination based upon religion, race, and so on, an injunction that the cabdrivers clearly violated by refusing to transport passengers with alcohol or pork products—or when religious laws are enacted at the expense of the taxpayers on a secular university campus, we have a problem. There is a big difference between respecting a person's religious beliefs and acquiescing to his or her demands, and essentially replacing secular laws with religious ones.

And one must keep in mind that not all people who come to America are here because they really respect this country's embrace of liberty, democracy, and human rights. There are people who come to this country because they want to undo it, to remake it along the lines of religious fundamentalism, or because they're anarchists, and simply want to destroy the United States, or because they want it to be like China, Cuba, and so on. Not everyone is here to take advantage of the opportunities for prosperity. Some actually want to undo our economy because they see it as the easiest way to destroy us. One must remember that Al Qaeda's goal on 9/11 was not just to knock down buildings and kill Americans but also to cripple our economy. And let's face it, they went a long way toward accomplishing that goal, at least for a short time. Our economy was already teetering, and their attacks gave it a near deathblow. We recovered, of course (well, relatively speaking, at least until recently), but one must keep in mind that terrorism also undermines economies, and that is typically part of their agenda, since nations with faltering economies cannot advance their vision of freedom across the world.

So, yes, as both foreign and homegrown terrorist threats continue, we must all be on guard and support our government's battle against Islamist terrorists. At the same time, we must also be on guard for that much more subtle threat, the propaganda arm of the Islamists, which is determined not just to establish enclaves of shariah law in America, but as part of that goal wants to directly influence and infiltrate our national legislature so that our nation is anesthetized to the threat of political Islam. It is for this reason that our diverse American Islamic Leadership Coalition (AILC) supported a proposed bill during the fall of 2011 in the Michigan State Assembly, HB 4679, intended to bar Michigan courts from enforcing any foreign law, if doing so violates any rights guaranteed by the U.S. Constitution or the state of Michigan's constitution. The AILC felt that the bill allows Muslims safety from being enveloped by the tentacles of medieval, man-made laws that have been falsely accorded divine status. We fully recognized that our own interpretation of shariah may guide our own marriage documents, last will and testament, and personal contracts. But the U.S. Constitution, the Bill of Rights, and the law of the land should never be violated. Until we recognize the threat of Islamism in all its forms, the majority of Americans will be gulled into recognizing only its most obvious form: terrorism. All these years after 9/11, it's time for us to finally see the threat in its complete form and fight back actively against it.

11

HOW THE QUR'AN IS MISINTERPRETED

To hear one side tell it, the Qur'an is nothing but a prolonged series of rants against infidels, the essential manual of hate for the 9/11 terrorists, with various verses in particular as the matches that started the flames. On the other extreme are those who claim that the Qur'an is nothing but one long lovefest in the name of God and that there is no way that anyone could ever interpret any of the verses as a genuine call to arms. The truth is that there are verses in the Qur'an that deal with war, but as we will see, the idea of using these particular verses as an excuse to attack innocent civilians is something that only an Islamist supremacist could justify. The centrality of Qur'anic scripture in the Islamic faith cannot be overstated. Its recitation, memorization, and details consume the majority of our five daily prayers and the evenings of our holiest month of Ramadan, and in its Arabic syntax and script is the common thread that binds all Muslims. Essentially, every Arabic Qur'an in the world is the same text and felt by Muslims to be God's authentic, unalterable word. However, it is the human interpretation and contextualization of those Qur'anic verses, along with varied interpretations of the example (*sunnah*) of the Prophet Muhammad, that separate and define so many variations in the practices and belief systems of Muslims. Islamists will insist that there is only "one Islam." The reality is that my Islam may not be their Islam. This is a simple recognition that Muslims may disagree about what is and what is not within the realm of "Islam"—a natural condition of any faith group. The reality is that Islamists will use their tribal techniques to marginalize any disagreement or new ideas from Muslims about Islam by basically painting them out to be apostates—those who have rejected the "truth" as the Islamists see it. One of the telltale signs of fanaticism and dangerous extremism is the proclivity of some Muslims, especially Islamists, to categorize other Muslims as "ignorant," "non-Muslim," or "unqualified to opine about Islam." As with any area of human interest, study of faith should certainly be based in a healthy respect for "*ilm*" (knowledge). But that respect should not in any way become prima facie evidence in any discussion. A genuine movement to modernize Islamic interpretations of our scripture will be realized when our discussions are centered on logic and reason and not on the preconceived qualifications of the discussants. Islamists paralyze growth and critical thinking by obsessing over the qualifications, training, or degrees of any Muslims brave enough to advocate religious opinions. It is far easier for them to dismiss reasoned arguments and interpretations with patronization and personal attacks of being "unorthodox" than with engagement and substance. Such is the obstacle of blind tribalism and groupthink that stifles real creativity, growth, and humanity.

Most extreme views are driven by particular agendas, the need to see things a certain way regardless of reason, and this is definitely true in relation to the Qur'an. Post-9/11, there appear to be those who want to hold Islam to blame for every terrorist act committed by Islamists, as opposed to holding Islamism to blame. For this side, Islam and Islamism are merely terms, and there are those who claim that Bin Laden and his ilk actually represent the real Islam, that Islam by its nature is violent and radical.

On the other side, you have those whose goal is to never utter a harsh word about any version of Islam, its extremists notwithstanding, and in some cases such people are driven by a PC agenda that considers any such criticism "racist" or "anti-diversity" or other such buzzwords. The Islamists, as we have seen, are great at manipulating such sentiments, managing to cast a pall (again to avoid substance) over respected counterterrorism investigative journalists like Steven Emerson and anti-Islamist academicians like Daniel Pipes, labeling them "Islamophobes." Never mind that Daniel Pipes's mantra is that militant Islamism is the problem and moderate Islam is the solution. In the midst of all this, both extremes want us to lose sight of the truth—that there is an Islam, a moral Abrahamic faith that can be the source of morality and righteousness for more than 1.3 billion people in the world, and there is Islamism, a theo-political movement that uses shariah to try to control society and prevent liberty.

One of the main problems that we deal with in relation to the Qur'an is that specific verses take on certain meanings depending on the particular translation and the particular mind-set one brings to those verses. All the difference can be made, for example, by simply separating history from religion. Do the phrases used in a particular passage relate to a specific battle in a specific time, let us say around 615 CE? Or does the phraseology profile all Jews, all Christians, all pagans, as enemies of all Muslims at all times? And even within those passages related to a certain time, do we use literal interpretations of the message from God to Muslims or are they allegorical and to be reinterpreted based upon the facts and the intellectual climate of modern times? This is not unique to reading the Qur'an, but is also true of other religious texts and many great works of literature.

Let's look outside scripture and reading God's word. For example, Friedrich Nietzsche, whose works I studied extensively when I was in college, was a greatly misinterpreted philosopher. His most famous book, *Thus Spake Zarathustra*, was filled with aphorisms whose meanings were often multilayered. His words in the original German were full of puns and double and triple meanings, and the symbolism was open to interpretation. Some things, though, are clear from Nietzsche's life and from his work. He was not an anti-Semite, he despised German nationalism, and his model for the superman was Goethe, not Hitler, whom he would have likely detested as a thug and a cretin. So how is it then that his work, which spoke so profoundly to the existential plight of man, was somehow used in part by the Nazis to justify their evil mission?

The answer in part is that his sister, Elisabeth, after Nietzsche's mental breakdown and death a few years later, used his work, which she only dimly understood, to try to curry favor with the Nazis. The Nazis wanted to promote the idea that Hitler was the embodiment of the superman, and in order to boost sales of her late brother's work (from which she benefited financially), she was more than happy to play along.

Both the Nazis and Elisabeth Nietzsche were conniving about what they did. They knew that many people would accept at face value what they were told. Then as now, that tends to be human nature, particularly in a totalitarian regime. Even more to the point, a myth is often more powerful for people than truth, so in this case the myth of Hitler as superman, and of the Germans as the "Master Race" who were destined to conquer the world, could be accepted by many Germans if fed to them enough times, as could the lie that Nietzsche had looked forward to just such a day, and had written about it in his works.

Add to this some of the bad translations of Nietzsche's work that have come down through the years, and the possibility of misinterpretation becomes even greater. And how does this all relate to misinterpretation of the Qur'an? The answer is that some of the very same criteria apply that have contributed to gross mis-interpretations of particular verses.

Instead of Elisabeth Nietzsche, Islam has the Wahhabists and the Salafists, whose translations of the Qur'an are the most common ones available to the world at large, and tend to cater to their anti-Christian, anti-Jewish agenda. There is an Italian saying that translation can be a traitor, and this is why it is so crucially important that the translator be extremely careful with how he translates particular words, and that he or she be as objective and scholarly as possible. With Arabic, this becomes even more of a challenge, since Qur'anic (classical) Arabic is very complex, with a broad vocabulary, far more so than conversational Arabic, and its words can have various meanings. Choosing the wrong one can completely change the context of what is said. Add to this the far more complex issue of explanation and interpretation (*tafsir*) based upon the history and context of the passage's timing and revelation, and one can see how easy it can be for an oppressive global network of well-funded petrodollar tribal theocrats to manipulate and push forward a dominant literalist (Wahhabi or Salafist) version.

For Muslims, the authenticity of the Arabic script of the Qur'an revealed to the Prophet Muhammad has the same sort of divine status as the Prophet Jesus has for Christians. My understanding is that in our belief, this was the language chosen by God in which to reveal the Qur'an, because this language was the one perfectly suited for it, a language of a pagan community that had not yet been exposed to God's revelation. So essentially, this is more evidence that Islam was not revealed to convert Jews or Christians to Islam but rather to pagans as an updated version of the Message from the God of Abraham. It was not only one of the most complex and rich languages in the world, but was a language through which God's message had not yet been revealed.

Hence, translations of this sacred work are something that should not be taken on casually, but with extreme attention to detail and the meaning of every word.

It is also important to know that for Muslims there is a significant theological difference between the hadith (sayings of the Prophet Muhammad) and the Qur'an, especially with regard to authenticity. So many of the passages portrayed as "authentic" hadith are actually rather "weak," and, many Muslims believe, were never the actual words of the Prophet Muhammad but rather were fabricated by theo-political power interests to advance a supremacist agenda of some kind. It saddens me to see so much in the public space about Islamic scriptural guidance that is driven by certain hadith that most Muslims intellectually dismiss in our daily lives as being false. Yet they do remain within some of the major known collections of *ahadith*. Why? Because the vast majority of those voluminous texts are maintained and financed by extremists from the Salafi or Wahhabi tradition originally fueled by petrodollars and their theo-political fascist bedfellows. But a fair assessment of what is and what is not Islam must not exaggerate the importance that most Muslims place upon those weak and contrived hadith. Honest analysis will show that the most extreme hadith are usually those that are very weak and can be traced back to illegitimate sources written down long after the death of the Prophet, sometimes over three hundred years after the fact. In fact, many scholars of Islam seeking to modernize our faith interpretations are starting with projects to find consensus among scholars on what their agreement is with regard to defining which are the "strong" hadith and permanently marginalize or discard those that are weak with "consensus" or *ijmaa*. Success in these endeavors will come only if they are guided by theologians who are genuinely dedicated to modernizing Islamic interpretations, especially with respect to the separation of mosque and state. If this modernization is led by Islamists, those dedicated to the ascendancy of the Islamic state, the hadith they keep will no doubt be biased to include those that legitimize the Islamist endeavor. This is why I have always believed that before we as Muslims even get down to the brass tacks of dismissing false hadith, we need to have a modern worldview of the role of scripture and theology in society and governance. Until we defeat theocratic impulses and see a victory of liberty and universal human rights over an Islamocentric worldview (Islamization), reinterpreting scripture and filtering out hadith will be an exercise in modernizing Islamism (Political Islam 4.0) rather than a modern, reformed interpretation of Islam compatible with modernity, the Enlightenment, and Western secular "Jeffersonian" democracy.

First, to me as a Muslim, there was a very good reason God told Muslims that only the Arabic script of the Qur'an could be called "Qur'an" (the recitation) and everything else was interpretation or explanation. So all of the English translations of Qur'an in cyberspace are not "Qur'an" but rather human attempts at interpretations or explanations of our scripture. This may seem like splitting hairs, but it is vital in the demarcation between God's religion of Islam and human interpretation of what each Muslim views as his or her "Islam." There are very good reasons God told Muslims in the Qur'an in one of the last revealed passages, "Today I have perfected your religion for you, and finished My blessings to you. I have certified My choice of Islam (submission unto Me) as a religion for you" (5:3). One of the foundational beliefs in Islam is the need to maintain the integrity and authenticity of the Arabic scripture of the Qur'an to the "comma." Thus, while certainly the Prophet's example (*sunnah*) and discussions (*ahadith*) are important to augment the details of our faith practice, their human transmission and reproduction are admittedly fraught with potential errors related to delays in preservation and reproduction.

Thus for many Muslims, hadith is felt to augment faith, not define it. I was always taught that where I felt that the hadith conflicted with the Qur'an's message to me, those hadith should be dismissed as invalid. Sure, the hadith can give us details on better specifics with regard to rules of prayer and personal practices (shariah) that may have been left general in the Qur'an, but the hadith is not supposed to come up with new laws unsupported in God's message to Muslims in the Qur'an. If it was important enough to charter new territory of daily guidance, it would have been expressed in the Qur'an. So many Salafi scholars use certain hadith to charter new domains for clerical influence in daily life that are just extra-Islamic, in my opinion, and beyond the scope of God's guidance to us in the Qur'an. For example, if the role of shariah in government and the type of government was so important to us as a faith community, it stands to reason that God would have spent far more time circumscribing these concepts and the role of government in the Qur'an. He did not. Instead, He left it that our affairs are our own to manage between ourselves, stating on consultation in 42:38, "Those who responded to their Lord and attended to their prayers, ran their affairs by advice and consent among them, and who spend in charity some of what We give them." That is the closest the entire Qur'an gets to telling us how to manage our affairs or our governance on earth. Thus to me, if God wanted us to establish theocracies led by religious scholars who determined religious legalisms, He would have taken the time to make that clear. He did not. Thus one of the concepts in the West that ultimately led to the Christian Reformation, "render unto Caesar what is Caesar's and to God what is God's," fits within the parameters of my reading of my own scripture and the reading of many modern Islamic scholars, such as Mohammed Al-Ashmawy and Abdullai Na-im.

Let's now look back at the issue of translation, and how that has contributed to misunderstandings about God's Qur'anic verse, as well as in what context particular verses are quoted. There are many websites, such as www.prophetofdoom.net, www.jihad watch.org, and www.religionofpeace.com, that are devoted to trying to prove that the Qur'an is anti-Christian, anti-Jewish, and that its overall messages encourage Muslims to be jihadists against the world. Part of the way those who run the different websites try to prove their point is to separate out quotations from the Qur'an related to Jews, Christians, and so on.

One of the most famous quotations that people have cited since 9/11 to prove that the Qur'an is anti-Jewish is this one from the second chapter, Verse 64, which prophetofdoom.net translates as:

But you [Jews] went back on your word and were lost losers. So become apes, despised and hated. We made an example out of you. (2:64)

This is the entirety of what is quoted. My father spent over ten years translating the Qur'an and based his translation and explanations on his knowledge of the classical Arabic in which it was originally written. I would also do my due diligence as the eternal student of my faith and vet his explanations with as many other modern Islamic thinkers as I could find in the public domain. The point here is not whether my father or my grandfathers, each of whom was a scholar in his own right, had the "street cred" to offer Islamic exegesis. I believe they did, but history will judge how what they taught me fits into Islamic modernization. The point is that my father's lifetime of rational work and daily conversations with me about our scripture, my grandfather Zuhdi Jasser's Islamic defense and advocacy of secular Western principles of democracy in Syria, and my other grandfather Subhi Sabbagh's modern leadership and interpretations of Islam from the bench of the supreme court in Syria empowered me to use my own free will and cognitive skills to complete my faith narrative and interpretations. For example, in my father's translation and explanations of that verse, he felt that it stated: "Even after all that, you still abandoned your obligations and if it were not for God's favor to you and mercy upon you, you would have been lost." Quite a difference from lost losers! After that, he follows with "You know those among you who violated the Sabbath, and We made them disgraced apes," and then follows with "We made their ending an example for those who lived with them and those who lived later and an appropriate reminder for those who are pious."

So what is being discussed here? Is the idea that Muhammad thought that Jews were simply apes? Hardly. The context is about how Moses tried to guide his people morally with God's laws and how some of them failed miserably to honor their commitments, the end result of which is that they became as savage as apes. The same thing, in fact, is discussed in the Bible, albeit with somewhat different language. Interestingly, Shelomo Dov Goitein writes that there is Yemeni *midrash* that first described the Jews who broke their own Sabbath as "turning into apes," unrelated to the anti-Semitism of many Islamist scholars. However, for the Islamist or for the person convinced that Muhammad was against the Jews, it is overly simple: the Qur'an says Jews are apes. I see these verses as clearly showing that piety is necessary for me not to be overcome by the savage within me, who could be seduced by sensual pleasures, wealth, violent impulses, and so on. If anything, reading the quotation in context reminds me once again of the debt all Muslims owe to Moses and to Judaism in general, and how their bedrock of laws and the moral examples of their prophets were such a vital part of God's message to the Prophet Muhammad in the Qur'an. God, in speaking to Jews through the

Talmud, to Christians through the Bible (*Injeel*), and to Muslims through the Qur'an, often used hyperbolic language to describe nonbelievers and those who refused His law. This is language of and only from God, not to be used by human beings as tools for control of one another.

Let's look at another oft-cited passage, from Chapter 8, Verse 65, which prophetofdoom.net translated as:

O Prophet, urge the faithful to fight. If there are twenty among you with determination they will vanquish two hundred; if there are a hundred then they will slaughter a thousand unbelievers, for the infidels are a people devoid of understanding.

Pretty stern stuff, to be sure, but again, what is the context? If one reads the chapter in question, one will quickly come to understand that God is referring to life during wartime, and is exhorting his troops to be brave, that they may vanquish their enemy. In the prophetofdoom website, they are called "infidels" in this verse, while in my father's translation the word "unbelievers" is used. While this may seem a small point, it is important to note that Muhammad's main military struggles were not with Jews and Christians but with pagan Arabs. One must keep in mind that Arabs did not all at once embrace the faith, any more than those in Jesus's time flocked all at once to his message. The violent resistance to Muhammad in certain Arab quarters was so great that it did lead to battles that pitted Muhammad and his followers against the pagans. Every religion has established in its history and theology principles of "just war" against those who seek to destroy and murder their faith community. Like most Jews and

Christians, Muslims are not pacifists. To most Muslims the verses that deal with battles are along those lines. This is especially relevant when we consider the need to separate historical situations from the general principles of the faith. The chapter in question in the Qur'an deals in part with military strategy, as well as with a group of Arab idol worshippers who had explicitly broken a peace treaty with the Prophet Muhammad and his followers, which resulted in Muhammad's exhortations to do battle with them as a last resort. War is not something any people has ever approached softly or passively. At the same time, the same chapter talks about the need to be merciful and wise with an enemy who has given up his arms, just as God is Merciful and Wise.

If one goes through other similar verses in the Qur'an, one will find that the military context is there with regard to a just war, quite distinct from advocating attacks on civilians. As a Muslim and also as a Navy veteran, I read such passages in their historical context. That Muhammad, just like any military commander, had to spur on his troops when they were at war does not mean that I am obligated to go and slay the "unbeliever," wherever I may find him. If wholesale war was formally declared on all Muslims everywhere, I would certainly have an obligation to defend myself and my family, but that is not the case in Phoenix where I live, or in the United States, or in the world at large, despite what the Islamists and the jihadists may claim. Nowhere in the Qur'an does God tell Muslims how to establish and run their governments. Nowhere in the Qur'an does God tell Muslims that they must repeat and thus emulate the Prophet Muhammad's role and actions as a military or governmental leader. Nowhere in the Qur'an does God tell Muslims that they must impose their beliefs, practices, and rituals upon others. And most certainly, nowhere in the Qur'an does God tell myopic automatons to instigate murderous, terrorist actions against civilians and other noncombatants who, by definition, are incapable of causing them harm. My interpretation of the Qur'an has always included the overriding idea that the Prophet Muhammad's example, spiritually and morally, is for all times—but that his political and military actions were an example that cannot be taken out of the context of the times in which he lived and its specific conflicts.

As contemporary Muslims, I believe we need to relegate to history the fact that our faith was established by a fighting force that defended a faith community that was also a nation-state, over fourteen hundred years ago. We need to acknowledge that living in a nation like the United States, with its Constitution written atop a foundation of natural laws, in which each citizen's faith rules (laws) are his or her own to practice, in a secular, individual, and peaceful fashion, is far preferable to living under a theocracy—Islamic or otherwise—in which one faith, and only that faith, guides the legal system of the nation. That becomes coercion no matter which way you slice it. Thus these verses:

They ask you about the lunar months, say these are timing devices for people and for pilgrimage. It is not piety to come to the houses from the back of them; but piety is to be God-fearing; so come to the houses by their doors, and fear God; so that you may succeed. (2:189) And fight in the way of God with those who fight you, but aggress not: God loves not the aggressors. (2:190) Kill them anywhere you find them and push them out from where they pushed you out, persecution is more grievous than slaying. Do not fight them in the Holy Mosque until they fight you there; then if they fight you, slay them—such is the consequences for the unbelievers who fight you. (2:191) But if they desist, surely god is All-forgiving, all-compassionate. (2:192)

In verse 2:190, God refers only to the tribe of Quraysh, and this cannot be extrapolated to any other group at any other time to justify any other war. Similarly, verse 2:191 refers to the earlier time in which the Muslims had been removed from their homes in Mecca before emigrating to Medina. With this interpretation of these verses, one could make an argument that Islam advocates peace and condones war only *as a last resort*, as a *defensive* measure, against annihilation. As an American I supported the wars in Afghanistan and in Iraq because they were protecting us from the imminent threat of Al Qaeda and Saddam Hussein, who would not reveal whether he had weapons of mass destruction. Similarly, the targeting of Osama Bin Laden was a moral and righteous attack upon the epitome of evil by SEAL Team Six. The targeting and killing of Imam Anwar Al-Awlaki was also a righteous mission. He called for violent attacks against our citizens and our soldiers and was a driving force behind a number of attacks on Americans, including the Fort Hood massacre committed by Major Nidal Hasan. Liberty-loving Muslims such as I wholeheartedly reject the notion that this verse or any of the others that refer to battles during the time of the Prophet Muhammad can be interpreted to justify commandeering airplanes, murdering their flight crews, and flying them into buildings occupied by innocent civilians. Similarly, I reject the entire notion that this passage can be used to justify the imposition of Islamism—or even Islam itself—upon anyone through any means at all, let alone through violent, offensive warfare. I reject the notion that our ummah can any longer ever be a nation-state. Yes, "ummah" can mean "nation" in the Qur'an, but that is history and we need to acknowledge that the better system in the modern world is one that does not equate any single faith community with citizenship in the nation-state. For we cannot modernize the concept of jihad without doing that also. As long as being Muslim is tied to being a citizen in the Islamic state, then jihad is tied to the function of that state's military. If we can separate mosque and state and relegate the nation-state of the ummah to the dustbin of history, then jihad becomes only a personal concept of struggle for God and righteousness rather than a concept of armed struggle for the community and nation.

The world has evolved beyond nations based in religion as the Prophet Muhammad's community was. The Times Square would-be bomber, Faisal Shahzad, told Judge Miriam Goldman Cedarbaum in June 2010 that he was a "*mujahid*" or "Muslim soldier." Shahzad was many things—a terrorist, a traitor, and an adherent to a supremacist ideology that has no place in modernity. But the most important question for the twenty-first century is whether he represents the "Muslim soldier." If we challenge and ultimately disprove this interpretation taken out of Salafi and Wahhabist theo-political ideology, then we can ultimately defeat the Islamist threat. As a devout Muslim and a former lieutenant commander in the United States Navy, I never felt myself to be a "Muslim" soldier even though I prayed five times a day and read the Qur'an. I always looked at myself as an American soldier who happened to be Muslim. I never had a split allegiance to any other military collective (such as a Muslim ummah)—even when fighting against other nations that happened to be Muslim. It is these concepts of ummah and jihad that need global movements of reinterpretation in the context of America and liberty. At the core of the difference between the jihadists and the rest of us Muslims who are loyal to our nations is our own personal interpretation of jihad. This discourse needs to go beyond the platitudes of definitions of the various meanings of the term and become a more frank discussion about what meanings and assumptions inherent in "jihad" in Islamic history are no longer relevant in the twenty-first century to Muslims.

While jihad has many meanings, one of the predominant ones for Islamists is armed conflict or war in their warped concept of the defense of Muslims and the "Islamic state." This is why AIFD's primary mission is the separation of mosque and state. "Ummah" as a faith community (for prayer, holidays, theological practice and education, charity, and socialization) for Muslims is no threat to modernity. "Ummah" as "nation-state" is a firewall against modernity. Ummah as nation is incompatible with our allegiance to Western nations such as the United States that are based in reason and secular law, like our U.S. Constitution, Bill of Rights, and especially its Establishment Clause. As long as Muslims have any way of defining ummah as nation-state, ultimately the head of that ummah can declare war and thus it must be defined as jihad, which will always end up fueling the Nidal Hasans and Faisal Shahzads of the world.

The core of our American citizenship pledge and my officer's pledge is to defend the United States against enemies foreign and domestic. Muslim leadership needs to openly reform the ideas that feed the development of such traitors as Hasan and Shahzad and others who slide down the slippery slope of political Islam to become agents of the "Islamic state," rejecting allegiance to the United States, the nation that gave them freedom. Simply placing roadblocks along that slope, as many who prefer political correctness over debate would do, is not enough. This involves recontextualizing those passages in the Qur'an that deal with battles, jihad, and the ummah. The whole of political Islam needs to be ideologically defeated in real debate within the House of Islam. Many if not most Muslims whom I know do not believe in the tenets of Islamism, but the reality is that we have yet to mount any palpable domestic or international movement against the ideas of political Islam, Muslim collectivism, and the "ummah" that feeds this supremacism and militancy. In fact, most evidence shows that Islamists are making gains around the world where anti-Islamists are not because of an absence of U.S. and overwhelming Western support for the ideas of liberty against the Islamic state and Islamic war. The obligations of jihad in the seventh-century Arabian Peninsula under the Prophet Muhammad's leadership are gone. The American Revolution proved that there was a far better, freer system of governance than the Islamist one. We now have a national obligation of citizenship only to our nation—the United States—and there are and can be no other competing obligations. Muslim teachers need to make that clear, with no qualifications about Muslims being in a majority or minority. If Muslims apply the true meaning of jihad today, they would start a "jihad against jihad," as Tarek Fatah of the Muslim Canadian Congress has stated. They would work to end the concept with regard to armed conflict, nation-states, and the ummah. The real jihad in the twenty-first century is within the House of Islam against the Islamists and those advocates of political Islam and its radical manifestations who have hijacked the spiritual path of Islam. The only Muslim soldier I long for is one who is an American soldier who happens to be Muslim. It is time for soldiers who happen to be Muslims to fight to protect the inalienable rights of all men and women to liberty and freedom rather than theocratic martyrdom or servitude. The guarantee of individual freedom and liberty in our Constitution is our greatest weapon against an enemy who holds power through the theocratic, despotic control of its people.

One of the Qur'anic passages most frequently cited by militant Islamists and jihadists is Chapter 9, Verse 5, sometimes called pejoratively the verse of the sword. The literal interpretation of the series of verses (9:4–9:7), from my father's translation, is as follows:

Those of the unbelievers (idol-worshippers) who signed treaties with you and did not violate them, provided no assistance to your enemies, and abided by their commitments to you, then by all means keep your commitments to them, God loves the God-fearing who keep their word. (9:4) Then, when the sacred months are drawn away, slay the idolaters (those who did not sign treaties) wherever you find them, and confine them, and lie in wait for them at every place. But, if they repent and establish worship, and practice charity, let them go their way, God is all-forgiving, all compassionate. (9:5) If an unbeliever (idolater) requests an asylum with you, grant it to him, so he may have the chance of hearing the word of God, then convey him to his place of security. That is because they are a people who do not know. (9:6) The idol-worshippers have no credibility with God or His apostle, but as to those who made the treaty with you at the Grand Mosque, honor it with you. God loves those who abide by what they promise. (9:7)

This passage again also refers to the "disbelievers," which refers only to the idol-worshippers of Quraysh, at that particular time in Muslim history when the Meccans were looking to destroy the Muslims, and then violated the treaty they had signed. After the violation, Muslims threatened war but came into Mecca peacefully by promising that if their enemies stayed in their homes, there would be no war. Thus, war was averted. War ethics teaches that a diplomatic threat of war can be necessary in order to prevent war. This passage also refers only to the idol-worshippers of Mecca, and to no other faith group at all, and to no other time in history.

Freedom-loving Muslims must help America and the free world fight against Islamists and jihadists. The only way for

Islamists to abort their dream of a theocracy under their version of Islam is for them to be overwhelmed with a better vision (interpretation) of an Islam and our Qur'an based in liberty: an Islam that articulates and defends pluralism, tolerance, free speech, free markets, and all the other fruits of a free society where all citizens are equally protected "under God," not "under Islam"; an Islam that rests at home with the freedoms that Americans claim as their birthright and will defend at all costs. Bassam Tibi, a noted Western Muslim scholar on Islam, stated, "The secularization of Christianity did not bring about its demise. I would argue that it brought about its liberation to the personal domain. This culture is still very Christian but it just doesn't have to coerce it in law to be so. Because the character of the people is Christian and Jewish and many faiths that is the culture, the character we see. Religion must simply be protected from state exploitation."

Again, a person's perception and intent are everything when it comes to reading a religious work. The jihadist finds verses in the Qur'an that he or she feels justifies their war with the West, while a non-Muslim who is convinced that Islam is a warmongering religion finds evidence of the same. There is a certain irony in that, while one claims to be embracing Islam, and the other is rejecting it, both claim that all the proof is there that the religion sanctions such violence. Perhaps Paul Simon put it best: "A man hears what he wants to hear and disregards the rest."

In fact, before and after the verse translated above in Chapter 9 that talks about fighting the unbelievers wherever one may find them, it is clear that this is another case where Muhammad is talking about a peace treaty and certain terms, including an amnesty period. It also makes clear in the chapter that as long as they honor the terms of the peace treaty, they should not be attacked. More to the point, in Chapter 9, Verses 11 and 12, the Qur'an can be translated:

If they repent and stand up in prayers and pay the alms-tax,
they become your brothers in religion. We detail the verses for
those who have knowledge. If they violate their treaties with
you, and attack your religion, fight the leaders of disbelief, for
you cannot turn your back to them and they must desist.

This, of course, is a far cry from encouraging indiscriminate attacks on those of other religions, but again clearly defines rules of
engagement as they relate to wartime. The reality is that militaristic verse can also be found in the Bible. There are plenty of biblical
verses that deal with the Jewish people at war where it is claimed
that they had God's favor and therefore won the battles, the same
claim that is made for Muhammad and his troops at various
points in the Qur'an.

The key for Christians, Jews, Muslims, Hindus, Buddhists, and
so on is: On what do we want to focus? On our differences with
those of other faiths or what we have in common? For the fanatic,
it is enough to quote a religious verse to somehow justify the
murder of the innocent or any other sort of unjust act. Even if it
doesn't reach the extreme of murder, perhaps it is something akin
to looking down on those of other faiths. Perhaps the Islamist can
find more than enough Qur'anic verses to somehow justify such a
position. For me, the focus has always been on respecting those of
other faiths, and I find plenty of verses to support such a position
in the Qur'an.

Let's look at another Qur'anic verse, Chapter 5, Verse 51,
which prophetofdoom translates as:

Believers, take not Jews and Christians for your friends. They
are but friends and protectors to each other.

Sounds fairly straightforward, right? And it certainly doesn't sound very open to other religions. And yet this passage runs contrary to other verses that allow Muslims to intermarry with Jews and Christians (People of the Book). If Muslims believe the Qur'an has one holy source, God, how could there be such inherent contradictions in message? How could God entrust a Muslim family to the leadership of a Christian or Jewish mother if we are also told that we should not be "friends"?

However, a more correct translation from the classical Arabic of the same verse is:

People who believe do not take the Jews or Christians as sponsors. They should sponsor each other, and whoever chooses their sponsorship becomes one of them, and God does not guide the transgressors.

The word in question, *awliaa*, is incorrectly interpreted by Salafists as "friend" rather than "sponsor." This is crucially important. If one reads the verse with "friend," it sounds like a swipe at Christians and Jews, plain and simple. But with "sponsor," the meaning changes substantially, since a sponsor refers to a legal protector within the faith. In that sense, the verse is saying that a Muslim needs a fellow Muslim to sponsor him if he cannot sponsor himself, which is something that both Christianity and Judaism both espouse, namely that one must seek guidance from those within one's own religious ranks as to the rules of our faiths. A Catholic, for example would naturally need to choose another Catholic to be the legal sponsor (that is, godparent) of his or her children if the parents are no longer around. The term *awliaa* is used in Islamic jurisprudence to discuss the role of legal witnesses to the legitimacy of a marriage. The witnesses are *awliaa*. Does this mean I cannot find spiritual common ground with a Christian or a Jew? Of course not. Wahhabis turned *awliaa* to "friends" in order to solidify a supremacist Islamist version of Islam. In this same chapter, God discusses in the Qur'an the debt Muslims owe to "People of the Book," and shows great respect to both the Torah and the Gospel as shown in Verses 68 and 69 of the same chapter:

People of the Book, you have nothing until you obey the Torah and the Gospel and what was revealed to you from your Lord. What God has revealed to you will increase the arrogance and the disbelief of many of them. Do not let the unbelievers bother you.

And then in Verse 69:

The believers, the Jews, the Sabeaens, and the Christians who believed in God and the Last Day and did good works have nothing to fear and shall not be sad.

Does this sound like the message of a faith that is anti-Christian and anti-Jewish? Again, I would ask those of you who are serious about reading the Qur'an to please keep in mind that a verse quoted out of context can have an entirely different meaning, and that in addition the translation of particular words will also make a big difference in the overall meaning.

At the same time, no matter how good a translation is, people's interpretations of certain texts are bound to vary, particularly if it is a work rife with symbolism that lends itself to different meanings. This is why you have right-wing Christians and left-wing Christians, and the same with Jews, Muslims, and those of other religions. Each of them reads the same Torah, Gospel, or Qur'an (albeit with different translations), and each interprets the book somewhat differently.

What really changes everything is the element of fanaticism. Charles Manson listened to the *White Album* by the Beatles and decided that it contained coded messages that directed him and his followers to slaughter innocent strangers in their homes in California. The Beatles, of course, never intended any such thing and did not even know who Manson was.

God-fearing Christians read certain biblical verses and decide that they justify their plan to blow up abortion clinics, or kill a doctor from such a clinic in his home, or even recently, in the case of Doctor Tiller, while he was at church.

Mohammed Atta and his henchmen were muttering prayers to Allah before they boarded the planes and then later on board, to give them strength to carry through with their actions. I don't have words to express just how horrifying this is for me as a Muslim.

At the same time, I have read that Joseph Goebbels at one point justified the persecution and murder of the Jews as an obligation of every German Christian, as a way to make the Jews pay for what he saw as their murder of Christ.

The list of atrocities committed in the name of God could fill another book. My point here is not to enumerate these acts one by one, but to make it clear that faith is no excuse for hate. Ultimately, if our faith, whatever it may be, is not guided by love, compassion, and generosity, it should lead to the inevitable question, what kind of faith is it that one has?

I believe parents have a huge responsibility in relation to their children's spiritual well-being. Had my parents and grandparents taught me that violent jihad was the responsibility of every God-fearing Muslim, or that other religions were inferior to mine, and that God desired a worldwide Islamic state—and justified all of this with Qur'anic verses that they said proved it was God's will—imagine how this might have influenced me as a child. Perhaps as an adult I would have reached different conclusions about my faith, but the fact remains that many children grow into adults who adopt their parents' beliefs to the letter. The child who is taught to hate Jews or other groups of people will often later pass on the same hate to his or her own children.

I can say that the Qur'an is very important, central, to my faith, but at the same time I don't rely strictly on this book for my decisions and beliefs. The Qur'an is *a* source of law and inspiration for me in my life but it is not *the* source. The fact is that in my heart I know the difference between right and wrong, love and hate, and barring some sort of serious pathology I believe the same is true for others. I truly believe that the greater part of who I am, what guides my conscience (my superego), and my relationship with God were set in my internal compass long before I had the skill or the knowledge to entertain Qur'anic exegesis and comparative religions. None of us should hide behind religious verse to justify bigotry, discrimination, or hatred and violence toward others that we learn inherently from the faith traditions transmitted over generations within our families. Socrates' famous maxim, that the unexamined life is not worth living, applies here. Our faith should act as a light to help us examine all the corners and crevices of our lives, and we should be relentless in our efforts to change ourselves for the better. Faith in that sense should be a verb, a call to action, and while the great religious works can guide us in our struggles to look within and begin that communication with God and change what must be changed, ultimately all of us have the great existential freedom to act or do nothing.

The Qur'an is a Muslim's confirmed communication from God. Even if I am left with no human rights, I still have God and my faith of Islam—that deeply personal submission to God. Islam to me is not a societal mandate but a personal one, a personal bond between an individual and God. The give-and-take from God between His gifts and challenges and my response to them are the ultimate test of my free will. The essence of Islam from a community perspective is thus the central part of this battle for the soul of Islam. Is it up to the individual, or is it a mandate of government, the state, and its law? I believe there can be no submission and thus no Islam without the freedom to sin, the freedom to live in a laboratory that gives God the opportunity to witness what kind of choices we each make when given the opportunity. Without the opportunity to choose faith or no faith, shariah or no shariah, all religion, all of Islam becomes negated in its very essence. That's what the Islamists refuse to admit when they play God in government.

The Qur'an has become my guide in my daily journey to look within myself as part of that conversation with God through prayer, meditation, and reflection, and one of my goals has always been the same, to have the words of God help me build a bridge with my fellow man, not just my fellow Muslims, for that I believe is the soul and essence of Islam.

12

AN ISLAM COMPATIBLE WITH AMERICAN PRINCIPLES

In his first inaugural speech, titled "Peace, commerce, and honest friendship with all nations—entangling alliances with none," President Thomas Jefferson summarized the essential principles of Jeffersonian democracy:

About to enter, fellow citizens, on the exercise of duties which comprehend everything dear and valuable to you, it is proper that you should understand what I deem the essential principles of our government, and consequently those which ought to shape its administration. I will compress them within the narrowest compass they will bear, stating the general principle, but not all its limitations. Equal and exact justice to all men, of whatever state or persuasion, religious or political; peace, commerce, and honest friendship with all nations—entangling alliances with none; the support of the State governments in all their rights, as the most competent administrations for our domestic concerns and the surest bulwarks against anti-republican tendencies; the preservation of the general government in its whole constitutional vigor, as the sheet anchor of our peace at home and safety abroad; a jealous care of the right of election by the people—a mild and safe corrective of abuses which are

lopped by the sword of the revolution where peaceable remedies
are unprovided; absolute acquiescence in the decisions of the
majority—the vital principle of republics, from which there
is no appeal but to force, the vital principle and immediate
parent of despotism; a well-disciplined militia—our best
reliance in peace and for the first moments of war, till regulars
may relieve them; the supremacy of the civil over the military
authority; economy in the public expense, that labor may be
lightly burdened; the honest payment of our debts and sacred
preservation of the public faith; encouragement of agriculture,
and of commerce as its handmaid; the diffusion of information
and the arraignment of all abuses at the bar of public reason;
freedom of religion; freedom of the press; freedom of person
under the protection of the habeas corpus; and trial by
juries impartially selected—these principles form the bright
constellation which has gone before us, and guided our steps
through an age of revolution and reformation.

The genius of Jefferson as a writer and a thinker can clearly be seen in these words, his ability to distill the essence of such profound democratic principles, so much so that the only president since who could potentially rival him for sheer depth and articulateness is Abraham Lincoln. Much of what Jefferson has to say here resonates with me as a Muslim. The Islam that I learned from my father, grandfather, and others at our mosque in Neenah, Wisconsin, encouraged me to think critically, and to respect others' religions and belief systems, as well as to be responsible for my own economic destiny. For me, there was never any inherent contradiction between Islam and liberty. In fact, as a Muslim born and raised in the United States, I saw myself then and see myself now as someone in an ideal situation. My faith gives me all the spiritual sustenance I need in that deep personal relationship and covalent bond with the almighty God, while my country gives me all the freedom and rights, including that of religion, that I could ever want as a human being.

Having friends of various faiths, I can easily see that one's religion doesn't ever have to be an impediment to living in a pluralistic, democratic society, as long as one is not an extremist or a supremacist and believes in the primacy of our Constitution, its Establishment Clause, and its legal system based in reason. While I am no expert on Judaism, Buddhism, Catholicism, and so on, it would seem to me from what I have read, and from friends I have of other such faiths, that the essence of these various teachings is to help one better connect not only with God, but with all people, regardless of their beliefs. The genius of our Founding Fathers was that they equated a moral and devout Christian nation with a government that stayed out of the business of religion.

The Qur'an itself did not contradict my own belief that I could embrace both my country and my faith, while at the same time keeping my organized religion out of the public arena, insofar as respecting the U.S. Constitution as the ultimate authority for governing. I could be proud of my faith publicly but I always knew that religion was real only when followed by choice; where I could accept or reject the rules of faith not by governmental imposition. Again, nowhere in the Qur'an does God insist that the Muslim religion must prevail as the governing authority or that God's conversation with me as a Muslim must be transposed onto government and society. This is an invention of the Islamist imams and clerics who abound in the madrassas and who gave us such figures as Yusuf Qaradawi and Ayatollah Khomeini.

One must keep in mind that over fourteen hundred years ago, when the Qur'an was revealed to Muhammad, there was no such thing as "separation of church and state." The imams who insist on theocracy and that Islam must be the ruling force throughout the world are operating out of a mind-set that confuses militarism, governance, and religion. While it is true that Islamic conquerors once held a good part of Western Europe in their sway, that does not mean that Muslims must try to repeat such history. For hundreds of years, Christian conquerors took over many lands throughout the world and insisted that the natives adopt their religion, but that does not mean that they are bound to repeat that history in the modern world.

The radical Muslims who mistake militaristic verse in the Qur'an for a mandate to take over the West suffer from ahistorical myopia. This is not the seventh century, when Muslims were part of a new religion and found their survival threatened by Arab pagans who did not want to adopt their faith. Such militaristic verse was appropriate then as Muhammad sought to rally his troops, in battles not only with the pagans, but also with certain Jewish tribes as well as Christians, protecting the Muslim community from complete obliteration. Now, with Muslims over one-fifth of the world population, somewhere over 1.3 billion people, such reasoning for invoking an Islamic state, a political ummah, or a jihad would be absurd.

The Qur'an, as we have seen in earlier chapters, is not actually a text that was written with the idea of conquering those of other faiths. Throughout the Qur'an, the debt to Christians and Jews, for their teachings and prophets, is acknowledged over and over again in their common origin from the God of Abraham. For the Muslim who is actually delving far enough into the Qur'an, the idea of free will, that one must freely choose one's faith, is also discussed.

With that in mind, can one truly say that Muhammad would have rejected the idea of representative democracy? There was no such thing in the Prophet's time, so how could one expect any such philosophy to be addressed in the Qur'an? One of the primary tasks we set for Muslim youths in our Muslim Liberty Project is to think and write about how a conversation would evolve about religion, law, and the state if the Prophet Muhammad had ever been able to sit with our Founding Fathers. Would Muhammad accept the Establishment Clause of the First Amendment in a Muslim-majority nation? Would he accept one law and a secular state? The philosophy of the Islam I know and practice depends on the affirmative. The future of Islam depends upon our youth pushing and selling this meme to other Muslims in order to defeat the Islamist response. In Muhammad's time, for example, there were also few of the medical advances we have today, and yet Muslims around the world now avail themselves of them whenever they can. So, following that trail of logic, does it not make sense for Muslims to take advantage of a system of government (advanced political science) that allows them the freedom to practice their religion the way they want and gives to all certain rights and freedoms?

Here is one of the greater ironies of the Islamist way of thinking when it comes to democracy. The Islamists, in their most bellicose rhetoric, have called for the overthrow of the "decadent," "Godless" Western world and for the replacement of secular laws with those of shariah. They want an Islamic theocracy to rule over all. And where do these Islamists have the most freedom to express such views? In the Western world, of course, particularly in the United States, where freedom of speech is guaranteed. They have to blame the West dishonestly, through contrived conspiracy theories, for the eternal failures of the Islamic state rather than acknowledge that it is a system doomed to fail since it does not recognize the primacy of universal individual rights and equal access to government and society for all. In many Middle Eastern countries, the call to overthrow secular leaders and replace them with Islamic religious leaders is not tolerated. Such views are best expressed underground, for one would have to risk one's life to express them publicly.

Just as we have seen how Islamist values conflict with basic principles of Americanism, that is to say, liberty and democracy, to move past the Islamist mind-set into a new day where such narrowness and bigotry are consigned to the junk pile of history will require Muslims to adhere to a very specific set of reformist principles, which we will now examine in depth.

One of the core principles of Jeffersonian democracy and of democracy period is the rights of the people, and that includes the right to speak out. Many of us American Muslims come from countries where no such rights existed. But what good is it to have such rights if we don't exercise them?

I am reminded of a friend who attended a self-improvement seminar in which two of the key questions posed (related to transformational thinking and action) were:

If not me, *who*?

If not now, *when*?

This is once again a case where the individual must break away from tribal thinking to make a difference. To a large degree, it all starts with changing one's way of thinking and from there changing one's actions. Very often, this process starts with one person or a small group of people. Some principles for us Muslims to keep in mind as we seek to reform our religion and form a tighter bond with the principles of liberty and democracy that have sustained America all these years were listed earlier in the book, which include universal human principles of liberty, separation of mosque and state, women's rights, antiterrorism movements, and the acceptance of pluralism.

We need leadership that does not shrink from promoting the right side of these conflicts in Muslim-majority nations. Many Muslims in America get a pass when they say they follow the laws of the land, since they are a minority, but in Muslim-majority nations or "Islamic states" they would not advocate for universal liberty but for Islamic law, since Muslims were a majority. That philosophy instills a dangerous dual identity in our children, telling them that Muslims accept the American secular ideologies because they are a minority or in effect just "visiting," but if Muslims were a majority they would advocate an Islamist system that is connected to our "Muslim" identity. The importance of what lies at the core of our identity with our society and our nation cannot be overstated. I personally teach my children and all Muslims I know that if we believe in the American system, we should advocate it as truly ours from the bottom of our heart, our identity, and as the best in the world whether we are 1 percent or 90 percent of the population. Until that consistency is seen in Muslim discourse, Muslims' identification with American nationalism will always be less than ideal and they will be ripe for radicalization as they seek the fictional and coercive "Islamic state."

Prime Minister David Cameron of Britain said it best in Munich in February 2011 when he talked about the lessons Britain learned from the failure of post-9/11 counterterrorism programs that ignored British Muslim identity and worked too closely with British Islamists. He said that the only way to bring Muslims to a genuine British identity is for the United Kingdom to begin a more potent advocacy of a "muscular liberalism" in Muslim communities and Muslim nations. He lamented the profoundly negative impact of "politically correct" multiculturalism on the ability of the British government to provide a winning narrative over the Islamists.

In the summer of 2010, I was nominated by U.S. Senate

Minority Leader Mitch McConnell (R-KY) to the State Department's U.S. Advisory Commission on Public Diplomacy, a bipartisan presidential commission. Yet after fifteen months of vetting and passing every high-level clearance with flying colors, including confirmation of a top-secret clearance, my nomination was suddenly removed from consideration in September 2011. When asked why, the White House told staff that I "was not qualified." It seems that the primary qualification for President Obama's previous two Democratic appointees to the same commision was their donation or bundling history to the Obama campaign, as they had little to no experience in public diplomacy or foreign policy. One was a homemaker. My qualifications had only improved during this period, and to have such an extensive process abruptly end that way demonstrated that something sinister was going on.

The administration chose to block a conservative nomination to a bipartisan presidential commission without explanation. The decision could have been political, due to my outspoken criticism of the Obama administration's perceived weakness toward Islamists. However, I was also relatively critical of their predecessors in the Bush administration on the same account. It could have been a dangerous lack of understanding about the battle we face within the Muslim consciousness globally against Islamism. It may have been undue influence in the White House by Islamists and Muslim Brotherhood legacy groups. We submitted a Freedome of Information act request to look at the paper trail, but the White House may choose not to comply.

Writing on the rejection and in defense of my work, James Woolsey, former CIA head, and Seth Leibsohn, author of *The Fight of Our Lives*, stated in *National Review Online* on October 6, 2011, "Clarity in the war of ideas, the ability to identify the ideology we are fighting, and expertise in the religion of Islam are precisely what we need. . . . It is a shame we will not soon be availing ourselves officially of Dr. Jasser's work." When people ask where are the voices of moderate Muslims speaking against the ideologies that feed radicalization, they need look no further than those responsible for blocking not only my appointment but the work of many other anti-Islamists that has been kept from the public eye. In order for us to move forward at this point in our history, the majority of Muslims must embrace such principles and be active, vocal proponents of them. The problem is *not* that most Muslims are Islamists. They are not. The problem is that most Muslims are passive, silent, and are not taking an active stand against the Islamists and in favor of principles of liberty and democracy. This, of course, is not something unique to Muslims. Many Americans take their liberty and democracy for granted. Many of us don't vote, or are not engaged with issues of the day in any meaningful way, and many of us don't know the names of our local, state, and federal representatives. My father used to tell me how much he and my grandfather loved America. I recall him often telling me it was sad how many Americans breathe liberty like oxygen and do not realize the gifts from God we have in this nation. I believe liberty and democracy should never be taken for granted, no matter what, but in the case of my fellow Muslims, the problem is made even more pressing by the crisis that confronts our faith and our country today—political Islam and the slippery slope toward radicalization, militancy, and supremacism.

When one looks closely at these principles, it is important to note that the call to action is a call not simply to defend liberty and democracy here in America, but to do so worldwide. While this may seem overly ambitious to some, the simple fact is that throughout the Middle East and most of the nations that have Muslim majorities, people continue to live in oppressive regimes where freedom of speech, the press, assembly, and religion are not rights accorded to all citizens. There are those throughout

Muslim-majority nations who dream of a day when their country might know real freedom and liberty. How will we ever know how many of those voices for freedom actually exist worldwide if we don't do everything we can to support them in their efforts and encourage our government to do the same—to speak out and be heard above the noise of the radical imams and the corrupt secular dictators? Over ten years after 9/11 our government is still sadly in a defensive posture against radical Islamism rather than an offensive one. The only effective offense is a forward movement of a narrative of liberty-minded Muslims into the domestic and global Muslim consciousness. Defense, or what is basically a sophisticated whack-a-mole program, will keep us safe for only so long. This requires a Liberty Doctrine. The Bush Doctrine was a freedom agenda that got lost in the muddle of the Iraq War. The Obama Doctrine is unclear at best and incomprehensible at worst. As Muslim nations transform, the only way to give liberty a chance against ascendant Islamism is to take sides for liberty and against Islamism.

For the sake of Islam, for the sake of our national security and of liberty and democracy, our voices *must* be heard over those of the Islamists as well as over those of the secular fascists and monarchs. The peoples of the Middle East are now in a state of profound flux never imagined possible in our generation. Few know with confidence where they are headed. I wish my grandfather and my father were alive to witness these cracks in the iron fist of the Assads, these profound convulsions against tyranny and for the will of the people. My grandfather would have felt such vindication to see the Syrian people wake up and attempt to control their own condition. As they shed the yoke of the secular fascism of Bashar Assad and his henchmen who followed the evil of his father, Hafez, the Syrian population desperately need the foundations, institutions, and instruments of liberty in order for real democracy to succeed. In 2011 and 2012 they paid an unfathomable price in their attempt to realize freedom. The Syrian people needed not only the departure of Assad and his tyrannical family but the entire military leadership who gave orders that murdered thousands of men, women, and children in cold blood and destroyed their homes. Until all the vestiges of that military are gone and with it the byproducts of corruption, hate, and radicalism, Syria will never realize genuine liberty. This is why our own opportunities here in the United States, living in the lap of freedom and its laboratory, require that we help them in whatever way we can. Without our efforts on behalf of liberty, supremacists like the Islamists will try to hijack their movements. This is not to say that we should simply throw cash at them. We should not. But we should work hand in hand in helping them build institutions, in partnership with liberty-minded Syrians, Egyptians, Libyans, Tunisians, Yemenis, Saudis, and others. We need to pick sides within the opposition and help freedom win in the contest of ideas. Islamism will not be defeated until we defeat it with a better idea from within the House of Islam—the idea of liberty from these emerging democracies in the Middle East. Those who label Islam the problem leave Muslims with no solution to Islamism and radicalization. If thought leaders in the West who recognize the ideological threat do not expect Muslims to convert in order to find liberty and free markets, then the problem is Islamism and not Islam, and the solution is the defeat of Islamism by anti-Islamist devout Muslims. But those Muslims will not achieve this on their own. They need the help of all liberty-minded peoples. The United States needs to take the side of the anti-Islamists. Without our intellectual involvement, we may see those emerging nations lost to Islamist movements, as we saw in the post-Shah Iran of 1979. Islamists have had a long head start, fed by petrodollars and fueled by an underground culture of victimization. The advocates of secular liberty and freedom have a lot of time to make up, but it is certainly possible and can be done. Is that not the history of the American Revolution, our Constitution, the Bill of Rights, and our Founding Fathers?

Domestically, many Americans still think of Muslims as being somewhat isolated from mainstream society and, more to the point, of being more loyal to Islam than to America. And are there not solid reasons that many of us are perceived thus? During the rise of Nazi Germany, there were many prominent Germans of conscience, such as Herman Hesse and Thomas Mann, who spoke out against the threat, and made it clear that these fanatics were a danger to the whole world. The problem was that not enough people spoke out, or acted to stop the Nazis. We have seen similar behavior over and over again throughout history. During the Cold War, the United States quickly developed a consensus that we were competing and fighting not only against the Soviets but globally against the ideas of communism. Regardless of the time, the voices of dissent are few, no matter how terrible the threat. Silence is the norm, not the exception.

But it doesn't have to be this way, not for those of us who have the luxury of liberty and democracy. American Muslims in particular must lead the way in dissent when it comes to Islamism, and embrace and exercise all the freedoms for which our country stands. As Peter Gabriel once sang in reference to the martyred South African civil rights activist Biko, "You can blow out a candle, but you can't blow out a fire. . . . Once the flames begin to catch, the wind will take it higher. . . ." Our example as Muslims who are defenders both of our country and of our faith can indeed light the way for other Muslims around the world, who will see from our courage and full exercise of rights how they too may be free of corrupt, secular dictatorships, totalitarian theocracies, and the overall antidemocratic, antiliberty agenda of the Islamists.

All of this in its own way must start at home. American Muslim children must learn from the very start the basic principles of liberty and democracy just as surely as they learn the basic tenets of Islam. They must learn that these principles and tenets are not mutually exclusive, but complement each other, and while it may sound like sacrilege to some, they must learn, in reference to society at large, how to be Americans first, Muslims second. The ideas of liberty are the only inoculum against Islamism and its inherent radicalization.

We certainly have many models of past courage to guide us in this struggle. The movement toward Indian independence actually started in South Africa when Gandhi (who was practicing law there at the time) and a small group of followers stood up to the government and its racial policies. Later, Gandhi and others took their nonviolent philosophy of civil disobedience back to India, where they sought independence from the British. While it took about half a century for Indians to attain their freedom from England, by the time the movement succeeded, it consisted of millions of people.

The same can happen with Muslims in relation to Islamism. The United States, in fact, can be the test laboratory, so to speak, to make that happen. It's not as though our country has not suffered from the various "isms" that have affected many other nations—racism, sexism, and so on—but what has distinguished us from so many other countries is an effort to recognize our wrongs and to right them. It is true, for instance, that the southern states practiced slavery. It is also true that our country fought a civil war to free the slaves. What other country can claim the same? Decades before apartheid was defeated in South Africa, the United States had passed laws to ensure civil rights for African Americans in the Deep South and beyond. We recognized how unfair segregation laws were, as was the mistreatment accorded African

Americans when it came to voting, employment, and general treatment in society. Along with all this, the rights of women to vote, and for equal treatment in the workplace, have also been recognized. The amazing thing is that these core principles were part of our U.S. Constitution and Bill of Rights but obviously took us many generations to realize. Muslims deserve the same maturation process, which will be possible with the right foundational principles of liberty-based reform.

With all this in mind, we American Muslims must become more active voices in U.S. politics, not only to expose Islamism for the threat it poses to our faith and our country, but to show the life-affirming side of Islam that is not nearly as visible to most Americans as it should be, and that consists of millions of free-thinking American Muslims who love their country just as much as they love their faith.

Muslims in the United States should also look at facets of the One Law movement in Europe, which is opposed to the institutionalization of shariah law in European society and makes a compelling case for how shariah courts undermine the rights of women, prescribe medieval punishments, and use a premodern tribalism, and for why, for society at large, standard, secular law must apply. Yes, shariah can have global personal faith-based meanings, much as the word "Islam" has to a devout Muslim. But with the separation of religion and state will come a natural defense of personal shariah and a strong marginalization of governmental shariah, keeping clerics and their interpretations out of our public lives and only in the part of our personal lives we choose.

Muslim voices against shariah are the most likely to be heard, for what makes a more compelling case for the need for secular-based law than Muslims who revere their Qur'an, but embrace the U.S. Constitution as the guarantee of equal rights for all people?

We must always keep in mind that the United States is a very young country compared to many other nations in the world, and that while our democracy has endured many struggles, and has always prevailed, it is not indestructible. Anything that is taken for granted is in danger of being swept away. For that reason, we must always remember that much of the rest of the world does not have the rights and privileges we have here, and moreover, in the history of the world that has largely been true as well. The United States *is* unique. One need only look toward South America, and the many struggles countries have had with dictatorships versus democracies, to realize that our relative stability over the last two hundred plus years is something exceptional.

The enormous diversity of our country is an exercise not in tolerance, but in pluralism. To truly be an American is to accept the increasingly wide array of religions and ethnicities that make up our country. But for the Islamists, as for any supremacist, that is not possible. At best, they may "tolerate" those of other religions or ethnicities, but always with the idea that they are part of a special group and therefore deserving of special privileges. This sort of exceptionalism and entitlement must end for true Muslim reformation to take place and for overall integration into American society. Without that, our children will always feel as if they are visitors in this society rather than bonded to it and its legal system along with their faith.

So far, the United States has in general not been nearly as conciliatory as Europe when it comes to the Islamists. However, that can change, just as it did in Europe, and that is why we must be ever vigilant when it comes to protecting the democratic ideals that the Founding Fathers gave us. It is not one nation under shariah, or Islam or Christianity or Judaism or under Yawheh, or Christ, or Allah, or Vishnu, but one nation under God, and it is up to each individual to define who that God is for him- or herself (if he or she indeed even believes in a Supreme Being) and to respect the fact that the basis of our government is a secular document called the U.S. Constitution, which clearly separates religion and state.

All of this discussion of secular versus religious laws brings back into clear focus just how wise Jefferson and other Founding Fathers were to push for a clear separation of church and state. It's bad enough to have a small but very vocal and active group of Islamists vying for a separate set of laws for themselves within the United States, but imagine what it would be like if Hindus, Jews, and Christians en masse insisted on their own religious laws as well? The chaos that would ensue would probably be unbearable, and such separate sets of laws for each group would definitely dismantle U.S. democracy as we know it. Jefferson and the rest may have not been able to envision just how religiously diverse the United States would become, but they planned for it in their own way, responding to Christian diversity by giving us all the right to practice our own religion in our own way, and at the same time giving us constitutional laws that apply to everyone. They were prescient to formulate a Constitution for our government that was under God and based in strong faith but intentionally left the word Christian out. Thank you, Jefferson, thank you, Adams, Washington, Franklin, Madison, Hancock, and all the rest for all you did to make that so, and may we never undo what so many others have given their lives to protect.

EPILOGUE

A Letter to My Children

Dear Zachariah, Zaina, and Zaid,

On occasion you have asked me, What is this book you're writing? What kind of story is it? An adventure? Is there a bad guy? Who wins?

All very good questions, of course. In its way, it is an adventure, but probably not one you will want to read until you get a bit older, since you are barely ten, eight, and four. With that in mind, I'm writing you this letter in a way that will also make more sense to you when you are older because some of the things it addresses are very much from the world of grown-ups. But what kind of adventure is the book, you may ask, and I will answer: the one of our country and our faith. You ask if there is a bad guy, and I tell you there are, in fact, many bad guys and bad women, and many good guys and good women.

Just over a year ago, members of our U.S. Navy SEAL Team Six killed a very bad man named Osama Bin Laden. You, Zachariah, have had questions about that. Who was this man? Was he bad? Why did they call him a Muslim? It would have been so much easier for me to just tell you, "He's not a Muslim." But that is between him and God. What I do know and have explained to you is that he was very bad, that he sent men to kill our fellow

Americans on September 11, 2001, a few months before you were born, and unfortunately, they were very successful in their mission. Thousands of innocent Americans died: fathers, mothers, even children of all faiths and national origins. It was a terrible day for this country and for the world. How do I explain why a man would send other men to do such a terrible thing? I can't, really, other than to say there is a thing called "evil" in the world. It is very real. All of us every day are confronted by evil. In the Qur'an God refers to *shaitan,* or the devil, as the source, a metaphor, of all evil putting those ideas into our head. It is all basically a sign of free will. We cannot understand good if we have never known evil. We cannot understand health if we have never known sickness. We all have to decide what is wrong and what is right. If we intentionally choose what is wrong, God sees and knows all. Everyone is taught right and wrong, but people have many different ideas about what makes something right and what makes it wrong. There is, however, a simple way for you to know if you are doing the right or the wrong thing. If what you do does more harm than good, then you can know you're doing the wrong thing, and if it helps people, then it is the right thing. If three thousand hungry people receive food, it is something good. If three thousand innocent people are killed, there is no good in that, only evil.

When Bin Laden was killed, millions of people around our country celebrated. That may strike you as strange. You have asked me, isn't it wrong to kill? Yes, of course, killing is a terrible thing, but in the case of Bin Laden his death may end up saving thousands of lives, because Bin Laden lived to kill. Why? Because he was evil. Our nation was at war since he had declared war on us. He claimed to kill others for the sake of Islam, and that he had God's blessing to do so. But the fact that people say that they do things in the name of God does not automatically make them good people. We judge others' goodness, or the lack of it, by their actions. Bin Laden prayed. He read the Qur'an, but it was almost as though he read a different book from the one you and I read and the scripture you and I recite when we do our daily prayers. He thought the Qur'an, which was dictated in our Arabic language to the Prophet Muhammad by God through the Angel Gabriel, gave him the words with which he could explain how he could kill innocent men, women, and children. But tell me, what kind of God would tell others to kill the innocent? Bin Laden may have thought he was a holy man, but his actions showed him to be pure evil.

Live your life so that others will look at you and say, there goes a good man or woman. There goes someone who is kind, who does not look down on others, who helps the unfortunate of this world and knows that God sees all we do and all we think. Live your life to love others, whatever faith they may have, whether they are Christians, Jews, Muslims, Bahai, Buddhists, Hindus, or if they have no religion at all, but love them, treat them with respect and charity, no matter how different they may seem from you, for God has made the world with many different people, and our challenge on any given day is to love and love still more. Our challenge is not based on our success in this world, but only that God knows that for any given day, you tried your best to meet all of our challenges with the gifts we are each blessed with having. You will know if you tried your best. But only God will know if and when you do it from humility or from arrogance.

Bin Laden believed that his faith was better than other people's, even other Muslims, that only he had the answers, and others did not have the right to disagree with him, that only he knew what was right for the world. Would you like someone like that for your friend? Probably not. Is that what God teaches us to be? Of course not. Stand up for what you believe to be right, but if what you are calling right is hurting many other people, it must be wrong.

In a way, that is what my book is all about: trying to do the right thing by our faith and our country, and in the process trying to help as many people as possible. Bin Laden was the worst example of what happens when Muslims depart from the part of our faith that is beautiful and personal and make it into a global political movement that it is not meant to be. Bin Laden was not just one man, and he was not crazy. He was a natural product of dangerous ideas. I know you are proud of my work as a doctor. Trust me. He was a sign, a symptom of a much deeper disease—Islamism. Know it. Understand it. Defeat it.

I want you to embrace your faith, to know that God is always with you, and at the same time I want you to love your country, to know that it is very special, like no other in the world, and that it gives you great freedoms just as God has given you many blessings. Please, never let your faith be something that you use to hurt other people, but rather let it be a bridge, something with which you build understanding and friendships and love. Learn your religion and be disciplined in its scholarship, but feel free to set your own path and rely on your own conscience once you've done all your reading and asking. Questioning leaders, imams, and scholars is central to Islam and being human. As much as I and your mother will always pray for you, in the end you will be judged by God alone without anyone at your side, even your parents. Show everyone you meet love, but some may need tough love. Don't let the pressure of the tribe sway you from what is right. If you love God, rely on Him, stay humble, and remain true to your values, all will work out. Don't allow anyone or any government to get between you and God. Never let anyone into that space.

As to your country, please always be willing to give something back. I joined the Navy when I was younger because I wanted to give something back. I became a physician because I wanted to give something back. I started the American Islamic Forum for

286

Democracy some years ago because I wanted to give something back, and because after 9/11 I thought it was important that American Muslims stand in defense of both their country and their faith and make it clear to the world that we as Muslims took responsibility for repairing our own house. It is great to live in a free country, and one in which there are many wonderful things to enjoy, but it is also important to stand up for something, and to fight against evil. Our parents, your grandparents, came to America not to bring Islam here, but rather to appreciate freedom and bring the values of liberty into our faith.

I hope you can understand, even at your young ages, that both faith and freedom call us to action. They are both gifts, but they must not be taken for granted. They must be cherished and defended, just as you would with those you love. You take care of them, stand up for them when you have to, and show your loyalty and love through your actions. Your grandparents and your great-grandparents knew what it was like to live without freedom, but fortunately, they never knew what it was like to live without faith. They believed that God would help them as they struggled to form a new life in America, and He did. Perhaps your motherland of Syria will begin to know and taste real freedom soon? Getting rid of an evil tyrant like Assad is only the first major obstacle. My hope for you is that your faith will always provide you with the inner strength to meet any challenge and that our country will always offer you the freedom you need to make your dreams come true. Know that already you are living lives that your grandparents and great-grandparents only dreamed of, and this is because of their brave actions, and all the actions of many men and women through the years, who make it their job to keep us safe and free. Some are soldiers, others police officers, or those who promote civil rights for all—the list could go on and on—but they all have one thing in common: They believe in the freedoms on which this country was founded, including freedom of religion. Here in the United States, we are more free to worship the way we choose as Muslims than we would be anywhere else on earth. Yet, we could lose all of our freedoms tomorrow, and we would still be Muslims and still be close to God. It would be all we'd have. But it would make it difficult for us to be human the way we are now, and have the opportunity to live, create, love, and enjoy each other. Our great nation and its great laws guarantee us our identity, our opportunity to live. Our faith can never be taken away and it is not for government to oversee, only to give us the freedom to practice it.

At your young ages, it may be hard to take all that in, but through the years I hope and pray that you will make it your mission in whatever way you choose to give back to the country that has given us so much and to hold close the faith that has seen us through so many trials. In order to do so, you must carry the mantle against political Islam and for a spiritual, free Islam. I have never had a conflict between my faith of Islam and my nation. I pray that I am able to give you that same gift that my parents gave me. Being a patriotic American, I worry deeply that most of the books on the shelves about Islam and being Muslim, whether written by Muslims or non-Muslims, could drive you away from that synergy and these ideas. I pray that you devote at least part of your own lives to helping Muslims in America and across the world advocate for liberty, and to seeing that my dream that political Islam wither on the vine of history and be replaced by an academic tradition of Islam that unequivocally separates mosque and state comes true. I hope and pray we can do our hajj to Mecca one day before our time on this earth is done. One of the ways that you may know that Islam has been liberated from the shackles of Islamism is when the world can see that the nation that houses the Grand Mosque of Mecca is free and represents an

Islam that embraces universal human rights and liberty. It saddens me so that the Kaaba, which is one of the central unifying spiritual symbols of our faith and history, the direction to which we all pray, is protected by a nation that violates most of the sacred humanitarian principles of life and our Islam. Instead they produce and toxically export Osama Bin Laden, Al Qaeda, Islamism, Salafism, Wahhabism and impose on their people one of the most oppressive xenophobic regimes in the world. The birthplace of Islam neither belongs to the House of Saud nor any single Muslim. It belongs to all Muslims, to God. No nation and its people should ever belong to a tribe. Countries and citizens should be free with unalienable rights and never owned by a family. When the citizens of Saudi Arabia are free and their petrodollars are used to spread freedom rather than Islamism, hate, and fascism, then our humanitarian dreams of liberty for all will finally begin to be realized.

Know that your mom and I and your grandparents are always with you in spirit in the depths of your heart, praying for your strength, clarity, and success. Success is neither measured in achievements nor material wealth but in your own sense of moral clarity and integrity. Always first remember God, and know that it is nations built upon values like those of our United States that give us the liberty and the opportunity to know Him and be Muslim or be any faith, equal before the law. I hope my story, my ideas, let you understand *why*. Your own stories will certainly be different. Chart your own course. The places you take your opportunities will be different. But I hope your morals, your values, and the context in which you place God, our nation, our law, and Islam are the same if not better. It is your responsibility to take our experiences, our ideas, and build your own upon them, and to leave this world a better place for your children than the one we left to you. There should never be a conflict in your heart or your mind between loving your country, the freest nation in the world, and loving your faith of Islam.

Your mother and I love you all more than we could ever put into words, and hope you can understand that more than anything else, my work and this book are for you.

ACKNOWLEDGMENTS

In many ways, my story is not my own. It is a combined product of not only my work but the support, encouragement, and nourishment of every individual who has believed in me and even those who have not but have had the courage to openly take on my beliefs on America, liberty, and Islam.

First, without my mother, Aiche, and father, Kais (M.K.), I would never have had any of the tools I needed to navigate the challenges of my life and to build upon the vision for my family's life that my mom and dad helped ground and instill. My mother's selflessness and my parents' love and support not only in my youth but throughout the travails of my work against Islamism gave me the space to plant the seeds that came to fruition in this book. I can never repay you, but I always pray for you. To my sisters, thank you for joining me in our journey when you did and especially to my youngest sister, Samar. You understand more than anyone my raison d'être.

Second, no one deserves more thanks and appreciation from the depths of my heart and soul than my wife, Gada, and my remarkable children, Zachariah, Zaina, and Zaid. You may not have exactly chosen this journey, but not one minute goes by that I do not thank God for your belief and trust in me and your acceptance of the road we have all had to navigate together. If not today, I hope someday you understand why we had to do this despite the price we continue to pay. I love you.

Crucially, this book would have never been a reality without my agent, George Hiltzik of N.S. Bienstock, Inc., who found a great home for it at Simon and Schuster with one of the best editors in the business, Mitchell Ivers. Thank you, George, for being the consummate advocate, and thank you, Mitchell, for your trust and confidence in helping shape this book and allowing me to tell my story on your pages. Thank you to my publisher, Louise Burke. And thank you to the rest of the world-class team at Simon & Schuster: Natasha Simons, production editor Al Madocs, cover designer Lisa Litwack, my copyeditor, Sean Devlin, and our publicity manager, Melissa Gramstad. A special thank-you also to Emilio Dabul, now a personal friend, whose editorial assistance from the very beginning of this project helped me gain clarity about the best elements of my story and vision to put on paper. Your counsel and guidance made this book a success.

And to Glenn Beck and Kevin Balfe, who were the first with a national platform to believe in my work, thank you for being so instrumental in making this book a reality.

I want to especially thank my dear close friends Mofied Kassab and Zakwan Alzein, whose loyalty, courage, and counsel gave me immeasurable support in the often rough waters of the American Muslim and Syrian communities. You kept me from ever feeling alone even at those moments of weakness when I sometimes doubted if it was "all worth it." You truly are the brothers I never had.

Thank you to Soul Khalsa, my confidant since the day we met in 2002 at the Arizona Interfaith Movement board; we quickly learned how much we shared not only between our Muslim and Sikh traditions but in our visions for America, family, and life. I think we may learn one day that your vision that in a previous life we fought together on some battlefield may have been true. Thank you for continually reminding me to lead—and especially when you challenged me to launch—our Muslim rally against terrorism in 2004, which set AIFD upon its historic path.

ACKNOWLEDGMENTS

Thank you is just not enough to say to our most selfless and devoted team at the American Islamic Forum for Democracy: Lea Benson, our director of operations, who teaches me so much; Courtney Lonergan, our director of community development; Norma Salas, my executive assistant; and our researchers, Jon Sutz and Raquel Saraswati. Also, our messages at AIFD have gotten out to the masses thanks to the untiring dedication of our media team, Gordon James and Gregg Edgar. God truly looked down upon our work and blessed it when he led each of you to AIFD.

To our future American Muslim leaders, our youth who have courageously joined us in AIFD's Muslim Liberty Project, thank you for renewing my faith in the American spirit and the validity of our ideas. I want to also thank all of the American Muslim leaders who helped us make the American Islamic Leadership Coalition a formidable and diverse group that finally gave Americans a palpable alternative to the Muslim Brotherhood legacy groups, giving my work a new life. Thank you for your inspiration, courage, and trust. Thank you to America's leaders who have long supported and lifted up my work, including Senator Jon Kyl (R-AZ), Congressman Peter King (R-NY), Congresswoman Sue Myrick (R-NC), Congressman Trent Franks (R-AZ), former congressman J. D. Hayworth, and John Shadegg, former secretary of education Bill Bennett, Seth Leibsohn, Attorney General Michael Mukasey, Admiral John Eisold, Foster Friess, Matthew Taylor, Kenneth Bialkin, Stan Richards, Harlan Crow, "Dr. Bob" Shillman, Nina Rosenwald, Dennis Miller, Steve and Rita Emerson, Daniel Pipes, author Steven Emerson, Frank Gaffney, Walid Phares, Andy Polk, and Tina Ramirez, to name just a few.

Words cannot express the gratitude I have for all those in my life who have made my story what it is and who have supported me and our work in this journey. To Rabbi Chuck and Barbara Herring and all my friends in our Children of Abraham dialogue group, thank you for giving us the personal support and foundations so early on back in 2000, when we locally started this complex interfaith work in Phoenix. To all my patients, whom I love, to my partners in my medical practice, Dr. Marc Lee and Amy Ingersoll, PA-C, who allowed me the freedom to undertake this work, thank you. It is a journey I may have chosen for myself, but affected many who may have not. To all of you, thank you.

Last, to my fellow Americans, thank you for giving my family a home and a nation that allowed us to be free and live in liberty that our motherland of Syria could not give us. You have taught us that there is no stronger human bond than the bond that ties us together as Americans under God.

For any readers interested in contacting the author:

M. Zuhdi Jasser, MD
Author, *A Battle for the Soul of Islam*
Email: Battle@ZLiberty.com
Web: www.BattlefortheSoulofIslam.com
Twitter: @DrZuhdiJasser
Facebook: Facebook.com/mzjasser

For any readers interested in contacting the American Islamic Forum for Democracy (AIFD):

American Islamic Forum for Democracy
P.O. Box 1832
Phoenix, Arizona 85001
Office: 602-254-1840
Email: info@aifdemocracy.org
Web: www.aifdemocracy.org
Twitter: @aifdemocracy
Facebook: Facebook.com/AmericanIslamicForumforDemocracy
YouTube: Youtube.com/AIFDtv